* Was Amelia Earhart captured by enemy troops —or does she live in obscurity?

* Is Jimmy Hoffa the victim of an execution, or is he in secret exile?

* Did Aimee Semple Macpherson, America's leading evangelist, stage her own kidnapping?

"Alan Landsburg, and his extraordinarily talented staff were out in the field collecting some of the most unusual images ever recorded on a television screen . . . More than a hundred people were scattered around the world recording pieces of data, clues, evidence which fulfilled Hamlet's promise that *there are more things on earth than you have dreamed of in your philosophy.*"

—Leonard Nimoy

IN SEARCH OF MISSING PERSONS
An Uncanny Exploration of the Unknown
by Alan Landsburg

IN SEARCH OF MISSING PERSONS
Alan Landsburg

Foreword by LEONARD NIMOY

BANTAM BOOKS · TORONTO · NEW YORK · LONDON

RLI: $\dfrac{\text{VLM 9 (VLR 8–10)}}{\text{IL 9+}}$

IN SEARCH OF MISSING PERSONS
A Bantam Book / February 1978

ISBN 0–553–11459–X

Published simultaneously in the United States and Canada

Bantam Books are published by Bantam Books, Inc. Its trade-
mark consisting of the words "Bantam Books" and the portrayal of a bantam, is registered in the United States Patent
Office and in other countries. Marca Registrada. Bantam
Books, Inc., 666 Fifth Avenue, New York, New York 10019.

PRINTED IN THE UNITED STATES OF AMERICA

To Julian Bach,
who has always believed.
Thank you.

To Elayne Sawaya and Jeanne Russo for their efforts in finding the real stories of missing persons, and to Barbara Wegher for her invaluable editorial assistance and sure eye for important detail.

The chronicle of discovery amassed in this volume is the work of many people. More than a hundred researchers, scientists, and skilled film-makers participated in the various quests. For simplicity's sake, we have combined our experiences into a single, first-person narrative so that we may share with you the essence and excitement of the hunt, without a clutter of personal introductions. As author and chief chronicler of this work, I owe an enormous debt of gratitude to those who aided me in the field to explore the world of mystery. To all those dedicated workers committed to *IN SEARCH OF* . . . , I say thank you. This book is as much yours as mine.

—ALAN LANDSBURG

Contents

foreword
by LEONARD NIMOY

My first working association with the television series
In Search Of . . . was a narration session in which
I was asked to read aloud the major objectives of the
various categories—Lost Civilizations, Strange Phenomena, Missing Persons, Magic and Witchcraft, Myths
and Monsters, and, finally, Extraterrestrials. The roll
call of subjects was mind-bending. I kept on reading
the sentences appended to the list but my mind was
focused on the prospect of walking the electrifying
path between what is scientific fact and what is considered far-out science fiction.

Alan Landsburg is a much-honored producer of
television documentary films, and his extraordinarily
talented staff of directors, writers, cameramen, and
editors were out in the field collecting some of the most
unusual images ever recorded for the television screen.
What appealed to me most was the very range of subjects. On one hand, we might be searching for Amelia
Earhart, lost on a trans-Pacific flight in 1937; on the
other, for the famed Count Dracula of myth and fact.
Who really did build Stonehenge? Where do UFOs
land? Is there really life after death? Do plants speak?
The quest and the questions presented a virtually unlimited source of adventure. More than a hundred
people were scatterd around the world recording data,
clues, evidence that fulfilled Hamlet's promise that
"there are more things on earth than you have dreamed
of in your philosophy."

I liked the experience of butting up against old ideas
and demonstrating the new explanations possible. In

pursuit of old and baffling mysteries, the programs opened new directions to pursue in search of more illuminating answers. For all these reasons, I immersed myself in the fascinating game. It's good to know that our television series *In Search Of* . . . has now become something of a byword for many viewers.

This book is a chronicle of the efforts that have gone into making the television series. It's a fascinating log-book to me, filled with the excitement of overcoming the seemingly impossible and with the fulfillment of discovery. I hope you find it as intriguing as I did.

—LEONARD NIMOY

PART I

THE ADVENTURERS

Prologue

The first mistake was trying to shout. I should have known that no one would hear me over the heavy slap of choppy, nighttime seas, but I had reacted instinctively to hearing my name called over the bullhorn aboard the diving barge. All I got for my trouble was a mouthful of salt water. In the first fit of sputtering coughs, I felt the prickle of panic. Suddenly I began to wonder just what had impelled me to voluntarily place myself in such jeopardy.

We were putting the finishing touches on a particularly difficult bit of underwater filming. The wrap-up was a night sequence. On the screen it would look wonderfully exotic, but shooting in the dark creates all manner of hazards for a camera crew. Divers are forever getting tangled in black electrical cable, which is nearly invisible in the dark. The narrow circle of light required for this kind of shooting is so intense that the divers and the crew are virtually blinded to anything taking place at the periphery of the scene. One particular terror is that sharks are drawn by the sights and sounds of our work.

As I supervised the filming I realized that I wanted the effect of glowing phosphorus torches. The problem was that they were back on our boat, some one hundred yards away. Rather than stop the cameras, I decided to swim back to the boat and get them myself. This was the second mistake. I struck out for the boat, breaking a cardinal rule of nighttime underwater work: Don't *ever* leave your buddy.

My action set in motion a chain of misadventures. About the time I reached the boat, my "buddy" noticed I was missing. Apparently he signaled the crew to stop shooting, surface, and begin to search for me. For my part, I picked up the flares, dived back in, and made for the wide pool of light that marked the filming area. My crew grouped frantically at the surface, and decided to kill the lights in order to obtain some night vision.

I couldn't believe I had lost my beacon. It never occurred to me that they had intentionally turned off the lights—I simply assumed that I had strayed. I struck off, seeking the spot where the illuminated circle had been, and wound up fighting a tidal pull strong enough to make swimming difficult.

Flapping around, lost, nearly choking on seawater, exhausted from fighting the tide, I found myself wondering why I was risking my life for such a silly enterprise or adventure. And I realized a simple truth: I couldn't stand the thought of not being part of all that action. Diving, filming, and discovering things I had never seen before was, to me, well worth the risk.

The *In Search Of* . . . television series and books are dedicated to that precept. *Exploration is worth the risk*. In this case, the quest was for people who also had been enamoured of the chase.

I decided to devote the first part of my search for missing persons to the phenomenon of adventurers who have disappeared. I began to wonder whether they had been propelled into "fate" by the very characteristics that had led them to place themselves in such potentially dangerous situations and why were their lives always filled with such intrigue and mystery even up to the end? Were their quests in life, their goals, part of the collective unconscious? Was it their bizarre disappearances that captured the public's attention and held them spellbound, or were these adventurers and explorers interesting figures in their own right? In short, why did their sudden disappearances pique the interest of the entire world?

I went in search of four famous missing adventurers in order to present the significant facts of their lives and their subsequent disappearance. I wanted to examine all the plausible theories concerning the fate of these missing adventurers. As a documentarian, I felt compelled to analyze the many facts about the disappearances, and to see if the facts would explain the mysteries.

In some cases I found that the popular beliefs were at odds with the official accounts of why and how each of the persons had disappeared. I wanted to know why. In one or two instances, i.e. Amelia Earhart, there seemed to be an enormous amount of evidence supporting any one of the popular theories; and yet these theories were diametrically opposed to "officially accepted" opinion.

In other investigations I witnessed a process by which the theories of the public, clinging desperately to a few grains of fact, ended up creating legends lacking substantial evidence and sometimes even basic logic and reason. Some popular legends had no basis in ated in order to pay homage to the adventurer-heroes.

And in still other stories, the adventurers' disapreality; they merely fulfilled a need to diminish uncertainty and chaos. Moreover, I found rumors that were so incredible that they seemed to have been crepearances generated speculations that were based on more than just a grain of fact; and still the official opinion obstinately held way. Why?

I looked for patterns in the backgrounds and personalities of my subjects. The heroic adventurers intrigued me. I was in search of a commonality peculiar to each's attitudes about life.

Who becomes an adventurer? What kind of families do they come from? As I investigated the biographies of the four missing persons—Richard Halliburton, Amelia Earhart, Percy Fawcett, and Michael Rockefeller—I continually asked myself what the pattern was.

As I worked, I noted some interesting similarities. Adventurers do not breed adventurers. Something else breeds their relentless drive for heroics. Something else compels them to consistently seek life-against-death situations. They seem driven to live intensely. Death-defying stunts become translated into triumphant adventure. They spoke and often wrote about their perilous feats of daring in dreary, love-struck ways. Why? Did they harbor an ultimate death wish? I think that is much too simplistic an explanation.

These men and women craved challenge and fame. They achieved no real satisfaction from normal, every-day life. Their only genuine satisfaction was in conquest and in the fame produced by their bold enterprises. They vanished or died in pursuit of their ultimate "high." Somehow, they even engineered their own mys-terious end. They didn't die peacefully—they vanished. And the searches generated by their disappearances are still going on, in some cases more than sixty years after the fact.

Interestingly enough, all the adventurers I focused upon came from rather rigid, righteously puritanical upbringings. They came from families where the practical and rational aspects of life were encouraged and stressed. Psychologists whom I spoke to ex-plained that traditionally in families such as these, the child's psychological needs and desires are not nur-tured much, if at all. As a result, the youngsters de-velop an extremely rich fantasy life as well as an elaborate conception of who they are in relation to the rest of the world. This in itself is not pathological, but in extreme cases can and often does cause some peo-ple to do some rather foolhardy things.

Adventurers stand apart from the rest of society. Their lifestyles stand as proof. Through their various exploits they can prove to the world that they are worthy of love. In their own view, they are nobler and more courageous. They do not live their lives on the level of the mundane.

There are parallels in the life stories of my subjects, particularly in their childhoods. They tended to be precocious, and always seemed more mature, more advanced, than their peers. Instead of playing with the gang, they would tuck themselves away in their rooms or in the library, reading history books and literature. Time away from their contemporaries meant more time to develop a thriving, rich fantasy life. Perhaps unnurtured by their families, their thirst for romance and their dreams of great heroic deeds were left to their wild imaginations. And so they created fantasy worlds, which continued into their adult lives.

As I read each of their stories, I was reminded of Nietzsche's statement: "I create in order not to die of the truth." I also realized that these supermen, unlike the mass of men, had not—in the words of Jean-Paul Sartre—"been born without reason, prolonged themselves out of weakness and died by chance." They seemed to exercise more control over their lives.

They turned their backs on the conventional world as much out of fear as out of love for adventure. They feared failure—failure in that their lives would be permeated with the mediocrity of routine. Thoreau wrote that the mass of men lead lives of quiet desperation. This was the fate these adventurers struggled, with equal desperation, to avoid.

In another sense, however, it is also true that it takes courage just to endure—to confront boredom and routine, and to shoulder responsibility for one's own actions and for the happiness of others. But the adventurers rejected the conventional world because it seemed to them that to embrace it would have meant failure. They wanted to succeed on their own terms and on their terms only. In the words of Richard Halliburton, they all seemed to be engaged in "a rebellion against the prosaic mold. . . ." They rejected what seemed to them the confining world of adulthood.

And in one sense at least, what is an adventurer but a seventeen-year-old kid who refuses to grow up and relinquish the intense narcissism and ideals of youth? The unconscious zone of the adventurer's soul dynamically asserts itself, driving them forward, on to ever-greater deeds.

It wasn't so much that they were self-destructive but that, perhaps, they were victims of a self-imposed exile—forever banished to an island of unfettered possibilities, a world not bound by the limitations and shrinking horizons normally imposed by adulthood.

I have recorded their fascinating stories in the following pages.

1

Richard Halliburton

The report that Richard Halliburton was missing at sea was accepted rather calmly. The search parties carried out their efforts in minimal fashion compared to the searches mounted for adventurers like Amelia Earhart and Percy Fawcett. A few rumors cropped up hinting that Richard Halliburton might have survived the typhoon and was living out his days on a remote island. The popular belief regarding his ultimate fate, however, was in perfect agreement with the official accounts of how and when he disappeared.

In March 1939 Richard Halliburton and a crew of fourteen set sail from Hong Kong in a lavishly decorated sailing junk christened the *Sea Dragon*. They were bound for the World's Fair at Treasure Island in San Francisco Bay. The voyage was to last two months, allowing the colorful oriental sailing vessel to arrive in time for the opening ceremonies at the fair. But Richard Halliburton, his crew, and the *Sea Dragon* disappeared in a typhoon. No remains were ever found. The sea tends to bury any such evidence very well. Six months after his sudden disappearance, Richard Halliburton was legally declared dead.

The fact that the *Sea Dragon*'s disappearance had not sparked the usual flurry of wild conjectures and numerous search parties normally surrounding famous-missing-person cases intrigued me. What kind of man was Richard Halliburton that his abrupt disappearance was almost taken for granted? He had been the great swashbuckling hero of American adolescents in the 1920s and '30s. He became almost a legend in his own time. He wrote seven best-selling novels documenting his romantic exploits throughout the most exotic countries. His syndicated articles appeared in fifty newspapers with a combined circulation of more than nine million. His first two books had appeared together on the best-seller list. He earned a thousand dollars a week on his lecture circuit alone. He was handsome, fearless, courageous, and virile. On the surface, at least, it seemed that Richard Halliburton was the most glamorous man-about-town of his day.

Halliburton gained his greatest popularity in the '30s. Travel to foreign countries was still a romantic notion, the reality of it reserved for the select few. Escape from the doldrums of the Depression was an end greatly desired. Halliburton provided a simple avenue of release, paved with the richness of his prose and his imagination.

He was one of America's serious, authentic heroes. The literature concerning his disappearance, however, was bereft of the sort of speculations normally accorded to such charismatic figures. At first, the report that Halliburton was missing was thought to be another one of his press agent's stunts. Newspaper reporters and other journalists were suspicious, and his "alleged" disappearance was reported only briefly and incidentally, minus all the reverence usually employed in such articles. Belatedly and somewhat reluctantly, search parties began only after continued prodding from Halliburton's family. Did he stage his own disappearance? Did his adventuresome lifestyle predict this kind of ending?

I wanted to gather new evidence in my search for Richard Halliburton. I wanted to find out not only how he disappeared but, even more importantly, why he disappeared. Jonathan Root, one of Richard's biographers, wrote: "Richard was the embodiment of daydreams, the public manifestation of private fancies.

He could have frolicked across the tapestry of history at any given point and mankind would have recognized him. He was what any of us like to believe we might have been."

Then why did that magnificent myth end in so much silence? Why did so few bother to probe? Was there something in Halliburton's character that made his dramatic disappearance inevitable? Just who *was* Richard Halliburton?

I had a wealth of information. There were Halliburton's books, his letters to his parents, a biography, relatives and friends bulging with anecdotes and impressions about the man, and a log of magazine articles criticizing and praising him from the day he began his global, larger-than-life adventures. I decided to begin with the letters he wrote to his parents.

Richard was born in 1900 in Brownsville, Tennessee. When he was still very young he and his family moved to Memphis. There he held the distinction of being the only male student in the Hutchison School for Girls. Nelle Nance, Richard's mother, was a member of the school's faculty and enrolled her son there for convenience' sake. Richard was very attached to his mother, as is revealed throughout the course of his some thousand-odd letters. Richard's father, Wesley Halliburton, was a descendant of early Scotch immigrants and had been described by those who knew him as "a caricature of the southern gentleman." He was a strict disciplinarian, and Richard continually craved his respect.

Richard came from a southern family. As I read Richard's letter to his parents, I found a man struggling with the concepts and ideals that his rather puritanical upbringing had imposed upon him. Richard was trying to break free of strong parental reins. He craved romance, adventure, and liberty. He had a good scholastic record but didn't excel in sports. His interests lay elsewhere. He spent his time reading the travel and history books that lined the shelves of his family's library. In marked contrast to Richard, however, Wesley, Jr.—Richard's younger brother—preferred baseball and football.

At the age of fifteen Richard developed a rapid heartbeat and was taken from school and confined to bed for several months. After his recovery his father constantly reminded him to lead a restrained life. I suspect that the restriction against overexertion nurtured Richard's scholarly interests as well as his growing desire to actually live the romantic and noble life he had read about. Most likely, the subsequent intensity with which he lived his life can be related to these persistent parental warnings against strenuous activity.

At the age of sixteen Richard was editor-in-chief of the Lawrenceville School newspaper. And in 1917, against his father's better judgment, Richard entered Princeton University. In that same year Richard's younger brother died of rheumatic fever, leaving Richard embittered toward what seemed to him life's gross injustices. By this time Richard's letters to his parents were beginning to show a restlessness and discontent with the "ordinary" things of life. He wrote:

The older I get, the more sadness there seems to be in the world. Maybe it's just because my emotions have become unusually sensitive in the last year or two. There seems to be something in turmoil inside me all the time. I intend to keep myself in control until the war is over and my education, and *then* I'm going to *bust loose* and let my restless, discontented spirit run its course. The idea of leading a monotonous, confined, respectable life is horrible to me. Someday the fires inside are going to break out and I'll push my working table out the window and just be a wild man. I've got in the habit of running instead of walking. Something keeps saying faster, faster—move! ...

And so he did move. He went to Europe, South America, the Orient, Russia, around the world. He copiously wrote his parents about all his adventures. His first book, *The Royal Road to Romance,* soared to the top of the best-seller list and remained popular for years afterward. He became the alter ego of every would-be adventurer of his time. In his twenties he lectured to two thousand members of the National Geographic Society. The Metropolitan Opera House in Philadelphia was brimming with members from the Philadelphia Forum who had come to hear Richard weave his romantic yarns. With tales of his fantastic, joyous exploits, he thrilled and titillated museum members, historical and geographical societies, universities, prep schools, and ladies clubs.

In an interview in *American Magazine* in 1926 Richard described himself:

> I hungered for the Romance of the sea, and foreign ports, the prow of a ship, any ship, and sail away, perhaps to China, perhaps to Spain, perhaps to the islands of the South Seas. I hungered for the mystery of great mountains. I wanted to float down the Nile in a butterfly boat, make love to a pale Kashmiri maiden, dance to the castanets of Granada gypsies, see the Taj Mahal by moonlight, hunt tigers in a Bengal jungle—try everything once. . . .

Richard did see the Taj Mahal by moonlight. He even swam in the lily-padded pool, or so he claimed. He also climbed the Matterhorn, hiked across the Pyrenees, swam the Nile at Luxor, scaled Mount Fujiyama in mid-winter, followed and compressed Ulysses' ten-year trail across Greece into five months, where he swam the Hellespont in the image of his hero Lord Byron, swam the Panama Canal, leaped into the Mayan Well of Death, spent a night on Devil's Island, marched with the French Foreign Legion, played Robinson Crusoe in a cave in Tobago for two weeks, and on and on, till the last glorious sailing of the *Sea Dragon.* His adventures spanned a brief twenty years.

During his travels he wrote his parents about his

accomplishments. And as Richard traveled to more and more exotic countries, his parents grew increasingly anxious. Root, in *Halliburton, The Magnificent Myth,* reported that these parental fears took the form of personal admonitions. "Beware the criminal minds and diseased bodies that proliferate in the unwashed corners of the world. . . ." As I read through Richard's letters I discovered a man constantly trying to justify his adventurous lifestyle to concerned, conservative parents. He wrote home to his father:

> Dad, you hit the wrong target when you write that you wish I were at Princeton living "in the even tenor of my way." I hate that expression, and as far as I am able I intend to avoid that condition. When impulse and spontaneity fail to make my "way" as *uneven* as possible, then I shall sit up nights inventing means of making life as conglomerate and vivid as possible. . . .

And Richard Halliburton was accused of just such flamboyant invention of his adventures. He admitted freely that he did employ poetic license, but denied, however, that he ever out-and-out lied about any of his feats of daring. Richard was not an athlete, and he took at least a few precautions against apparent risks (i.e., he swam the Hellespont under the watchful eye of a Turkish boat, etc.). Yet, he was prone to publicity stunts and at one point asked a journalist friend to report that he had drowned in the Hellespont in midswim. That stunt failed, somewhat to Richard's chagrin.

His adventures inspired parody and satire. There were many cartoons and caricatures about his frivolous and adolescent writing style. *The Bookman* of March 1930 contained "A Series of Parody Biographies" by H. W. Hanemann. One of the biographies exemplified the skepticism with which his self-aggrandized exploits were viewed. Richard is portrayed in conversation with an East Indian: " 'I've got to do something,' I said. 'Are there any mountains around here?' 'The best mountain we have is Mount Everest away off to the southeast. It's the highest mountain in the world. Nobody can climb it. Nobody will ever climb it.' That was enough for me. 'Which way is southeast?' I asked."

On the surface it seemed that Richard was numb to such slings and arrows. But that was just on the surface. Later his letters home began to show a change. And he himself was beginning to note that change. His "joyous wonder" disappeared from his later letters. Richard was getting older and perhaps growing weary of his adventurous lifestyle. He started to reflect on life more and more. And he slowly began to realize that he had very few really close friends. He wrote to his father:

> In the first place there's just no helping my unsociable nature. I've always been wearied by the company and minds and hearts of most human beings ever since early childhood. But this in no way comes from sourness or misanthropy. I'm not in the least antagonistic—just not interested. . . . My life will always be too full of activity and ambition for anything of the sort. But I also know that I shall never have more than a few friends. I've never had, and I shall always stand apart. This is the inevitable result of the international, wide-experienced life I've led. I can't be interested in John Jones and his local affairs. . . .

Richard didn't view his lack of close friends as a problem. And, in a way, he was right—for his unsociable nature was merely a symptom of a problem. Yet, he interpreted it as merely the result of his cosmopolitan nature. However, I believe that it was part and parcel of his need to keep traveling, and thereby placing himself in virtuoso, life-against-death situations—situations not encountered by the common man.

I realized after having read all his letters that the bulk of them seemed to lack any real emotion or passion, making them radically different from his books.

His letters seemed somehow a bit too intellectual to be believable. The sheer number of his letters home was blatant evidence of his deep devotion to his parents. But to me the letters seemed almost a compulsion. Normal emotion was deeply lacking in the text of Richard's letters. Sure, there were the "be assured I love you" type of phrases, but somehow they seemed too perfunctory. They came too automatically, too frequently, to be taken only at face value.

What was it that drove Richard on and on to adventure after adventure? Some writers have described it as a self-destructive impulse. Others have said that he was a reluctant adventurer driven by financial troubles. Those notions both intrigued and bothered me. I decided to call a few of the friends and relatives who had known Richard and listen to what they had to say about him. Maybe they could help clear up some of the quirks in Richard's personality that appeared throughout his letters.

The first person I interviewed was Irving Hockaday —one of Richard's roommates at Princeton, and his traveling companion in Europe. Mr. Hockaday had some very fond memories of Richard, and in the course of our conversation he provided me with an insight into the real Richard Halliburton. Hockaday said that Richard had always been different. He had a tremendous imagination and never wanted to be one of the crowd. As a freshman at Princeton, he was called "irresponsible"—a rebel who broke all the rules just for the sake of breaking them. I asked Irving whether he thought Richard had a secret death wish. He answered flatly in the negative and gave a little chuckle at my attempt to psychoanalyze. He replied, "Dick just wanted to get people to go out and experience the joy of life. He just wanted to go around the world and live a life of fun and adventure, as simple as that." In one sense, I think maybe it *was* just as simple as that. For I really do believe that we end up doing what we need to do. Irving Hockaday gave me a clue.

I talked to other roommates and relatives, many of whom wished to remain anonymous. I don't presume to know why they asked me not to mention their names, for they all pretty much agreed with what Hockaday had said. They described Halliburton as a charming, alluring adventurer who succeeded in stealing the hearts and fancies of young and old alike. He fulfilled their fantasies. But, more importantly, he succeeded in fulfilling his own fantasies and needs.

Richard was not a reluctant adventurer. He adored traveling. He needed to be an adventurer—a hero. And to say that Richard had a self-destructive impulse is too simplistic.

I had begun to question why Richard had never made any reference to romantic relationships with women. When speaking to his relatives and friends, they assured me that even though there had been rumors that he was homosexual, they felt that it was unfounded. In the final analysis, the composite image of Halliburton is clouded by the possibility of the label "homosexual." Obviously it was untenable for the American hero of adolescent boys to be a homosexual. It must have been hard to deal with the nasty little rumors maliciously whispered at dinner parties. Most people in the 1930s staunchly believed homosexuals to be lepers and social deviants. Was Richard a homosexual? I don't know. It would become a matter of importance only if Halliburton performed his larger-than-self feats of adventure and romance in order to mask his homosexuality. I wondered to what degree his adventures might have been undertaken to fulfill a need to certify his masculinity. His adventures would allow him a means of escaping the guilt that our society at the time imposed upon homosexuals. As an adventurer, rumors of homosexuality could be quelled.

The next person I wanted to speak to was William Alexander, the architect who had designed Richard's Hangover House in Laguna Beach. Though the house is one of the architectural monuments of California, Richard's parents had never approved of it. I wanted to find out what William Alexander knew about Richard.

William Alexander studied architecture with Frank Lloyd Wright and is a rather well-known celebrity among California architecture enthusiasts.

I met him in his antique and novelty shop, The Mart. Mr. Alexander was extremely cordial. Clearly, he enjoyed reminiscing about how and why he designed Halliburton's house. His impressions of Richard in the last seven years of his life were important ones, for they described an older man. Mr. Alexander seemed to believe that Halliburton's letters to his parents were a sham—that he did what most obedient, respecting children would do: he wrote what they wanted to hear. Mr. Alexander's point of view differed sharply from accounts I had been given that painted the traditional image of devoted son and doting parents. William Alexander told a different story, however—a story that seemed to contain more than just a grain of truth when I checked against the unedited (Richard's father had edited all of the correspondence), unpublished versions of Richard's letters to his parents.

According to Mr. Alexander, Richard's father was milking him for money and was partially to blame for Richard's constant debt. In the undoctored version of a letter to his parents, Richard wrote: "Just forget, of course, about the bank loan [Central Hanover]. It's down to $3,000 now, only $150 a year interest. And I'll reduce this by half before long. I'm going to keep nibbling away at your insurance debt too. When this is paid up, it will be a solid block of capital for us to draw on if ever necessary. . . ." Interestingly enough his father edited this letter to read: "Just forget about *my* [father's insertion] bank loan," etc. The second half of the doctored letter reads: ". . . keep nibbling away at your insurance, too." His father, it seems, was making a concentrated effort to hide the fact that he had been taking money from his son.

Mr. Alexander claimed that Richard's father had detested Dick's roommate Paul Mooney. I looked back through the letters and noticed that all references to Paul Mooney had been deleted. An idea was slowly coming into focus. It was beginning to look as if there were deeper complications to be found in Halliburton's personal relationships. I was now getting conflicting opinions as to what Richard Halliburton was all about. Just before I turned off the tape-recorder I asked Mr. Alexander whether rumors were correct: "Was Richard Halliburton a homosexual?"

He responded with a question. He asked whether homosexuality would have infringed upon Richard's writing. "It wouldn't take away from the man's charm or greatness."

I said that I realized that, and began to pack up my equipment.

He was right. Being a homosexual would not infringe upon one's ability or humanity. I don't mean to dwell on the question of whether Richard Halliburton was gay, for I most assuredly agree with Mr. Alexander that it would not have altered the man's achievements or fame. I just wonder what price, if any, he would have had to pay in order to prove that fact to his peers and his family.

I was beginning to learn the whereabouts of other people who had known Richard during the last decade of his life. In his thirties, he was beginning to realize that he couldn't continue the daring, death-defying stunts forever.

From all indications, he had decided to write a serious novel. It was to be a biography of the poet Rupert Brooke, another of his heroes. He had even made a pilgrimage to Brooke's grave on the island of Skyros. Rupert Brooke died at the age of twenty-eight while serving in the British navy. He is best remembered by the phrase: "If I should die, think only this of me: that there's some corner of a foreign field that is forever England. . . ." Rupert Brooke, an impassioned man of letters, had left his mark on the world and Richard was duly impressed. Halliburton's fame now trapped him. He knew that his audience would not want the serious novel under his own name. To pay his chronically overdue debts, he would have to "adventure." Moye Stephens, the pilot who flew Richard around the world for eighteen months, confirmed that Richard was aware of his own artistic predicament. And during those months together Richard had often complained about being a slave to a writing style that no longer amused or enthralled him. But he pressed on and wrote another travel thriller, *The Flying Carpet*, based on his experiences with Moye Stephens and his around-the-world jaunt.

Halliburton's life changed slowly. His popularity gradually declined. Lecture audiences were dwindling. Book sales were down. His father's debts needed paying. Despite his economic troubles, Richard had commissioned William Alexander to design and build the Hangover House in Laguna. He needed a new idea that would launch another adventure book. Walter Gaines Swanson, a San Francisco publicist, proposed that Richard go to Hong Kong, buy a junk, and sail it across the ocean, arriving in time for the opening of the San Francisco World's Fair. The feat demanded a handsome chunk of financing, and Richard encountered a bit of trouble obtaining it. He finally formed a corporation of young, semiexperienced sailing enthusiasts, some of whose well-to-do families put up a large portion of the money. Out of the entire crew of young men, only two—Bruce Potter and Gordon Torrey—had previous sailing experience. Strangely, both Potter and Torrey decided to leave the junk before its final sail. Today, both are still well and living on the East Coast. I decided to ask them to recount the events leading up to Halliburton's last glorious adventure.

Bruce Potter, who now lives in Miami, is quite an experienced yachtsman. His opinion was going to be a valuable lead toward discovering the ultimate fate of Richard Halliburton. We had a rather lengthy interview over the telephone. At the outset he warned me that his impressions were based on only one segment of Halliburton's life. The flashbacks streamed forth. Pot-

ter knew Halliburton when he was presumably under
quite a bit of stress. Halliburton couldn't find an ap-
propriate junk to purchase and so decided to build his
own. As the building of the junk got under way, the
difficulties began. The final price increased and money became more and more scarce. Potter knew that
Richard had mortgaged his new house and was in grave
financial trouble. "Dick was probably depending on
this voyage to get him out of debt," Potter guessed.
Strikes by Chinese laborers were frequent and caused
loss of valuable time. Richard's mooring at the fair
could not be reserved indefinitely. He had to reach San
Francisco pretty close to schedule.

The crew was totally inexperienced—they didn't
know the first thing about sailing. Halliburton signed a
Captain Welch to come aboard, in the hope that he
could shape up the crew. Potter described Welch as a
"sardonic, apoplectic" individual who had some experience as a tramp-steamer captain. Henry von
Fehren, a former ship's engineer, was hired as the *Sea
Dragon*'s engineer. Thus, there were only two really
professional sailing men on board.

When I asked Mr. Potter for his impressions of
Halliburton, he told me that Richard was quiet, not in
the least aggressive, and in fact almost introverted.
"Maybe he had a foreboding of the difficulties to come.
He never laughed and seemed to be deeply worried
about the trip." He continued to explain how time was
running out. They had missed their first scheduled
starting time, due to all the building delays. Mr. Potter
went on to say that from reading Richard's books he
had expected a completely different sort of person. His
image was of a lighthearted, untroubled, devil-may-
care individual. But the person he encountered seemed
worried.

Mr. Potter had only gratitude and respect for Richard. It seemed that Potter had had an accident shortly
after they set sail. He explained how Dick had saved
his life when he ordered the ship back to the mainland
hospital in order to enlist medical help. This return

voyage further delayed the ship. In the end, Potter was advised not to continue on the sail.

I asked Potter what he thought happened to the *Sea Dragon*. It had been my impression that junks were extremely seaworthy vessels and I didn't understand why Halliburton's ship did not survive the typhoon. Mr. Potter agreed: ordinary Chinese junks are indeed very seaworthy. But this was no ordinary junk. Richard wanted to make it as colorful as possible. He added poop decks, and a big heavy diesel engine, which rendered the boat unstable. Potter explained how when the boat was first lowered into the water, the portholes were underwater. After the first shakedown cruise, they began to realize just how unseaworthy the junk was. To compensate for design instability, they added a fin keel. "I guess it didn't do much to counterbalance the weight of the engine," Potter said.

"So you think they sunk in the typhoon?" I asked.

"Yes. From the last radio message, it seems pretty obvious that that was the case. Anyway, Richard Halliburton was a kind, gentle man. He just miscalculated, that's all."

I examined the last radio message the *Sea Dragon* sent. It read: "Southerly gales, squalls, lee rail under water . . . wet bunks, hard tack . . . bully beef . . . having wonderful time . . . wish you were here instead of me. Welch, Master."

"I see what you mean."

"Yeah," Mr. Potter said quietly.

Sometime in July 1940, Captain Charles Jokstad of the *President Pierce* liner reported seeing passing driftwood that resembled the rudder of a Chinese junk. He thought it was Halliburton's rudder. "What do you think?" I queried. "Well, I went out to inspect those pieces of driftwood, and the bolts were of brass. We didn't use brass bolts. That wasn't the *Sea Dragon*."

Gordon E. Torrey, the other crew member who did not set sail with Halliburton on his final voyage, had gone into the hospital for treatment of an illness and decided to remain in Hong Kong. I called him, and asked about his relationship with Halliburton. He told me that, unlike Potter, he was a paid hand and was not a friend of the Halliburton family, so his view would probably be a little different from Potter's. It was. Mr. Torrey liked Captain Welch. He didn't find him dictatorial at all. With a slight tinge of a Maine accent, he said: "Now, his qualifications were that he was a chief mate, and how much sailing background he had other than merchant vessels . . ." The question hung unanswered. In Torrey's opinion, Welch had little or no practical experience. "Anyway, he knew how to handle a crew," Torrey said, "and he also knew how to navigate and how to rig. So, in that sense, he was a very practical choice. His judgment in going I'd have to question."

"What do you mean?" I asked.

"Well," he said rather quickly, "it wasn't a typical junk for offshore purposes. It was a mixture of all types of junks that were found on the China coast. It was designed to be colorful, not practical."

"What was impractical about it?"

Torrey explained in great detail why the diesel engine would render the boat unseaworthy. He said that people had warned Halliburton that he would never make it in such a vessel. But Halliburton was stubborn, almost bullheaded. I asked the obvious question: "Did he seem bent on self-destruction?"

"That would be about it, yes. In other words, I am quite sure many people had made the observation that it wasn't a smart move to sail it across. It should have been carried across. That must have been obvious from the number of people who pointed that out—that the risk element was certainly very definitely there."

Pause. An uncomfortable silence began. Then he said he'd rather not disturb the good memory people had of Halliburton. He had read all of Halliburton's books before he'd met the man. He had formed an image of someone sensible, someone who knew the risks involved in adventure. Suffice it to say that he was disappointed when he met the real person.

Torrey mused on: "Halliburton seemed driven to make the trip despite everyone else's advice that it was too dangerous a trip on that particular junk. He seemed irresponsible. He took people along who couldn't know the real dangers in sailing the Pacific in such a vessel." He was silent again, then added, "You see what I mean. Why spoil his image?" Torrey was an extremely thoughtful man. He did not want to be involved in anything that might harm anyone. I understood his concern and felt it admirable.

His concluding remarks were very interesting and fit in with my hunch about the almost artificial, always a bit too intellectual tone of Richard's letters to his parents. It seems that Richard's mother had contacted Torrey after the tragedy and asked him to verify some of the things that Richard had written about the boat's seaworthiness. I began to remember that his letters home constantly reassured his parents about the boat's safety. He never hinted in the slightest that there was a possibility of any danger due to instability. Torrey said: "I gathered they couldn't understand, in view of all these assurances, how anything could possibly go wrong." I bade Torrey good day.

Richard was writing to calm his parents' nerves. He was telling them what they wanted to hear. All his letters seemed to carry this same ingredient. He craved their approval and at the same time rebelled against their staid lifestyle.

Richard wrote: "After weeks of discouraging delays and false starts, our junk was ready, definitely and at last, for its great adventure. Two thousand gallons of fresh water were aboard, enough oil to fuel our auxiliary engine for ten days, and a three months' supply of food for twelve men." What happened then?

Curiously, the last letter Richard wrote to his parents began with the phrase "One more—one last— goodbye letter." Did Richard have a foreboding? William Alexander had seen one of the last letters Paul Mooney (he was on the *Sea Dragon* when it sailed) wrote to a friend. It read: "You can't imagine the utter resignation and despair we feel in the voyage and nothing to look forward to except the end. G'Bye." I don't know when these words were written. But they sound as if they knew they were doomed. Richard's radio messages home provide some clues.

March 5, 1939. RADIO JUNK SEA DRAGON VIA SAN FRANCISCO SAILED AGAIN TODAY SOUNDER SHIP BETTER CREW FINE WEATHER RADIO SEA DRAGON SAN FRANCISCO POSTAL TELEGRAPH HURRYING HOME LOVE

March 13, 1939. RADIO JUNK SEA DRAGON VIA SAN FRANCISCO 1200 MILES AT SEA ALLS WELL

March 19, 1939. RADIO JUNK SEA DRAGON VIA SAN FRANCISCO HALFWAY MIDWAY ARRIVING APRIL FIFTH SKIPPING HONOLULU WRITE CARE PANAMERICAN MIDWAY AIRMAIL LOVE

March 24, 1939. RADIO CAPTAIN JOHN WELCH OF THE SEA DRAGON TO LINER PRESIDENT COOLIDGE SOUTHERLY GALES RAIN SQUALLS LEE RAIL UNDER WATER WET BUNKS HARDTACK BULLY BEEF HAVING WONDERFUL TIME WISH YOU WERE HERE INSTEAD OF ME. . . .

That was that. After this last message, the entire crew of the *Sea Dragon* vanished, never to be heard from again.

The *New York Times* carried the story. They reported the findings of the rather scant search parties. On March 30, 1939, S. W. Fenton, marine superintendent of the Mackay Radio Commission in San Francisco, expressed fear for the *Sea Dragon*'s safety. He asked ships in the vicinity to watch out for the junk.

The Navy Department radioed the commandant at Pearl Harbor, Hawaii, and at Manila to watch out for Halliburton. This was on March 31, 1939.

On April 2, 1939, the *New California Clipper* joined other ocean craft to search for the junk. Still no sign.

But all these searches seemed rather casual and very unofficial. They were incidental rather than planned.

Finally, on May 16, after much prodding, the navy agreed to have the *Astoria* "unofficially" look for Halliburton on its way back from Japan.

On June 1, 1939 the *New York Times* reported the *Astoria*'s findings. After searching 152,000 square miles of ocean, no trace was found. The *Astoria* was equipped with four planes.

In the United States Naval Institute Proceedings of June 1939, this report was filed by Mr. Albert Wetjen: "If the *Sea Dragon* encountered such weather as we did on the night of March 23, and she undoubtedly did, there is small chance that the little craft survived."

On October 4, 1939, Halliburton was legally declared dead. A jury verdict decreed that he had died on March 23 or 24, thus noting that he was near the international dateline.

But some people, including myself, see October 4 as a relatively short amount of time from March 23 or 24. I don't really think there is much weight to be placed in favor of theories that Richard is alive today. But why the rush? Why was everyone, including his parents, so willing to concur with the official accounts? I don't know yet. But there are a few more pieces of evidence to explore.

One theory was that the ship could have been captured by Japanese warships. Richard had prepared for this eventuality, however, and had procured a safe-conduct-of-passage paper before he sailed. Not that papers ever meant much to "enemies," but there was never any evidence to substantiate this theory.

Was he captured by Chinese pirates? No one I talked to, including Potter and Torrey, was able to lend much credence to that possibility.

On June 11, 1939, The *New York Times* wrote in memorial: "One wished that he could be one day rescued from a South Sea Island with a new book written entirely on tapa cloth with ink made from the juice of the sea urchin." Rumors that he might still be alive today probably emanated from just such a musing. Did Richard end his days incognito on some remote island?

Was this how he would choose to finally escape the demands of his fans?

Richard's escape was through adventure and the subsequent fame that surrounded each escapade. It was in his travels that he felt liberated. It's been said that all of us attempt to escape painful situations in one way or another. We try to create a space in which we can successfully deal with our environment. We design lifestyles that facilitate and enhance our ability to cope with unspoken fears and hidden dreads. Some people eat themselves to death. Others drink. Others work nonstop. And still others, like Halliburton, carve a singular path unique to their desires.

I have tried to divine Halliburton's innermost needs by examining what he wrote about himself as well as what others felt compelled to say about him. I wondered what floated beneath his mysterious and joyous addiction to adventure and romance and his funny set of noble ideals. The *New York Times* of October 6, 1939, wrote this obituary: "He was an amusing fellow who told many tall tales and wanted to be talked about, but he did not expect to be taken seriously. . . ."

They were only partially right. Richard did indeed want to be talked about. He once told a roommate at Princeton that the worst thing that could happen to him was for people not to talk about him. But the question that needs asking is, why?

Richard created a fantasy land of romance and noble ideals where he was the shining star. He wanted to stand apart. He wrote in his first book, *The Royal Road to Romance:*

I looked behind me at my 4 roommates bent over their desks dutifully grubbing their lives away. . . . What futility it all was—stuffing themselves with profitless facts and figures, when the vital and the beautiful things of life—the moonlight, the apple orchards, the out-of-door sirens—were calling and pleading for recognition.

A rebellion against the prosaic mold into which all 5 of us were being poured rose up inside me. I flung my book away and rushed out of the apartment on the throbbing shadowy campus. . . . A wave of exultation swept over me. Youth—nothing else worth having in the world . . . and I had youth, the transitory, the fugitive, now completely and abundantly.

In our youths we all rebelled against the establishment. But after a while the rebellion softens and we proceed to live in a less desperate manner. Richard never did stop living intensely. What was driving him in the face of approaching age? He admitted that he was growing weary of all these feats of daring, yet he continued. What propelled him? What was he running from?—or to?

I can't presume to know the ultimate answer to that question. I do believe that Richard was truly an adventurer. Through his escapades he fulfilled a personal need to think of himself as different, unique, unconventional, and therefore worthy of his family's respect and ultimately the world's admiration. He didn't have many friends. People tended to bore him. He lived for godlike ideals while seemingly maintaining that other people lived on the mundane level. Perhaps there was something in Halliburton's character that made his dramatic disappearance inevitable.

The adventurer is a symbol. He is a symbol not of courage but of a posture resembling courage, an intellectualization of courage. Richard's letters are an example of intellectuality in the extreme.

The questions persist. Was his last trip an unconscious suicide mission? He had always said he wanted to die young. Maybe he had unconsciously fulfilled that desire. Other people say that he was a man who kept up a front—a man who was subject to depression. Others deny this. They claim they never saw him sad— he was always gay and charming. But Moye Stephens said that in the eighteen months they flew with each other he never really got that close to him.

Richard Halliburton was probably all of these things.

He was a hero and a legend in his own time. He didn't perform his stunts of daring in order to die; on the contrary, I think he had always believed that only through adventure would he finally begin to live.

2

Percy Fawcett

In 1925, at the age of fifty-eight, Colonel Percy Harrison Fawcett, his son Jack, and Raleigh Rimmel set out on an expedition in Brazil in search of the lost city of "Z." They never returned. During the next thirty years, more than half a dozen search expeditions were launched in order to discover the fate of the Fawcett party. Then rescue parties searched for rescue parties. Rumors still persist. To the present day, no conclusive evidence concerning the ultimate fate of the Fawcett expedition has been uncovered. Myriad stories regarding their end are still being proposed by spiritualists, anthropologists, eccentrics, and explorers.

What was it about Fawcett that prompted this worldwide investigation? Was it the exotic nature of his search for a lost city that intrigued people, or was the fascination generated by the romantic nature of the man himself? Endless stories developed around the fate of the Fawcett expedition, but uncertainty surrounds even the most tentative conclusions. Of the possible fates, "killed by hostile Indians" receives the most attention. Death by disease is given little credence, perhaps because it seems wholly unfit to consider so mundane an end for such an extraordinary man. Romantics —and I number myself in their camp—favor the notion that in some way Fawcett found Shangri-La and had no reason ever to return to our mortal coil.

I gathered all the available data. The *New York*

Times had carried stories on the Fawcett mystery from 1925 up until 1965. A colorful conglomeration of magazine articles and books written by interested "searchers" were at my disposal, begging for review. I wanted to amass all the oddities surrounding the Fawcett story. As a starting point, I delved into the background of the explorer. What kind of man stimulated such global commotion? Who was Percy Fawcett?

Brian Fawcett, Percy's only surviving son, once said that many people branded his father a dreamer, an eccentric, someone easily dismissed. But Brian took issue with that facile tag; he said "dreamer" could describe anyone whose imagination is vivid enough to envision the infinite possibilities of discovery—anyone whose imagination is unfettered by the shackles of accepted, sound, scientific truths. "Dreamer" connotates an investigator, an explorer, one whose ceaseless thirst for knowledge impels him toward the mysterious horizons of man. But as I read about the colonel's life, I discovered that the word *dreamer* only partially described Percy Harrison Fawcett.

Percy Fawcett was born in 1867 in Torquay, England. His father was an officer in the British army and passed on the mantle of military life to his son. Percy attended the Royal Military Academy in Woolwich. After graduation, he served in Ceylon, Hong Kong, Ireland, and Malta. First and foremost he was a military officer, and apparently he was a good one. Fawcett used his free time to write travel articles. As his writing skills increased, he began to dabble in the occult. Time and again in his various works he mentions the prospect of discovering buried treasure and lost cities.

Beyond his military skills and his writing ability, Fawcett also was an accomplished engineer and sportsman. In his twenties he built two successful racing yachts, patented the "ichythoid" curve, which added knots to the speed of a cutter, and was offered the position of design consultant by a well-known company of yacht builders.

Fawcett was a rare mixture of the mystic and the man of action, thirsting alternately for knowledge and for adventure. He served for approximately seven years as a subaltern in the Royal Artillery at Trincomalee, a seaport in Ceylon. There he became interested in Buddhism, and also spent all his available time and money on a futile quest for the buried treasure of Ceylon's ancient Kandyan kings. He was, in addition, a Founder's Medallist of the Royal Geographical Society, an award given to him for his efforts in mapping Ceylon's wilderness.

From 1906 to 1909 he was the boundary commissioner for the Bolivian government. He accomplished the delimitation of the disputed borderline between Bolivia and Peru, and during this time he made several expeditions into the Brazilian/Bolivian frontier, where he learned the rigors and rewards of exploration in the tropical jungles of that region. When World War I erupted, he returned to England to serve with distinction on the Western Front. After the war he revisited Brazil and began to concentrate all his energies on a quest for the lost city that he called "Z."

In 1925 he set out with his son Jack and Mr. Raleigh Rimmel, Jack's friend, on an expedition into the Mato Grosso to find this lost city and clues to its civilization. This was to be his eighth and final expedition into the Brazilian hinterlands. He never returned: The Mato Grosso had swallowed three more men. I had traveled enough in that incredible jungle wilderness to understand how simple it is to disappear. Tributaries of the Amazon provide passage into remote back-country areas. The Mato Grosso covers 350,000 square miles of jungle. In the so-called Fawcett area, no two maps agree; information reported routinely for other regions of the earth is, for large sections of the Brazilian jungle, marked "Unknown," "Doubtful," or "?".

Crocodiles and anacondas, twenty- to thirty-foot constricting snakes, guard the riverbanks. Panthers prowl the jungle floor. Macaws and monkeys howl a raucous song. For the explorer, the real hazards are the damp-borne fungus that erodes the skin, the malarial mosquito, and the encephalitis-carrying fly. If exploring the Mato Grosso is adventure, it is an adventure in pain.

As Fawcett entered the Mato Grosso, it was in every sense of the phrase virgin territory. The headquarters of the great northward-flowing tributaries of the Amazon—the Araguaia and the Zingo—bracketed unchartered territory. Between the Xingu and the Tapojós there were huge tracts of forest jungle that no white man had ever attempted to enter. Prehistoric monsters, white Indians, the ruined city of Atlantis, the Lost Mines of the Martyrs, each and every one of these had been thought to exist in this exotic region. But Fawcett was after the lost city of "Z."

Almost everything written about the Fawcett story suggested the explorer's strange, overwhelming obsession with finding an ancient culture that would predate Egyptian civilization and ultimately solve the riddle of Atlantis. Fawcett had made an exhaustive study of the regional folklore and discovered that all the stories he had collected agreed in one important respect: This was the location of the lost city. In all cases the information seemed to point to an unexplored region known as the Xingu country.

Fawcett's papers collected in *Lost Trails, Lost Cities* reveal him to be a man of unlimited courage and endurance. Jungle hardships, insects, fever, and privation did not seem to faze him. Where his companions would falter and pale before the exacting challenge of exploration, Fawcett would rally. He was self-reliant and fearless, yet never foolhardy. He was a thoughtful and philosophical man with a rather progressive perspective on the Mato Grosso jungle Indians. His extreme open-mindedness enabled him to learn effective folk cures from the Indians, which later greatly facilitated his expeditions. He was amused by both the anthropologists' and the general public's frequent use of the term *savages* when referring to the Indians.

He caught himself using the term and mused on the irony of the nomenclature that "civilized folk" employed. Finding himself in Brazil during the rubber boom, he witnessed the atrocities that the whites committed against one another in their hungry acquisition of fortune, and most of all those they committed against the native Indians of Brazil.

Critics have said that Fawcett combined the discipline of the scientist-engineer with the imaginative daring of a man unafraid to gamble his life on bold, innovative conjectures. He was not afraid to believe that the improbable was possible. He told the story of a basalt figure Sir Rider Haggard had given him. It seemed that whenever Fawcett held this object he felt a strong electric current. Wanting to know the figure's secret, he took it to scientists, who, after examining it, were at a complete loss for an explanation. He then went to a psychometrist, who, while holding the object in his hand, began to tell Fawcett of the lost city of Atlantis, almost completely forgotten, living now only as rumor and myth. This story was strangely similar to other stories he had collected. Fawcett vowed to carry this basalt figure with him on his 1925 expedition, as he believed it to be somehow connected to "Z."

In his journal Fawcett also described the existence of poltergeists. He wrote that he heard something roaming about his room at night, but only later did he find out that the hut he stayed in was believed by the townspeople to be haunted. He never made too much of these psychic phenomena, just accepted them, minus the awe which could have dangerously hindered him from his ultimate goal. He respected the beliefs of the Indians as realistic possibilities until they were proved otherwise. He got along with the "dreaded savages" where others failed. The Indians always accepted and helped him during his expeditions. Thus, the hypothesis that he was murdered by them in 1925 is difficult to accept.

His wife was one of the key forces that kept the searches alive for almost thirty years. She claimed that she was in touch with him telepathically and that he was still alive, but detained and could not get away. Conflicting stories that piled up over the years did lend some substance to her claims, but, of course, conclusive evidence of their fate is yet to be found.

Fawcett wasn't a die-hard fanatic. He sometimes had his doubts about the many rumored "lost" cities, but he always made enough progress to keep him going. And when in 1911 Hiram Bingham discovered Machu Picchu, in Peru, Fawcett was strongly encouraged. (Bingham uncovered the fabled lost city that he first called Villacabamba, thought for centuries to be just a myth.) Fawcett knew the risks he faced better than did most men, and he admitted that there were tremendous odds against his party returning. In *Lost Trails, Lost Cities* he stated:

> If we should not come out . . . I don't want rescue parties to come in looking for us. It's too risky. If with all my experience we can't make it, there's not much hope for others. That's one reason why I'm not telling exactly where we're going. Whether we get through and emerge again or leave our bones to rot in there, one thing's certain. The answer to the enigma of Ancient South America—and perhaps of the pre-historic world—may be found when those old cities are located and opened up to scientific research. That the cities exist, I know. . . .

"It is certain," he wrote not long before his disappearance, "that amazing ruins of ancient cities, ruins incomparably older than those in Egypt, exist in the far interior of Mato Grosso."

Francisco de Orellana was the first explorer of the Amazon. In 1541, while serving as a lieutenant with Gonzalo Pizarro's Napo expedition, Orellana was sent ahead with a brigantine and fifty soldiers to find provisions for the troops. When he finally reached the junction of Napo and Marañon rivers, he decided not to return to Pizarro but to continue down the Marañon River.

During the course of his voyage he encountered various tribes of river Indian who told him of a village populated by female warriors. Later, Orellana claimed to have met these warriors near the mouth of the Trombetas, a tributary of the Amazon. The main river derived its name from this story.

Orellana reached the Atlantic Ocean in 1542 and proceeded on to Spain. There he told the Royal Court of the hoards of gold and cinnamon that he had seen while on his voyage. He sought the right to explore and loot the lands he had just discovered.

His return to the Amazon proved a disaster. Ships and men were lost on the passage. Orellana's vessel capsized near the mouth of the Amazon and he was never seen again, but the legend of gold had been seeded.

Fawcett had maintained his belief in lost cities for a long time and based it specifically on a document he found in the archives at Rio de Janeiro. This document was the log of a 1743 Portuguese expedition that set out in search of lost silver and gold mines. The expedition went north from Minas Gerais and never reappeared. It was rumored that they had made an incredible discovery. One account told of their finding a jagged mountain range. Climbing up a crevice in one of the precipitous sides, they emerged on a rich tableland and saw before them the outlines of a city—a city massively built with huge blocks of stone, and absolutely deserted. It appeared to have been devastated by an earthquake. Most astounding of all, its buildings and monuments bore hieroglyphic inscriptions seemingly inspired by Egyptian texts.

Fawcett felt that the story was too compelling to be dismissed, and that "uneducated adventurers could hardly invent an account so closely corroborated by the cyclopean remains now familiar to so many."

High above the central arch characters of some sort were graven deeply into the weatherworn stone. . . . On either side were two-storied houses built of great

blocks fitting together with mortarless joins of almost incredible accuracy, the porticos, narrow
above and wide below, decorated with elaborate carvings of what they took to be demons. . . . In most
cases inner walls had collapsed, covering the floors
with debris, and the bat droppings of centuries
formed a thick carpet under foot. . . . Bats in
countless thousands winged in circles through the
dim chambers and the acrid reek of their droppings
was suffocating. . . . Here in the center was a huge
column of black stone, and upon it the effigy of a
man in perfect preservation, with one hand on his
hip and the other pointing towards the north. . . .
The figure of a youth was carved over what seemed
to be the principal doorway. It portrayed a beardless figure naked from the waist up, with shield in
hand and a band across one shoulder. . . . Below
were inscribed characters remarkably like those of
ancient Greece. Raposo [the name that Fawcett ar-
bitrarily chose to identify the unknown discover-
er] copied them down and reproduced them in his
narrative. . . . I know that Raposo's lost city is not
the only one of its kind. The late British Consul at
Rio was taken to such a place in 1913. . . . It, too,
was distinguished by the remains of a statue on a
great black pedestal in the middle of a square.

According to Fawcett, its general location and surrounding topography were known to only three men:
a Frenchman who had made several unsuccessful attempts to find "Z"; an Englishman who before he
left the country was suffering from cancer and probably died in the search; and the writer (Colonel Fawcett).

Fawcett was an interesting and romantic figure, and
he possessed inexhaustible knowledge of Indians, their
customs and country. It seems more than likely that he
could have survived where others would certainly have
perished. In 1925, on his eighth and final expedition,
he was traveling lightly. This was in keeping with his
theory that a few select men, living off the land,
would have more chance of survival than would a

more cumbersome expedition. Fawcett wrote: "All exploration across, as opposed to expeditions into, these regions depends for its success on the selection of a limited personnel, and if need be, to do without transport under extremely trying conditions." Therefore, pack animals were not advised, for drinking water was scarce, the jungle was dense, and the insects were harmful to all beasts of burden. One couldn't depend on porters either. According to Fawcett, most of the tribes feared and hated their neighbors, causing the Indians to be reluctant to accompany explorers beyond the limits of their own tribal territories. Moreover, food was a problem; "game," wrote Fawcett, "is nowhere plentiful in this country; there is usually enough to feed a small party, but never a large one." So, Fawcett departed in 1925 accompanied only by his son Jack and Raleigh Rimmel. They carried their own provisions and equipment.

Financed partially by the North American Newspaper Alliance, Fawcett and his two companions, on April 20, 1925, set off from Cuiabá with two guides. They went north over the same trail that Fawcett had followed in 1920, and on May 29 they reached a place called Dead Horse Camp, where one of Fawcett's animals had died on his previous expedition. Fawcett told his friend W. S. Barclay, a fellow member of the Royal Geographical Society, not to be concerned if he did not return for five years; he had intended to cover up his tracks, and would indicate his objective only vaguely; obviously he was anxious to discourage anyone from following him. On March 14, 1925, Fawcett sent a letter to Mr. Ahrens, the German consul back at Cuiabá, in which he wrote, "I'm not giving you any closer information as to locality, because I don't want to encourage any tragedy for an expedition, inspired to follow our footsteps under the impression it is an easy matter. . . . For the present *no one else* can venture it without encountering certain catastrophe."

From Dead Horse Camp, Fawcett sent back his last dispatch to the North American Newspaper Alliance.

It is dated May 20, and it ends: "Our guides go back from here. They are more and more nervous as we push further into the Indian territory. . . . I shall continue to prepare dispatches from time to time, in hopes of being able to get them out eventually through some friendly tribe of Indians. But I doubt this will be possible." As it turned out, it was not. Other than a rash of wild rumors, no authentic news of Fawcett has materialized since that last message.

In the subsequent years Fawcett's fate offered a fascinating field for speculation. Spiritualists, worldwide, took an interest in the colonel's destiny. Some claimed to have received communications from him, telling them that he was being held captive by an Indian tribe. Speculations abounded. Was he alive? Had he been made a god? Had he been killed by savages? Had he voluntarily renounced civilization in favor of the jungle?—a speculation that Mrs. Fawcett was inclined to believe, because she knew that her husband had always loved the "primeval sweetness" of the jungle and its natives. During his twenty-four-year marriage, fourteen years were spent in the Brazilian jungles.

Mrs. Fawcett believed that her husband had survived. Her faith was strengthened from time to time by telepathic communications she allegedly received through various intermediaries. On September 13, 1927, the *New York Times* reported that Mrs. Isacke, Colonel Fawcett's sister, had said, "It is very likely he is settled in Brazil. . . . Mrs. Fawcett isn't worried and is in daily telepathic touch with him and knows he will not come home 'til he succeeds." Mrs. Isacke added, "All his life he has been a mesmerist. He has tremendous will power which seems to awe the Indians. Even if they come to attack, they are soon overcome by his will. He has even pacified cannibals." According to other telepathic messages, the explorer was not only safe but had reached his lost city. Francis Gow Smith, an American explorer, told reporters that he believed Fawcett was really looking for the Mines of the Martyrs, discovered in the early eighteenth century by Bartholomew Bueno.

In 1955 Brian Fawcett, Colonel Fawcett's younger son, made a reconnaissance flight over the supposed city of "Z" and another lost city, "Sete Cidades." Brian claimed that what his father and others believed to be remains of man-made courses of masonry turned out to be merely an illusion—a freak erosion of nature. When referring to the Sete Cidades he stated, "My father had believed implicitly in its genuineness, and I wondered if he would have pursued his quest to his undoing had he visited it before the fatal expedition." The answer is unknown. Recognizing that "Z" was only an illusion of nature, did Fawcett continue his quest in search of yet another location of "Z," refusing to abandon his dream?

In the epilogue of his father's work *Lost Trails, Lost Cities,* Brian wrote:

> . . . They may have managed to penetrate the barrier of savage tribes and reach their objective. If that were so, and if the tradition is true that the last remnants of the ancient race had indeed protected their sanctuary by ringing themselves round with fierce savages, what chance would there be of returning—thus breaking the age-long secrecy so faithfully preserved? . . . It is possible that the riddle may never be solved. . . .

Prior to the final expedition, Fawcett had told his friends that a prolonged absence was more likely to mean success than failure. But by 1927 grave anxiety regarding his whereabouts was beginning to emerge. On June 21, 1927, the *New York Times* reported that the Royal Geographical Society (R.G.S.) would aid any competent explorer who would go in search of Colonel Fawcett. They stressed that the expedition was not to be one of relief but one of inquiry, due to the circumstances of Fawcett's mission.

According to the *New York Times* of September 11, 1927, a Mr. Courteville claimed he had seen

Fawcett little more than a hundred miles from his starting point (an easy dispatch distance). He said he had spoken to a mysterious, bearded white man sitting by the side of the road. Mosquitoes were biting the old man's legs. Courteville said that they exchanged a few words on insects in general. When Courteville returned to Cuiabá, he was told that this man must have been Percy Fawcett. However, the R.G.S. never confirmed this story. And after meeting and questioning Courteville in Lima, Brian Fawcett thought the story to be another frivolous rumor.

The first official search expedition supported by the R.G.S. was led by Commander George Dyott in May 1928. It was financed partially by an American newspaper syndicate. Dyott traced Fawcett from Dead Horse Camp down the Rio Kuliseu to a village of the Anauqua Indians, where the chief's son had a small brass plate hanging around his neck, stamped with the name of a firm that had sold Fawcett some supplies in 1924. Aloique, the chief, guided Dyott on a three-day journey across country to the Rio Kuluene, the banks of which are inhabited at that point by the Kalapalos Indians. Here Dyott was told, via sign-language communication, that Fawcett and his two "lame" companions (according to the last dispatch, only Raleigh Rimmel was lame) had been murdered. The Kalapalos Indians were convinced that they had been murdered by the Anauqua Indians, but Aloique said it was the nearby Suy Indians who had murdered them.

Dyott suspected Aloique himself to be the murderer. Aloique said that the bones lay only four or five days' march east of their present position and offered to show Dyott evidence to verify his story. Impending trouble with surrounding Indian tribes, however, made Dyott reluctant to take Aloique up on his offer.

No bodies were ever found, and no conclusive evidence was discovered to support Dyott's theory. Yet, the R.G.S. accepted this story as final and official.

Many people, including the Fawcett family, found

the theory highly questionable. The equipment that Dyott found could have been from Fawcett's 1920 expedition. Communication through sign language leaves much to the imagination; and it has never been proved beyond doubt what route Fawcett followed after he left Dead Horse Camp.

On September 27, 1928, the *New York Times* reported that the Brazilian press denied that Fawcett had been killed by the Indians, but claimed that Dyott had fabricated a romance for the newspaper syndicate that had financed him. Further, the Brazilian press said that Dyott had followed only the customary route that travelers use and that Fawcett had headed for unexplored areas.

In 1930, A. H. Morris set out on an expedition in search of the missing party. Morris was led to believe that the colonel was being held captive by the Indians, because Lampeo, a famous South American bandit, had given him a revolver, compass, and leather pouch that bore the initials P. H. F. No further evidence was ever found to prove his belief.

April 21, 1931—Julian Duguid began another search expedition. He believed that Fawcett was a prisoner of the Indians and compared Fawcett's fate to that of a German explorer who had been a captive of the Indians for fifteen years. Again, nothing of any consequence was discovered.

In 1931, Vincenzo Petrullo, an anthropologist at the University of Pennsylvania Museum, corroborated Dyott's theory as to the location of Fawcett's murder by Indians, thereby strengthening this officially accepted theory.

No further light was shed on the Fawcett mystery for some time. Sporadic expeditions followed but revealed nothing. Captain Vladimir Perfillieff of the Mato Grosso undertook an expedition in 1930 and found nothing. Elizabeth Steen of the University of California went into the jungle with her maid and an Indian guide. Leonard L. Legter, a Philadelphian missionary, reported that he had found traces of Fawcett's death—but he had no conclusive evidence.

As the years passed, the chances of Fawcett still being alive became more and more remote. Then suddenly, in March 1932, a Swiss trapper named Stephan Rattin came out of the Mato Grosso with a very curious story, which he related to the British consulate at São Paulo. Rattin claimed that Fawcett was a prisoner of an Indian tribe north of the river Bomfin, a tributary of the São Manoel River. He said he had spoken to an old man clad in skins, with a long yellowish-white beard and long hair. Rattin claimed he was a white man. He spoke English and told Rattin that he was an English colonel. According to *Lost Trails, Lost Cities,* the old man who was thought to be Fawcett said:

"Go to the English consulate and ask them to tell Major Paget, who has a coffee farm in the State of São Paulo, that I am a captive here. . . ." The old man enquired whether I [Rattin] had any paper, and took me to his tent. . . . He showed me four blocks of wood on which he had made rough sketches with a sharp stone. I copied these as best I could. . . . He wore four gold rings. He was about 65, approximate height 5′ 11″ and powerfully built. . . . I never heard of Col. Fawcett until I arrived at Barretos.

Rattin later identified Fawcett's photograph from among others submitted to him. The mention of Major Paget lent some credence to his report. But Brian Fawcett doubted that the man Rattin had spoken to was his father. He said that his father knew that Sir Ralph Paget had long ago returned to England and that he even had visited him in Sittingbourne, Kent. He claimed his father had never worn such a collection of rings and was well over six feet tall. He also wondered why the man hadn't identified himself and why he had spoken English. Rattin's English wasn't very good, but presumably they both were fluent in Portuguese. Be that as it may, Rattin made no financial demands, nor did he seek publicity. And in 1932 he set out to find the old man once more. Rattin was never heard from again.

I think Rattin's story might have been too easily dismissed. The portrait derived from the tale does not fit the image most people held of Fawcett. How could a swashbuckling adventurer be reduced to a babbling old man? I couldn't help thinking of what might have happened to the mind of a man who had dedicated a quarter of a century to finding a grail called "Z" and found in the end nothing but endless jungle.

Percy Fawcett had always loved the jungle and its pure exotic nature. He was restless with family life and subject to deep depression if forced to refrain too long from exploration. Of the twenty-four years he was married, he spent only ten years with his family.

If he had failed to find "Z" after his last arduous hunt, what might he have done? I tried to put myself in his place. Past sixty, plagued by ebbing strength, and deeply attached to a goal that was becoming unrealizable, would I have returned to so-called civilization? I was forced to conclude that I might have chosen to live out my days in the familiar environs of the jungle.

No one ever did follow up Rattin's story. Everyone assumed that the real Colonel Fawcett would be totally rational and sane. The possibilities of senility or psychological flight from reality were never even suggested. Another return to civilization might have been too much for him to bear; after all, he was nearing sixty and approaching the end of his venturesome lifestyle.

Rattin's story sparked another flurry of expeditions initiated by scientific explorers as well as adventure-seeking opportunists and eccentrics. In December 1932 an Italian explorer named Michael Angel Trucchi said that he had found Fawcett three years earlier, in November 1929, at the junction of the Manso and Araguaia rivers in the state of Mato Grosso. He said Fawcett was the Guida Indian chief and that he had saved his [Trucchi's] life from the Guidas, provided that Trucchi would promise to keep the secret of Fawcett's whereabouts for three years.

In 1933 *The New York Times* reported that Fawcett was alive and held captive by the Cuicuru tribe.

In 1934 a Paulista constructor said he knew that the Fawcetts were alive. They reportedly lived near the Xingu River. Jack had married the daughter of an Indian cacique and had two children.

The *Geographical Journal* of September 1942 reported that Miss Martha Moennich, a missionary just arrived from the Xingu, sent Mrs. Fawcett a group of photographs of a white boy named Du-ri-pe living with the Kuicuro (perhaps another spelling of "Cuicuru") tribe. He was believed to be the son of Jack Fawcett. Duripe was later proved to be an albino Indian. George Dyott claimed that just prior to Jack Fawcett's birth, an Indian witch doctor prophesied that Jack would eventually marry an Indian chief's daughter and that he and his father would be captives of the tribe. This could explain many of the popular theories. However, all the rumors were just that—rumors—there was no proof, and were all later substantially discounted by Brian Fawcett, who thoroughly investigated all of these claims.

Life magazine reported that in 1951, Orlando Vilas Boas of the Central Brazil Foundation won a "confession" from Izarari, chief of the Kalapalos tribe. Izarari confessed to having slain the explorer. But after collecting the promised reward, Izarari admitted that his story was a hoax. But Vilas Boas persisted, and after the death of Izarari he won the "truth" from the new chief, Comatzi. The new chief disclosed the grave of the murdered explorer and the bones were unearthed. Upon examination by the Royal Anthropological Institute in London, the bones were pronounced not to be those of Fawcett. The Vilas Boas theory was still a favored tale, but this time by the Brazilian press. Even after the Royal Anthropologi-

cal Institute's findings, the Brazilian press asked Brian
Fawcett to make an expedition into Mato Grosso with
Vilas Boas in order to satisfy the irate Brazilian au-
thorities who claimed that their Indians "do not lie."

According to Brian Fawcett in *Ruins in the Sky,*
in 1955 a Brazilian writer who published articles in a
popular weekly magazine claimed that Fawcett and
his son were "advanced souls" alive in a subterranean
city called Matatu-Aracauga in the Roncador region of
Mato Grosso. The writer said that there were several
such underground cities in Brazil where dwelt great
spiritual avatars who ruled the world's events. From
these secret places Fawcett and others issued flying
saucers to make reconnaissance flights.

In 1965 Fred Salazar of Queens, New York, left
for Brazil to meet with the Indians and, he told reporters, try to gather more details about Fawcett's disappearance. He believed that Fawcett had died without
violence.

The number of search expeditions launched for
Fawcett runs into the hundreds—testimony to the excitement that the Fawcett story provoked. But to this
day the riddle remains unsolved.

Why did relief explorers insist that Fawcett's route
followed the Xingu territory? Fawcett himself had
been very vague about his plans, in order to discourage
any relief expeditions. Moreover, Mrs. Fawcett insisted that he would not have gone to the Xingu in
1925. She was convinced that he wasn't going to explore any territory that he had previously explored.
On still another count, why were there such insistent
claims that the Fawcett party had been killed by Indians? In 1928 the R.G.S. accepted as final, without
any conclusive evidence, Dyott's hypothesis of "murder by Indians." Explorers like Petrullo went out of
their way to corroborate that theory. In 1951 this same
kind of theory was again pushed. It was believed that
certain British societies or the government itself had
offered a substantial reward for the finding of Faw-

cett's remains. This could answer why the Brazilian authorities were so adamant about the skull-and-bones theory. But this alleged promise of a reward has never been substantiated.

Other Fawcett-trackers have wondered why the colonel chose such inexperienced travel companions. They conjectured that only with inexperienced explorers would Fawcett have been able to impose his every wish.

The *Saturday Review* of June 11, 1953, reported: Fawcett was a decent, intelligent (if somewhat warped) human who threw off the shackles of modern scholastic dogmatism. . . . His book—obviously the disciplined revelation of a tortured soul—indicates why his family may well have thought that he voluntarily disappeared: throughout he displays a yearning for the simple primitive life—and at times even an envy for the several civilized people—educated university-bred Englishmen—whom he met after they threw off all civilization.

Could Fawcett have disappeared voluntarily? Could it have been a conscious decision?

Very few solid facts can be gleaned from the mass of jungle gossip. The din of ambient rumor blurs the real signals from the noise and rattle. History and legend become one and the same. Official opinion of "death by Indians" was never proved and served only to inflame popular opinion. The public's imagination soared to new heights. Fact became fiction. Fiction became fact. Fawcett became legend.

Concluding the last paper he wrote before his final expedition, Colonel Percy Fawcett stated:

If the journey is not successful my work in South America ends in failure, for I can never do any more. I must inevitably be discredited as a visionary, and branded as one who had only personal enrichment in view. Who will ever understand that I want no glory from it—no money for myself—that I'm doing it unpaid in the hope that its ultimate benefit to mankind will justify the years spent in the quest?

Percy Fawcett's last words to his wife were: "You need have no fear of any failure. . . ." Perhaps he was right.

3

Amelia Earhart

On July 2, 1937, slightly after 2:45 A.M., Amelia Earhart's voice, faint and faraway, interrupted the radio static on wavelength 3105: "Cloudy and overcast . . . headwinds." Amelia Earhart was on the last leg of her round-the-world flight.

The coast-guard cutter *Itasca* picked up the message. The radioman quickly sent out a long series of *A*'s, the homing signal on which KHAQQ (Earhart's call letters) could obtain a position bearing. *Itasca*'s Commander Thompson felt relieved and settled down to wait for Amelia's next radio message, scheduled for 3:15 A.M. But it did not come until 3:45: "*Itasca* from Earhart . . . *Itasca* from Earhart . . . Overcast . . . Will listen on one hour and half hour at 3105."

Amelia hadn't given any position bearings, the key code was not used, and the standard marine 500-kilocycle frequency was ignored. The message was muffled, abrupt, and incomplete. The crew in the *Itasca* radio room tensed. It was now apparent that the *Flying Laboratory,* as Amelia's plane was called, was having radio trouble.

At 7:42 A.M. Earhart broke through, her voice frazzled and weary: "KHAQQ calling *Itasca*. We must be on you but cannot see you. Gas is running low. Been unable to reach you by radio. We are flying at altitude of one thousand feet."

Sixteen minutes later, her signal now strong and

clear: "KHAQQ calling *Itasca*. We are circling but cannot see you. Go ahead on 7500 either now or on schedule."

Itasca confirmed: "We are receiving your signals but are unable to get a minimum bearing. Please take a bearing on us and answer with voice on 3105."

A series of dashes followed. But the plane's signal was lost, making it impossible to obtain a bearing. Commander Thompson tried to guess where the fliers were. He estimated that they must be within a hundred miles of their target, Howland Island, a tiny dot in the south-central Pacific Ocean.

At 8:34 A.M. the *Itasca* radio crew heard Earhart for the last time. Her voice, now high-pitched and frantic: "We are in line of position 157-337. . . . Will repeat this message. We will repeat this message on 6210 kilocycles. . . . Wait . . . Listening on 6210 kilocycles. We are running north and south. . . ."

All at once the signal faded. Commander Thompson feared the worst. Earhart was down. Within minutes the greatest air-and-sea search in history was under way. Admiral William "Bull" Leahy, chief of naval operations, ordered naval ships and planes to take up the search. *Itasca,* the coast-guard cutter, was joined by the battleship *Colorado,* the aircraft carrier *Lexington* with sixty-three planes, four destroyers, a minesweeper, and a seaplane. Together these ships and planes combed an area of more than 250,-000 square miles of the Pacific Ocean. The search lasted for sixteen days.

Amateur ham-radio operators from Honolulu, Los Angeles, San Francisco, Seattle, and even Cincinnati reported hearing signals from the downed plane. The ships moved to positions given by the ham operators' messages. They found nothing. An heroic effort ended with a cryptic official report.

In the early morning of July 2, 1937, during the final leg of a grueling round-the-world flight, westward-bound over the lonely mid-Pacific, Amelia Earhart and her navigator, Fred Noonan, were lost at sea without a trace.

The news that Earhart was lost shocked Amelia's devoted, worldwide following. She had come within days of achieving her goal. For many, it was hard to accept that so courageous a woman could be gone so suddenly. A welter of rumors began.

From all over the Pacific, ham-radio operators continued to report signals that the navy claimed they had not picked up. On July 7, 1937, a woman's voice purportedly was heard saying, "Earhart calling . . . On coral southwest of unknown island. Do not know how long we will . . ." Perhaps Amelia Earhart was still alive at that time. But the navy said these signals were the result of mass hysteria—cruel hoaxes. No "official" SOS had ever been received from the *Flying Laboratory* since the morning of July 2, 1937. Amelia Earhart, the greatest aviatrix of the era, had crashed in the Pacific. The public would just have to accept that simple, hard fact.

But the public has never been able to accept it. Amelia Earhart was their heroine. She was one of the romantic pioneers in expanding the capability of the airplane, and her personal magnetism had captured the admiration and respect of many. She was one more of the great American adventurers to vanish in mid-air, never to be heard from again.

The deeper I pressed my search into the lives of missing adventurers, the more certain I became that there was a pattern in common. They all seemed compelled to risk their lives. Each moved with a restless fury into ever more dangerous exploits. I wondered what gave rise to their compulsive drives. In the case of Amelia Earhart, I found my quest tangled by the web of rumors regarding her disappearance.

Amelia Earhart was born in Atchison, Kansas, in 1897. Her mother, Amy Otis Earhart, daughter of a judge, came from a prominent Atchison family. Edwin Earhart, Amelia's father, was a struggling lawyer who could never quite prove himself worthy of his father-in-law's respect. The Earhart children, Amelia and Muriel, spent a great deal of their childhood at the home of their maternal grandparents. Apparently, the family felt that the children should be raised in more enriched surroundings than Edwin and Amy could provide.

Earhart biographers say that Edwin was unhappy with his job of settling railroad claims. He had other plans, but dealing with railroad claims was the price he paid to satisfy his father-in-law, Judge Otis. The marriage between Amy Otis and Edwin Earhart would have to be made secure before Edwin could pursue his dreams of reaching the U. S. Supreme Court. Ed Earhart's goal proved unreachable: he spent his entire career mired in the unrewarding torts of railroad-damage claimants.

Perhaps Amelia's search for challenge and achievement in later life was, in part, a reaction against her father's failure. During her childhood, Edwin's unhappiness became increasingly apparent, and he slowly turned to alcoholism for consolation. He lost job after job, causing the family to move from town to town in search of new employment and still another start.

Amelia attended six schools in the course of four years. Perhaps her way of conpensating for the nagging insecurity of her life was to reject the conventions of the day. Marriage, children, and household chores were not part of the future she envisioned for herself. She stood apart. And in her high-school year-book, captioned under her photograph, was the phrase "The girl in brown who walks alone." John Burke in *Winged Legend* stated:

In her late teens she was coltish, not nearly so obsessed by her appearance or by her effect on boys as most of her contemporaries. . . . Amelia's mind was focused on finding a career for herself; she pasted clippings in a notebook telling of the achievements of various women throughout the world who were taking over jobs previously reserved for men. . . . [She] maintained, "Women will gain economic justice by proving themselves in all lines of endeavor. . . ."

In 1917 Amelia dropped out of the Orgontz Finishing School in order to work for the Canadian Red Cross as a nurse's aide, caring for the war wounded. Her varied career had begun.

In 1919 she began a premed curriculum at Columbia University in New York, and there excelled to the extent that one of her professors remarked, "She had great curiosity and fine ability to synthesize. She'd often be through with an experiment by the time I had set it. With her stamina, determination, and ability to concentrate, who knows what she would have discovered if she had chosen the research laboratory rather than aviation as a career." Perhaps the professor was right. But a more interesting question remains: Why did aviation capture Amelia's respect so completely?

During the summer of 1920 Amelia attended her first air meet, in California. The planes were wartime biwings, canvas-and-wood fighter planes like the Jennies and Canucks. The commercial airline industry had not yet begun. It was aviation's most romantic era. The skies were one of the last great challenges; the empty, vast reaches of space beckoned Amelia, and she answered the call. After her first airplane ride, Amelia was reported as saying: "When I came down I was ready to sign up at any price and have a try at the air myself." Amelia kept her word.

She worked as a commercial photographer, a teacher, a telephone-company employee, and a social worker in order to finance her dreams of flying. She held a total of twenty-eight jobs before she finally had flown enough hours to qualify for her pilot's license. Shortly afterward she set a new women's altitude record of fourteen thousand feet. And in 1922 her family gave her a Kinner Canary—a small yellow biplane—for her birthday.

Career possibilities in aviation were virtually nonexistent. Amelia was soon persuaded to give up flying temporarily and accompany her mother (Amelia's mother and father divorced in 1924) and sister to Boston, where she would work as a social worker and teacher. But hopes of somehow earning a living in aviation never left Amelia. On weekends she would pilot demonstration flights for prospective airplane buyers. She joined the Boston chapter of the National Aeronautics Association and began to organize a women's flyers association, culminating in the formation of the '99ers Club. Like everyone else in the United States, Amelia anxiously followed Charles Lindbergh's epic solo across the Atlantic. She had no way of knowing that Lindbergh had paved the way for an event that would deeply affect her future.

In April 1928, Amelia received a phone call that changed the rest of her life.

Press agent Hilton H. Railey asked: "Miss Earhart, would you be willing to do something important for the cause of aviation?"

Unsure for a moment, Amelia paused, then asked: "Like what?"

"Like participating in flying a plane across the Atlantic."

At first she thought the call was a hoax. Warily she asked Railey for more details. He explained that Mrs. Amy Guest, a well-known socialite, had just purchased a trimotor German Fokker called *Friendship*. Mrs. Guest had wanted to fly the Atlantic herself, but because of family objections she had decided against it. However, Amy Guest was determined that a woman should fly the Atlantic and was now busily recruiting prospective female flyers who might be interested. Mrs. Guest contacted George Putnam, of the

G. P. Putnam's Sons publishing house, who had just scored a journalistic coup by persuading Charles Lindbergh to write the story of his flight. Putnam in turn contacted his friend Railey, explained the problem, and prompted Railey to begin combing Boston airports in order to find any suitable women flyers.

Railey was alerted to Amelia Earhart. Her understated sense of personal determination reminded Railey of Charles Lindbergh, and this convinced him that he had found the ideal woman for the task. Amelia was not so sure.

She wrote: "I was interviewed by David T. Laymen [a friend of Railey's] and John S. Phipps [a relative of Mrs. Guest's] and found myself in a curious situation. If they did not like me at all or found me wanting in too many respects, I would be deprived of the trip. If they liked me too well, they might be loath to drown me. It was, therefore, necessary for me to maintain an attitude of impenetrable mediocrity. Apparently I did, because I was chosen."

In reality, she was wrong. Amelia so impressed Putnam that he later asked her to marry him. She did.

In 1928 Amelia Earhart became the first woman to fly the Atlantic Ocean as a passenger. The plane was a trimotor Fokker equipped with floats. The crew consisted of famed pilot Wilmer Stultz, mechanic Louis "Slim" Gordon, and "A. E." as she was fondly called. The *Friendship* flight from Trespassey Bay, Newfoundland, to Burry Port, Wales, marked the beginning of Amelia Earhart's adventurous career. Overnight she became a heroine. Newspaper headlines screamed her name. She was an instant celebrity. President Coolidge sent her a cable of congratulations, to which she cabled this reply: "SUCCESS ENTIRELY DUE GREAT SKILL OF MR. STULTZ STOP HE WAS ONLY ONE MILE OFF COURSE AT VALENTIA AFTER FLYING BLIND FOR TWO THOUSAND TWO HUNDRED FORTY SIX MILES AT AVERAGE SPEED ONE HUNDRED AND THIRTEEN M.P.H." It was evident that Amelia Earhart was not about to accept her instant fame without having actually earned it.

In 1931 she set the altitude record for autogyros, a contraption that later was modified to become today's helicopter. Although she continued to break record after record, Amelia always seemed to have something else to prove.

She wrote, "I wanted to make another flight alone." Success and fame without real achievement apparently disturbed Amelia. "I wanted to justify myself to myself. I wanted to prove that I deserved at least a small fraction of the nice things said about me. . . . I already had the credit heaped up and running over. I wanted to deposit a little security to make that credit good." (*Soaring Wings* by George Putnam.)

She plunged into the study of celestial navigation, dead reckoning, and radio communication. Thousands of flight hours later, she felt satisfied that she was ready.

On May 20, 1932, Amelia climbed into her single-engine Lockheed Vega at Harbor Grace, Newfoundland, determined to accomplish what no woman flier had done before—the trans-Atlantic solo. Fourteen hours and fifty-eight minutes later, Amelia Earhart touched down in a cow pasture near Londonderry, Ireland.

Her achievement paralleled Lindbergh's historic crossing. Amelia returned home triumphantly. She had become the first woman to fly solo across the Atlantic Ocean, and it earned her singular place in aviation's archives.

The aftermath of her Atlantic solo brought her a windfall of honors, medals, and fame. Hailed as the new Queen of Aviation, welcomed back to New York with a massive ticker-tape parade, she received offers for personal appearances, lecture tours, and writing assignments. She was flooded with advertising-endorsement requests. Amelia Earhart became a household word. Earhart appeared on the labels of women's clothes and children's hats. And, or so it seemed, each new honor drove Amelia toward achieving another flying first.

In 1935 she was the first to solo from Honolulu to the U. S. mainland, at Oakland, California. On April 20 she soloed from Los Angeles to Mexico City. Her drive for new achievements seemed never to falter.

She was an adventurer driven toward dreams of ever greater accomplishments and glory. Halliburton, Fawcett, and Earhart seemed compelled to place themselves in life-against-death situations even though their accomplishments had already assured their immortality through fame. And somehow all of them carried a subliminal foreboding that death or extreme danger lurked just around the corner. Was that foreboding also part of the pattern? I continued to research Amelia's life. There was still a great deal to discover about this fearless aviatrix.

The onset of the '30s marked the beginning of the end of one part of aviation history. The quaint "flying by the seat of the pants" days were beginning and the smaller competitors were on their way out. Amelia continued to fly. She also showed some interest in politics, and campaigned for Roosevelt and for women's rights in the 1936 election. She accepted a job as women's career counselor at Purdue University. There, with financial aid supposedly from the Purdue trustees, she was given a Lockheed Electra, which she planned to fly around the world at the equator—a distance of 27,080 miles—another first in aviation history. She would pilot the *Flying Laboratory* ostensibly to test long-distance–flight effects on the human body.

Just before her 1937 round-the-world flight, Amelia made a curious remark to a reporter. "I have a feeling that there is just about one more good flight left in my system, and I hope this trip is it." Joe Klaas and Major Joseph Gervais in *Amelia Earhart Lives* reported still another version of that remark: " 'You know,' she had in confidence told newsman C. B. Allen just before takeoff on her final round-the-world at-

tempt, 'I am not coming back from this flight.' "
Curiously enough, Amelia Earhart was right.

On the final leg of the flight—with little more than
seven thousand miles to go—she and her navigator
vanished over the mid-Pacific, without a trace. But
America could not accept the official, simplistic account of her death by drowning. They were certain
that something was missing from the story.

The disappearance of Amelia Earhart was one of
the ten biggest news stories of this century. The navy
spent $4 million in the largest air-and-sea search ever
conducted. Why? Death at sea seemed so likely, so
logical, yet the navy continued its search. And when
they finally issued their official conclusion, they felt
compelled to specifically deny all other conjectures.

Rumors about other missing heroes were rather
casually dismissed as mere wild-eyed speculation from
a crazed fringe of the populace, but the Amelia Earhart story warranted something different. The official
navy statement is intriguing, for it did nothing to quell
the rumors—indeed, it only added more fuel to the
fire of speculation, by directly denying some possibilities and endorsing others.

The statement made by the navy, titled "The Flight of
Amelia Earhart," is filled with inordinately cautious
language. It reads:

Navy files . . . show . . . that Amelia Earhart and
navigator Fred J. Noonan departed from New
Guinea at 1000, July 2, 1937, for Howland Island.
The ill-fated flight of approximately 22,000 miles
was recorded by the USS *Ontario* at approximately
mid-point along the route and by a Coast Guard
cutter at Howland Island. The USS *Swan* was on
station at mid-point between Howland Island and
Honolulu to guard the next leg of the flight. Except
for the services of *Ontario*, *Swan*, and the Fleet Air
Base at Pearl Harbor, the Navy had no official connection with the flight. The disappearance of the
flight naturally caused great concern and the Navy
responded quickly with search efforts. Careful evalua-

tion of all available flight data indicates that Amelia Earhart's plane came down at sea to the northwest of Howland Island. . . .

The next-to-last paragraph also is of interest: "Finally, the files contain no information to substantiate allegations that Amelia Earhart was or ever had been engaged in any type of espionage activity for the U.S. Government. The Navy plans no further public statements on this matter. . . ." Apparently the release was intended to squelch "fanciful" speculation about the intent of Amelia's flight.

Fred Goerner, in *The Search for Amelia Earhart,* reported some interesting items he found when examining the National Archives file on Amelia Earhart. The information he uncovered was not classified and therefore was readily available to the public. He claimed that everything in the file pointed to the "drowned in the drink" theory: "Everything, that is, except a set of facts that apparently had no reason for being included in the file at all." For example, there were copies of dozens of requests, dating back ten years or more, from the State Department to numerous foreign countries for permission for U. S. Navy planes to fly over their territory. Almost without exception, the countries, including many that had been allies of the United States in World War II, had replied negatively. In the Earhart file there was an entire history of the navy's frustration with the State Department regarding foreign overflights, and not one of the incidents seemed in any way connected to Amelia Earhart. Why include in Amelia Earhart's file documents that, superficially at least, had nothing to do with her?

Even Amelia's mother doubted the official version of the story. In 1949 she said: "Amelia told me many things but there were some things she couldn't tell me. I am convinced that she was on some sort of government mission, probably on verbal orders." This comment was part of a letter to the U. S. State Department in which she asked them to question the Japanese government regarding Amelia's fate. Fred Goerner had discovered Mrs. Earhart's letter in a classified State Department file. When he asked why the State Department had classified this letter, its very existence was denied.

Snippets of circumstantial evidence keep appearing that underline the possibility that Amelia Earhart's disappearance was linked to an espionage mission. The evidence takes on some credibility when seen in the context of the late 1930s political arena. If Amelia was on a photographic spy flight over the Pacific, the international tensions of the time could reasonably have been considered the catalyst.

Undoubtedly, the Japanese attack on Pearl Harbor had been in the making long before 1941. The political rationale for espionage would have been easy to understand in light of America's foreign relations. U. S. military intelligence was suspicious of the Japanese using Pacific islands mandated to their care by the League of Nations after World War I. It was believed that the Japanese, without authorization, were preparing for war by building military bases on these islands. If the Japanese were preparing for war, how far advanced were they? The Japanese would not allow U. S. Navy planes to fly over the mandated area. Information on the extent of the Japanese military buildup was difficult for the United States intelligence agencies to obtain. President Roosevelt wanted Congress to allocate additional funds for defense but could not prove any concrete need for it. Caught amid the 1930s—the Depression—it was impossible to generate enthusiasm for military spending. Roosevelt knew that if he could prove that the Japanese were building major naval bases on Saipan Island and on the the Truk Islands, he would get his defense bill passed. Earhart and Noonan's mission had not succeeded, and most people felt that their disappearance would justify a massive sea-and-air search—which, Roosevelt knew, would enable the U. S. to peruse the entire mandated area.

Perhaps by accident, perhaps by plan, that is exactly what happened. Ironically, following the navy's sixteen-day search for Amelia, Roosevelt, in January 1938, was awarded the largest peacetime naval budget of his first two administrations.

Were the round-the-world flight and the subsequent disappearance really part of a cleverly constructed bit of espionage stagecraft? Amelia's sense of duty to her country was so strong that she would willingly have participated in a scheme considered so forthrightly patriotic. She had met Roosevelt and was well known to him. The President, in fact, had agreed to build a landing strip on Howland Island expressly for her venture. So much cooperation from the White House seems logical when viewed in a political context.

In his book, Goerner wrote that the National Archives contained many letters from private individuals requesting naval assistance on long-distance flights in various areas of the world. The requests were always denied with the curt comment: "The United States Navy would not and could not cooperate on a private flying venture." But the situation was different with Amelia Earhart. She had the cooperation of the President of the United States. There is an excellent chance that this occurred for one or both of the following reasons: Because Amelia was such a heroine, Roosevelt considered the move politically popular; or because he needed an excuse to build an airstrip in the Pacific that would facilitate surveillance of the Japanese-held islands.

Almost immediately after her disappearance, the news reports bristled with hearsay and speculation. The plane, designed expressly for buoyancy, was said to have floated to an isolated reef. Another account claimed that the flyers, safe on their inflatable life raft, with adequate provisions to sustain them, had reached an uninhabited atoll near Howland Island. According to other sources, the Japanese had shot down the plane when it had mistakenly soared over the Truk Islands and Saipan. Another speculation was that the flyers had been captured by the Japanese and executed or imprisoned after they had completed their secret spy mission of photographing Japanese military installations in the Pacific. Hard-headed aviation experts, on the other hand, swore that the flyers must have drowned when their plane underwent the impact of the ocean crash.

All the hypotheses were intriguing. Certainly it provided reams of Sunday-supplement copy. Every theory seemed to draw a handful of advocates. In addition, government evasion, classified files—the political context of the whole idea—served to lend credence to some rumors.

Hollywood also speculated. Five years after her disappearance, the film *Flight for Freedom,* starring the late Rosalind Russell, did much to keep alive rumors about the Earhart mystery. The cinematic view depicted a famous woman flyer whom the U. S. Navy asks to deliberately ditch in the vicinity of a small Pacific island. The subsequent search for the aviatrix would be the perfect pretext for navy reconnaissance planes to photograph the suspect Japanese mandated islands. But when the heroine of the film discovers that the Japanese know of the plan, she courageously ditches where no one can find her. The film, produced during World War II, encouraged the rumors that Amelia had been captured by the then-detested Japanese enemy. Some investigators believe the film might have been more than dramatic invention.

As I began to review all the different theories and examine the evidence that various searchers had amassed, I was struck with how thoroughly convincing were all the different hypotheses. Retired Air Force Major Joseph Gervais has devoted nearly twenty years of research to what he believes is the answer. He and Joseph Klaas wrote the book *Amelia Earhart Lives.* Gervais was one of the searchers I interviewed on the TV episode *In Search of Amelia Earhart.*

When I went to meet him at his home, I found

Major Gervais surrounded by photographs of Amelia Earhart from childhood to adulthood. Obviously he had immersed himself in his subject, and when he talked about Amelia he did so with a simple, quiet assurance.

"The last flight was a military flight," he explained simply. "Two civilian people flying a civilian aircraft on a mission for the then-President of the U. S., Franklin Roosevelt. The purpose of the flight was to overfly the Truk Atoll in the Pacific, which the Japanese were secretly fortifying, to take pictures of it, and to return to the U. S. with the photographic evidence to present to the League of Nations that Japan was in violation of the treaty. . . ." He explained how a Japanese aircraft carrier stationed between Canton Island and Hull, together with a Japanese Zero, intercepted Earhart and forced her to make a crash landing on the island of Hull.

This part of the theory seemed very reminiscent of the Hollywood film. But Major Gervais explained that his belief that Amelia Earhart landed on Hull Island is based largely on his interpretation of civilian radio direction reports received during the Earhart flight. He then showed me a photograph of Hull Island which he believes reveals the Japanese flag flying near the wreckage of Amelia Earhart's aircraft.

Gervais's book contained many eyewitness testimonies. I asked him about Ramon Cabrera, a former Japanese soldier who had confessed to Gervais that in 1937 he had interrogated a woman pilot before she was taken captive to Japan. Gervais confirmed the story:

In Japan she was a very important political prisoner. She was held captive in the Imperial Palace for a period of approximately eight years. At the close of World War II, two weeks before MacArthur occupied Japan, Jacqueline Cochran [another famous aviatrix] and a group of other people went in there and secretly removed Amelia Earhart, disguised as a nun, from Japan before the occupation.

When Gervais's book was published he believed that Amelia Earhart was alive and well. I was a little surprised to learn that he still believes this. My search for answers, I felt, would now focus on other independent investigators each of whom now believes he has a final answer close at hand.

The Pacific leg of Earhart's last flight was by far the longest and most dangerous. Her first destination was a refueling stop at Howland Island—a tiny, two-square mile atoll in the mid-Pacific jutting only fifteen feet above the sea. World-record-holding pilot and navigator Captain Elgen Long has carefully studied a wealth of detailed information about that last leg of the flight.

He analyzed such things as the fuel consumption of Earhart's plane, the strength of radio signals received by the cutter *Itasca,* and the effect of crosswinds on the flight—a condition of which Earhart was not even aware. From this data, Captain Long has reconstructed a sophisticated navigational model of Amelia Earhart's final flight.

Captain Long was very cordial and agreed to appear on the *In Search of Amelia Earhart* TV show. The cameras were rolling as he began to talk. "Actually I think everything went smoothly in the flight—up until they reported over Howland Island at seven-forty-two. At that time they said, 'We should be on you but we cannot see you.' In other words, they thought they were at Howland. They didn't think anything was wrong until then. Now, there's no evidence, or I can't find the evidence to indicate any single mistake that anyone made that caused them to miss the island, which they obviously did. Rather, it was a series of small errors, which compounded themselves and unfortunately all in the same direction, which caused it all to happen, and indeed they did miss the island.

"Of course, once they couldn't find the island—and they searched for it for over an hour and their fuel was exhausted—they were forced to ditch the airplane into the sea." That sounded like the official opinion concerning Amelia. But Captain Long went one step further.

From the information he has gathered, Captain Long believes that he has pinpointed the exact place where Amelia Earhart crashed into the sea. The location, according to Long, is about forty miles northwest of Howland Island—an area where the water is over sixteen thousand feet deep.

Captain Long continued: "Actually the airplane is almost perfectly preserved. You know, this is something we weren't familiar with. Just a few years ago of course we didn't know that things are preserved in deep water, and we have recovered planes that have been underwater for almost thirty years; and as long as they were in deep water, everything in that airplane and the plane itself is just as it was the day it went down there."

The possibility of recovering the *Flying Laboratory* fascinated me. Is it really possible that advanced deep-sea exploration equipment could locate the Earhart plane? If we could recover the plane we might be able to see whether Earhart had bailed out in time. We would be able to judge from the structural damage how much impact she and Noonan would have had to survive, and thereby learn whether survival was possible. I asked Long whether he gave much credence to ham-radio operators' signals reportedly received up to five days after the plane went down. He said that it was extremely doubtful that Earhart ever sent signals after 8:34 A.M.

Long prefers not to deal with the theory that Amelia was captured by the Japanese. He said: "In order to really put it all finally to rest, we've got to get an expedition together. We have got to get out, search, and locate her airplane, and recover it, and then I think finally once and for all the Amelia Earhart search will reach its conclusion."

I can understand Captain Long's position. If the plane is down there and can be recovered, the questions regarding the Earhart mystery could be quickly answered. In Captain Long's point of view, there's really no reason to speculate on the aftermath of the crash until the plane is dredged up from its watery grave.

From my years of association with the TV show *The Undersea World of Jacques Cousteau,* I am very familiar with the problems of deep-water recovery. The difficulties are immense and the expense is outrageous. I doubt that such a mission will ever be undertaken. Other theories will have to suffice.

"We believe the navy missed Earhart in the search in 1937 perhaps by only a few miles. Radio messages were received after her disappearance by amateur radio operators along the West Coast of the United States, and they were also received by navy radio stations. If we had looked in the right area in 1937, Amelia might be with us today."

I was talking to CBS radio broadcaster Fred Goerner, author of *The Search for Amelia Earhart.* Goerner has spent more than sixteen years investigating the disappearance of Amelia Earhart. His belief that she survived her crash into the Pacific is based on his analysis of information in civilian and military radio reports. Goerner had painstakingly uncovered these reports while researching navy archives in Washington, D.C. He has made four separate trips to the South Pacific in order to record eyewitness testimony concerning the possible presence of Amelia Earhart on the island of Saipan.

"It began in 1960 with CBS," Goerner said. "I was a correspondent here in San Francisco. We received information there was a possibility that Amelia Earhart might have reached Saipan in the western Marianas. And I was sent by CBS news to Saipan to find out if there was supporting information."

Saipan is nearly fifteen hundred miles northwest of Earhart's destination, Howland Island. Yet, Jesus Salas, a Saipanese farmer, told Goerner of an incident in the Garapan Prison on Saipan, which Goerner later retold in his book. In 1937, while a prisoner of the occupying Japanese army, Salas saw a white woman in the cell next to his. She was held there for several hours. Prison guards told Salas that she was a captured American pilot. Salas never saw her again.

José Pangelinan, a grocer on Saipan, remembered seeing a white woman several times on the second floor of a compound hotel. He had heard that she was a captured pilot and spy.

Saipanese natives Joaquin Seman and Ben Salas told Goerner that they heard that an American woman was buried in a cemetery sometime in 1937.

Goerner excavated several graves during his four visits to the Pacific island but was never able to substantiate the natives' testimonies. Goerner continued: "The strongest evidence is the eyewitness reports on the island of Saipan. To me it is inconceivable that these people were not telling the truth, and it is inconceivable to me that anyone else answering those descriptions was on that island at that time."

I asked Goerner about the classified government documents he had tried to obtain in Washington. He believes the files prove that the Japanese did capture Amelia Earhart. He replied slowly, taking his time, "Amelia landed on a small reef between Howland Island and Canton in the northern Phoenix group, was picked up, after search, by the Japanese, and taken to Saipan. She died in Japanese custody, and the proof of her Japanese custody is contained in records of the Counter Intelligence Corps, captured from the Japanese at the end of World War II. Those records are today classified in Washington. They are records of Japanese interrogation of Earhart and I think that a final answer to the mystery is going to be written."

Fred Goerner shared one quality with many of the other investigators with whom I talked in filming *In Search of Amelia Earhart*. When they talked about the facts they had uncovered, they gave their information with an assertive straightforwardness. But when they talked about Amelia the adventuress, the woman, their voices softened. Like all good researchers, they knew their subject. As I learned during my quest, there was a special quality about Amelia that caused those who knew her to fall in love with her. I had seen it with Major Gervais, with Captain Long, and it was there for Fred Goerner as well. It came out on the final line of our interview. Somewhat wittily Fred said, "Alas, Amelia Earhart is not alive and well and living in New Jersey. I wish that she were."

I had collected enough material for the *In Search of Amelia Earhart* TV show—all of it compelling, intriguing, and satisfying. I was puzzled, though. I was ready to believe Gervais, Long, and Goerner equally; yet I knew they couldn't all be right. What was the real story?

I was faced with a fairly broad array of evidence, eyewitness testimony, and the searchers' convictions. None of the theories seemed out of line with what I had surmised of Amelia's personality and lifestyle. She was, after all, a flyer. She had chosen aviation as a career. Roy R. Grinker in *Men Under Stress* wrote:

> The flier's opportunity to master his environment and to dominate a powerful machine represents an attraction which is emotionally satisfying to the average young man in our civilization. . . . Truly godlike, the flier soars above the earth and the little men confined to its surface. . . . This super-toy, this powerful, snorting, impatient but submissive machine enables man to escape the usual limitations of time and space.

Perhaps flying was the only career that could satisfy an adventurer like Amelia Earhart. Would she have accepted the awesome responsibility of a spy mission for the government? Based on my research, I would say *yes*. And, in light of Watergate, espionage, secret files, official government denials, etc., seem to be part of the political way of life. Nothing seems too surprising today.

It is forty years since Amelia Earhart vanished—

and the cause of her disappearance is still an enigma. There is a vast amount of convincing, and sometimes contradictory, evidence which can support any one of several explanations. But who is right?

For at least three men, Gervais, Goerner, and Long, the search will continue. It will go on until someone proves, without the slightest doubt, the fate of this daring and charismatic woman.

Before the takeoff on her last flight, Amelia wrote to her husband: "Please know that I am quite aware of the hazards. I want to do it because I want to do it. Women must try to do things as men have tried. When they fail, their failure must be but a challenge to others." (*Soaring Wings.*)

4

Michael Rockefeller

November 18, 1961. Off the southwestern coast of primitive New Guinea—an immense, steaming jungle of impenetrable swamp and endless mud. It is a hostile wilderness known as the Land of the Lapping Death by the primeval headhunter-cannibals who live here, suspended in time between the Stone Age and the twentieth century. Great rivers dump torrents of yellow silt into the treacherous Arafura Sea, home of crocodiles, sea serpents, and sharks. A native catamaran has capsized in the choppy waters at the mouth of the Siretsj River. High tides clash with strong currents and drive the boat, already hopelessly adrift, farther and farther from land. Michael Rockefeller abandons what is left of his sinking ship and begins a desperate swim for the muddy shore, many miles away. He is never seen again and his fate remains a tragic mystery.

Michael Clark Rockefeller, the most adventurous and high-spirited of the children of Nelson Rockefeller, was an heir to one of the greatest fortunes in the world.

The first U.S. oil well was drilled in 1859 and within twenty-five years John D. Rockefeller controlled ninety-five percent of the oil-refining business in this country. As president and founder of Standard Oil, he was perhaps the richest and most powerful industrialist of the time, with vast holdings in oil, lumber, iron ore, manufacturing, transportation, and other enterprises. In the early 1900s he retired from active business pursuits and devoted himself to the establishment of philanthropic institutions that supported education, medical research, public service, and social welfare. It is estimated that by these means John D. Rockefeller gave away over $600 million.

His only son, John D. Rockefeller, Jr., followed in his father's footsteps. He created and developed the Rockefeller Institute for Medical Research, the Rockefeller Foundation, the General Education Board, the International Education Board, and Rockefeller Center. Contributions from John D. Rockefeller, Jr., were in the range of $400 million.

John D. Rockefeller, Jr., had five sons, all of whom carried on the family tradition of prominence in public and political affairs as leaders of the various Rockefeller philanthropies and enterprises.

Nelson Rockefeller, the second son of John D., Jr., rose to great prominence in U. S. politics. As governor of the state of New York, his became a familiar face on the American scene. With strong presidential ambitions and much popular support, he exemplified the ultimate of his family's tradition.

Historians of the dynasty have remarked: "The Rockefellers do not consider themselves ordinary men." And fourth-generation Michael was no exception. Born in 1938—along with twin sister Mary—Michael was the youngest and perhaps the favorite son of Nelson Rockefeller. Daring and intelligent, he had a driving curiosity about other peoples and cultures. Encouraged by his father to explore the world, Michael combined a traditional education at Phillips Andover Academy and at Harvard University with extensive travel and a wide variety of summer jobs that ranged from ranchhand in Venezuela to supermarket clerk in Puerto Rico.

Michael graduated, with honors, from Harvard in 1960—a tall, handsome, fair-haired, athletic young man of twenty-two, born to the best things in life and with a very bright future ahead of him. He left the halls of ivy and enlisted in the U. S. Army Reserve to serve a six-month hitch as a private. And then, in search of adventure and knowledge, he joined an anthropological expedition to one of the most remote lands of the world: New Guinea.

Michael first visited New Guinea early in 1961— not long after his father's unsuccessful bid for the Republican presidential nomination—as audio technician and still-photographer for the Peabody Museum-Harvard University expedition to the Baliem Valley in the interior of New Guinea. Accompanied by his best friend and college roommate, Sam Putnam, the expedition was to be their last fling together before Michael went off to Harvard Business School and Sam to Harvard Medical School. As Michael said, "It's the desire to do something romantic and adventurous at a time when frontiers in the real sense of the word are disappearing." The trip was also to be the culmination of the photographic work they had done together. As Sam recalled later, "We wanted to bring back a visual image of another culture and of people with different values, yet show that they were human and that it was a very small world that we live in."

"The overall aim of the expedition," according to Robert Gardner, leader of the group, "was to make a comprehensive study of a single community of neolithic warrior-farmers. . . . Our plan was to choose a community of villages that would allow a group of as many as eight of us to stay for an indefinite period doing anthropological and photographic studies. . . . We intended to document verbally and visually the whole social and cultural fabric of this community. We were interested in its natural history and were equipped to scrutinize it from the standpoint of behavioral scientists, naturalists, photographers, and filmmakers. Our specific goals included an ecologically oriented account [*Under the Mountain Wall,* 1962], a feature-length motion picture [*Dead Birds,* 1963], anthropological monographs [Ph.D. theses in 1963 and 1967], and a book of photographs [*Gardens of War*, 1968]. . . . When the possibility of sending an expedition to do film and anthropological research first arose, perhaps the most difficult task was to choose among several areas urgently requiring such studies. Michael Rockefeller, then still a senior at Harvard, was the most enthusiastic and generous stimulant to our venture. It was my own hope to make a study of a society still practicing what in anthropological annals is known as 'ritual warfare.' For this reason, I was eager to go to New Guinea and into the central highlands where men from villages separated only by their gardens have been killing each other for as long as we have known that they have lived there."

It was off to the wilds of New Guinea, then, for this highly civilized team of Ivy Leaguers. During the months ahead, one of Michael's most frequent expressions was "It's unbelievable!" And indeed it was.

Over ten thousand miles away from New York, the fifteen-hundred-mile-long island was a vast, untamed terrain, a world of prehistory, with broad rivers snaking through thick tropical jungles, and ribs of tall, jagged mountains checkering the landscape into hundreds of narrow, nearly impenetrable valleys.

The world's second largest island (after Greenland), New Guinea's land area totals 304,000 square miles, including the main island and some six hundred outer islands and chains of archipelagoes. Located in the South Pacific Ocean one hundred miles north of Australia, New Guinea forms part of the circum-Australia mountain system and was probably connected to Australia in the Pleistocene Age. It is a country of diversity: majestic mountains, active volcanoes, gigantic swamps, high valley plateaus.

New Guinea's climate is mostly tropical, though the highlands tend to be cooler and drier. Hit by northwestern monsoons from December through March and southwestern monsoons from May through October, yearly rainfall varies from sixty inches in some places to over three hundred inches in others. Temperatures are usually torrid and humidity is high. The coastal areas are the most uncomfortable for Westerners. But in the highlands the days are often pleasant and the nights cool.

Although the soil is badly leeched by continuous, heavy rainfall and high temperatures, flora is abundant. New Guinea is classified botanically as part of the Indo-Malayan region, but the vegetation has much in common with nearby Australia. And, being an isolated island chain, evolution has followed unique endemic patterns as well.

Luxuriant rain forest covers much of the lowlands with a wide variety of tropical trees and exotic flowers. Along the saltwater coastal areas of poor drainage, this forest gives way to a muddy morass of mangroves and palms. Above two thousand feet, the rain forest is replaced by highland forest, farmlands, and meadows of tough, sharp grass.

Though flora is abundant, animals are scarce and the inhabitants rely mainly on a vegetarian diet. The fauna that does exist, however, is similar in many respects to that of Australia, with over a hundred species of marsupials, such as cuscuses, wallabies, and red bandicoots. There are more than seventy species of snakes, leeches in the rain forests, crocodiles in the tidal swamps and rivers, and swarms of insects everywhere (especially malaria-carrying mosquitoes). Unusual birds such as the ostrichlike cassowaries and the exquisitely plumed birds of paradise are unique to the land, while hordes of chattering parrots, cockatoos, and parakeets came to New Guinea from Australia.

First visited by the white man (Portuguese and Spanish sailors) in the sixteenth century and claimed alternately by the Dutch, British, and Germans, New Guinea is now under the divided rule of Indonesia and Australia. Though "civilization" had invaded many areas by the 1960s, some of the interior highlands and nearly all the western wilderness areas remained virtually "untouched" except by a few missionaries in isolated spots.

Michael's letters to Sam Putnam about his arrival in New Guinea were full of awe and enthusiasm:

> We flew in over Lake Sentani, jungles, mountains, the huge swamp of the interior, more mountains—and then finally the Baliem Valley opening up like a giant fertile cavity before us. . . . The Baliem is a thing of magnificent vastness, decorated with the greens of the valley floor and the blues of the surrounding mountains. The mountains rise over ten thousand feet on all sides and are constantly hidden and altered by the clouds that gather about them.

According to Peter Matthiessen, the naturalist-novelist of the expedition:

> The Baliem Valley was discovered from the air in 1938, but no white man came to live there until 1954, when a government post was established on abandoned lands of the Wukahupi tribes. Dutch patrols have now explored much of the valley, which supports more than forty thousand people, and the last large blank on the most recent maps is a region of perhaps thirty square miles under the northeast wall.

It was into this "last large blank" that the Peabody expedition ventured. The *New York Times* of April 5, 1961, reported that the group had:

> . . . discovered in the heart of Dutch New Guinea a savage tribe whose culture is focused on war—the Willingiman-Wallalua (tribe of the Dani) people in the lofty Baliem Valley. . . . The tribe's warriors are judged by the number of enemies slain, the number of pigs stolen, and the number of wives captured. Apparently they have no qualms about killing enemy women and children; these seem to add as much to their prestige as a slain male adult. . . . Even their music is unconsciously aggressive. A good deal of it consists of grinding their teeth in

harmony . . . [the recording of which was to be Michael's job].

Expedition leader Robert Gardner described the first meeting of Stone Age man and Harvard man:

We were on the edge of a swamp when we first saw the natives. They were observing us from watch-towers twenty feet off the ground which they had built by lashing long thin trees together. They climbed down from the towers as we approached. Broekhuyze, who speaks the language of the Dani group quite well, began to talk to them. He opened with a traditional greeting and then explained why we were there. . . .

The men became curious and put down their fifteen-foot spears. We crossed a swamp up to our knees in muck to some high ground where they were standing. There were about fifty warriors, some of them magnificent specimens 6′ 3″ tall.

We found that they were not of the Kurelu, but an allied (Dani) people. We explained that we wanted to live with them and motioned to three or four hamlets we had observed up against a hill. We talked for half an hour. Finally, a young warrior who was acute enough to realize he had much to gain— we had shown him the sea-snail shells (a prized native currency)—led us to one of the hamlets.

The expedition pitched tents—watched warily by the amazed tribe—and proceeded to set up shop. For the next half year, they would film and record a culture "entirely untouched by civilization."

Michael wrote home that he was having an exciting time. Gardner recalled that Michael would delight the natives with his wiry strength by walking ten yards on his hands. He was the undisputed champion at Indian wrestling. Some members of the expedition thought he seemed to be moving toward a career as field anthropologist and photographer. And Nelson Rockefeller felt that his son seemed happiest during his stay in New Guinea.

Life among the Dani people fascinated Michael, who set about his photographic and sound-recording work with great enthusiasm and dedication. It was a world both natural and supernatural, mankind living in delicate balance with ghosts and spirits.

As discovered by Gardner and reported in *Gardens of War,* Dani villages are collections of grass huts surrounded by a fence—to keep pigs from escaping. On one edge of the settlement is the largest building, a circular men's house, where all the men sleep. On both sides of the central courtyard are long rectangular cooking and family houses, where women and children sleep. In smaller circular houses, husbands and wives mingle. And in other houses, subdivided into stalls, the pigs are kept.

Basically, the mode of dress is nudity or near-nudity. Men wear only an enormously elongated gourd, known as a horim, over the penis, tied in an erect position to the chest. For decoration, they also wear bird-of-paradise feathers in their hair and bib-collars of seashells. Women wear three loose fiber nets: one for the baby, one for small pigs, and one for sweet potatoes. The standard make-up for the Danis is pig grease mixed with soot, daubed on the face and hair in great gobs.

The Dani diet consists mainly of sweet potatoes, which are diligently cultivated in elaborate terraced and irrigated gardens. The men generally do the heavy work of garden construction and upkeep, while the women do the daily work of cultivation and harvesting.

When the women leave in the morning for the fields, young boys take out the village pigs. Pigs are considered the most important beings besides humans, for they are the foundation of wealth, male pride, social importance, and polygamy. Only a man of many pigs is respected and has many wives. At ceremonial feasts the men eat steamed pig, with carefully chosen portions assigned according to status. Pigs are often stolen out of greed or revenge. Pigs are exchanged in marriage and peacemaking. A man without pigs, wife, or power is considered *kepu*—or worthless. Daily care of the pigs falls to the women and children, for the major occupation of the men is warfare.

Dani life is founded upon profound belief in ghosts, spirits, and magic. Their society is sustained, they believe, by acts of revenge for the spirits of lost loved ones and by avoiding the ghosts of enemies. To this end, the people constantly practice magic ceremonies and engage in intertribal wars.

The life-force is symbolized by the *etai-eken*, or "seeds of singing." These "seeds" are thought to be located near the solar plexus and are similar to the Western concept of soul. When a member of a warring tribe has been killed by an enemy—either directly or by magic, for it is believed that no one dies naturally—the spirit of the dead person must have revenge or else the ghost will weaken the *etai-eken* of its former relatives and tribe.

As Gardner explained, the Danis believe that:

> . . . until the ghosts are avenged, the people themselves will suffer. The ghosts may trouble them with accidents, sickness, blights upon their crops, droughts, floods, or any of a multitude of other distresses. For Dani warriors—and all Dani men are professional fighters—the risks involved in fighting an occasional battle . . . are not nearly as great as those to be enountered were they to ignore the demands of unavenged ghosts.

The whole society, therefore, is geared for warfare. The boundaries of the villages are no-man's land, guarded by watchmen on high towers. Men must spend much of their time making weapons and serving guard duty. The grass must be kept short to protect villages against ambush. Artificial ponds must be maintained with ducks, which will rise, quacking, in warning if an enemy approaches. Men must always carry weapons, travel in groups, and search everywhere for clues of potential enemy aggression. No man, woman, or child is ever safe anywhere, so powerful magic must be practiced constantly—defensively and offensively.

Warfare comes in two forms. Deadliest are the raids in which small parties of warriors sneak behind enemy lines and murder anyone in sight. Whereas these raids are brutal surprise attacks, ritual battles are prearranged affairs of martial protocol. Hundreds of shrieking warriors—facing one another in lines—hurl insults, spears, and arrows at one another across no-man's land. Few are killed immediately; however, often many are injured and die later. Ritual battles are called off as soon as someone is killed, or if it rains, or if the men tire of fighting. Whichever tribe feels itself the winner dances and whoops in victory.

Overall, then, Dani society is organized around the ceremonies of ritual battles and the grisly realities of raids. As Gardner observed, "war is one of the paramount institutions of Dani life. With agriculture and pig raising, it constitutes one of the few major focuses of all the people's interest and energy. Without it, the culture would be entirely different."

Although tribal warfare was a fascinating subject for the Peabody expedition, native violence was intolerable to Dutch officials and missionaries. They had devoted their energies to "pacifying" and "civilizing" the natives and were critical of the anthropologists. "After the expedition's arrival," one Dutch official claimed, "seven warriors were killed and one hundred twenty injured in a sudden flareup of tribal warfare." Although the Dutch government eventually conceded that the violence could not be linked directly to the activities of the expedition, some authorities remained suspicious. Local missionaries also complained that they suspected the anthropologists of inciting tribal violence in order to record it on film. The expedition denied the charges. But, much to the missionaries' dismay, the scientists openly admitted that they would do nothing to interfere with tribal practices.

Michael and Sam split off from the other members of the expedition for two weeks in late June, to make a trip of their own to a southwestern coastal area known as Asmat. The Asmat is essentially an immense mud-plain covered by tidal swamp and steaming jungle rain forest. Crisscrossed by countless muddy rivers—on which travel is by wooden canoe—it is a torrid, hostile wilderness called Land of the Lapping Death by the local natives, who also are known as the Asmat.

These people subsist almost entirely on sago palm and use wood almost exclusively, for the land is virtually without stone. What stone there is is imported from other tribes across mysterious trade routes and is used to form axes. By tradition, the Asmat are headhunters and cannibals. They are also woodcarvers. They produce some of the finest primitive art in the world. It was the art of the Asmat that lured Michael to the area and hooked him on New Guinea.

He wrote home later:

The key to my fascination with the Asmat is the woodcarving. The sculpture which the people here produce is some of the most extraordinary work in the primitive world. And equally as remarkable as the art is the fact that the culture which produces it is still intact; some remote areas are still headhunting; and only five years ago almost the whole area was headhunting. The Asmat is a land of jungle, winding rivers, and mud. You wouldn't believe it but there are no hills and no stones in the entire region. . . .

Michael also observed, with a keen and compassionate eye, that the land was doomed by the onslaught of civilization.

The Asmat trip was equal to my wildest dreams. I was very quickly elevated from a slight case of depression deriving from considerable disappointment over the first results of my photographic efforts in the Baliem. In retrospect, my approach to the problem of photographing the extraordinary life we have found was quite naïve. Photography like other artistic mediums requires a very particular combination of talents, and I now know that an eye sensitive to aesthetics assures little. . . . The Asmat is filled with a kind of tragedy. For many of the villages have reached that point where they are beginning to doubt the worth of their own culture and crave things Western. There is everywhere a depressing respect for the white man's shirt and pants, no matter how tattered and dirty, even though these doubtful symbols of another world seem to hide a proud form and replace a far finer, if less concealing, form of dress. Yet much more ominous is the economic and spiritual future of the Asmat. The West thinks in terms of bringing advance and opportunity to such a place. In actuality we bring a cultural bankruptcy which will last for many years and, what is more, poverty. Poverty after all is a relative thing. The Asmat is a land of great winding rivers, tropical forests, and mud. Literally nothing else. The people have for centuries lived on little besides the pulp of sago palm and fish. There are no minerals; and not a single cash crop will grow successfully. Nonetheless, the Asmat like every other corner of the world is being sucked into a world economy and a world culture which insists on economic plenty in the Western sense as a primary ideal. . . .

Fortunately for the morale of our trip, the bitterest symptoms of the Asmat's future were seldom seen. What we saw were some imposing remnants of a marvelous past. I suppose not so marvelous from a Christian point of view, for the Asmats were a ferocious headhunting people constantly engaged in inter-village war and raids of varying degrees of deadliness. However, the sculpture that has been and (in some areas) is being produced by Asmat artists is unquestionably some of the greatest to come from a primitive culture. . . .

Unlike the Dani people, those of the Asmat do not live in a region where soil and weather are suitable for agriculture. Nature is hostile and the living is subsistence level. Mankind, like trees, lives rooted in mud. As stone is nonexistent and wood is the dominant resource, the whole culture is based on wood. All tools (except imported stone axes) and shelters are made of wood. The only effective means of travel is by wooden canoe. Almost all food comes from trees. Indeed, the Asmat could be said to exist primarily in the Wood Age. Their very name, Asmat, means Tree People.

The Asmat world is, like that of the Dani, a universe of ghosts, spirits, and magic. No one is thought to die a natural death. Only evil spirits and enemies account for the passing of life. Once dead, the omnipresent spirits of relatives and allies must have their deaths avenged.

The Asmat, therefore, are also a people of warfare. But their wars take the form of raids and ambushes. And rather than return the bodies of enemies—as the Dani people do—the Asmat behead and eat them. For as mankind (man, woman, or child) is a tree, so is his body like a tree—to be eaten. And so is the head like the fruit of a tree—to be plucked.

Asmat villages are stark and simple—a row of wooden houses along a river, supported and lifted above the mud by housepoles. Multifamily dwellings are the norm, but each family has its own fireplace area. Villages are divided into quarters—each centered around a large ceremonial house (the Yeu house)—which serves as a community bachelors' house, men's club, and ritual center. Most ceremonies take place here. The dead are buried in front of it, but their spirits live inside—in the form of ancestor poles and other symbolic woodcarvings.

Wonderful symbolic woodcarving is at the foundation of Asmat culture. Their sculptures are a link between the material and the spirit world. The ghosts of the dead are thought to dwell inside some carvings, to be frightened away by others, to be won over by others. And, as nothing can be done without magic, woodcarvings are a necessity for "real life."

Only one or a few men per village become the artist-woodcarvers, the Wow-Ipits. Though they carve a limited range of objects with a limited range of symbols, they are often true individualists and creators, expressing their personal as well as their cultural views.

According to experts of Asmat art, two fundamental symbolic themes dominate: images of man as tree, and images of headhunting.

To understand Asmat art, it must be seen as it is used in daily life. One of the most important Asmat ceremonies has to do with the dedication of a new Yeu house—an event that takes place every few years because wooden buildings deteriorate so quickly in the humid jungle.

After the construction is completed, all the men—except for a few village leaders and drummers—leave it, and the women enter. They dance in the new Yeu house for a whole day (afterward they will be denied admittance except for rare ceremonial occasions).

In the center of the dancing women, a huge cylindrical wooden container—a "tree of life"—is constructed. When the women leave, the men enter and fill this "tree of life" with the ultimate Asmat delicacy —large squirming grubs of the capricorn beetle.

A month and a half before this, another ceremony takes place—the growth of these larvae in the special sago trees. As described by A. A. Gerbrands in *Wow-Ipits*:

> For the Asmat, the sago tree is not just a human being—it is specifically a woman. As sago comes out of the inside of the tree, the child comes out of the woman. . . . An especially beautiful sago tree, strong, tall, and magnificent, is selected. Preferably it is a tree about to bear fruit and die: in short, a tree in its final burst of life. Stems of fallen leaves and the lower part of the trunk are removed. The trunk will then be "dressed" in a skirt made from the same leaves as a woman's skirt; the tree is thus transformed into a woman. . . . Once the sago tree is dressed, it is called the "mother tree" of the feast.
>
> The ritual of cutting down such a tree incorporates many references to the slaying of a human being during a headhunting raid. Important men from the

community are invited there to give a public account of their brave deeds, especially in relation to
headhunting. This recital, which is called Dewen, is
also performed when men prepare themselves for a
headhunting raid. As a magical act, it is supposed
to frighten the enemy before an actual attack oc-
curs, to terrorize him from a distance. . . . As soon
as the tree has fallen, it is attacked with terrific
yelling and shouting, as if it were a fallen enemy.

The tree trunk is cleaned and a leaf from the crown
of the tree is made into a special container, called
the An. Holes are bored into the tree to help the
beetles penetrate the woody interior for egg laying. A
small replica of the village Yeu house is placed on the
tree and it is left alone for six weeks—the time necessary for the larvae to mature. The mature sago worms
are then harvested by warriors, who cut open the
tree and collect the grubs in their cocoons, amid much
screaming and whooping.

When it comes time, then, for the filling of the "tree
of life" in the Yeu house, the men deposit their white
grubs in the special sheathed An leaf. The An is then
carried into the Yeu house, where it is welcomed as if
it were the body of a slain enemy.

"Once everyone has given his share of sago worms,"
Gerbrands continued, "the container is slit open by a
guest of honor or a prominent community leader while
the onlookers sing him songs of praise and honor. The
larvae pour out of the cylinder and over the floor,
their abundance symbolizing new life emerging from
the female body." (The grubs are then lightly roasted
and eaten.)

Both the Yeu dedication ceremony and the headhunter symbolisms are strongly based in fertility
myth. As Gerbrands describes:

The An is [also] used to collect the brains of a
headhunted enemy. With the pointed end of a stone
axe a hole is made in the temple of a freshly
cleaned skull. The brains are removed from the

skull with a bamboo spatula, and collected in the
An. The An filled with brains resembles amazingly
the An filled with sago worms. In this connection it
should be noted that the An is identified with the
vagina in Asmat culture. Brains and grubs also have
a strong fertility aspect, and it seems likely that the
grubs are identified with sperm.

Equally as important symbolically as the fertility
themes are the themes of wood. The Asmat creation
myth, as collected by Father Zegwaard, a Dutch missionary, goes as follows: Fumeripits—the primordial
hero—was the first to build a Yeu house.

He created it simply by drawing an outline of it on
one of the rare sandy spots along the coast. Suddenly, there it stood, made of wood, with palm leaf
walls, and covered with a thatch of palm leaves. . . .
But it was an empty house. So Fumeripits began to
carve statues of people from trees he found nearby.
He carved men and women in abundance until the
Yeu house was completely occupied with the wood-
en figures. But there was no life in them; they were
nothing but lifeless pieces of wood. So Fumeripits
decided to make a drum. After he had finished the
drum, Fumeripits began to play it, and lo and behold! the wooden statues filling the Yeu gradually
came to life and began to dance. Fumeripits was
then attacked by a monstrous crocodile which tried
to destroy the newly created Yeu houses (Fumeripits
created six Yeu houses). And every day the crocodile destroyed one house. But every day Fumeripits
wounded him more and more severely, until finally
on the sixth and last day, he succeeded in killing the
primordial crocodile before it destroyed the last Yeu
house. He then cut the crocodile in pieces, cast the
pieces in different directions. From these pieces
sprang the different kinds of men: the brown, the
black, and the white.

In these myths, Fumeripits is not only the creator of
man. He is also the First Woodcarver, the First Drum-
mer, and a warrior who dismembers his enemy. As

Gerbrands interpreted, "This myth expresses a fundamental Asmat conception—to create life one has to kill, or the destruction of life is a prerequisite of life itself. And it is an explicit statement of the identity of man and tree. Man was actually created out of wood: 'Wood thou art and to wood thou shalt return.' "

As Fumeripits was the First Woodcarver, so the Wow-Ipits of each village is his descendant. All important objects of Asmat life and ceremonies require the Wow-Ipits to add symbolic carvings to items such as shields, drums, war horns, boat paddles, canoe prows, spears, sago pounders, bowls, soulships, ancestor figures, and ancestor poles.

Since man and tree are interchangeable, "man's feet are the roots of the tree, the trunk of the tree is the human trunk, its branches are his arms, its fruits the human head. The equation of fruit with the human head has particularly important consequences for the whole of Asmat art. Any animal which is a fruit-eater becomes the symbol of a headhunter, especially when the animal is a flying one": black king cockatoo, flying fox, heron, hornbill, cuscus.

Spiral designs may represent the tusks of a boar, for the pig also symbolizes a human being. A pig hunt is like a headhunt and a pig feast is like a cannibal feast. The tusks are as highly valued as human heads. Symbolic tusks made of large pearly shells are inserted in the nose to make man become like the wild boar.

Another favorite symbol is the Wenet, or praying mantis. The movements of this insect seem to resemble those of humans. The mantis is admired, for it is a voracious predator and a cannibal. (Often during copulation, the female mantis eats the live male, beginning with the head.)

Other symbols are obvious fertility images, with humans represented in coitus. The elongated prows of Asmat canoes are called the Tjemen ("penis"). Bowls are often designed to be symbolic receptacles, formed from the spread legs of carvings of women.

Ancestor spirits figure in the designs of many Asmat

objects. Ancestors reside in paddles, spears, shields, masks, ancestor figures, and ancestor poles.

The ancestor pole, or Bis pole, is the most spectacular achievement of Asmat art. Made from a mangrove tree with a single huge root preserved, the ancestor poles are from fifteen to twenty feet high. They represent ancestors (and other symbols), with an enormous Tjemen emerging from the top of the pole.

Bis poles are constructed when the spirits of dead ancestors call out for revenge. The Bis pole serves as a pledge from the living to the ghosts that the enemies who slew them will be slain. After the poles are carved —which takes about six weeks, the time of sago-worm maturation—a ceremony is performed by the men. They dance in mock battle around the pole, followed by a dance in which the women attack the men —to expel from the village the spirits of the dead.

After being on display in the village for a while, the Bis poles are usually returned to the jungle. They are left there to decompose and, by their supernatural powers, to fertilize the growth of the sago trees. Sometimes, however, the Bis poles are kept in the Yeu house and used to replace the supporting poles around fireplaces. The smoke from the fires turns them dark brown and prevents woodworms from destroying them.

Michael kept a detailed journal throughout the trip. In it he recorded observations about the Asmat and its culture. Though mainly anthropological in nature, some sections of the journal vividly record his images and feelings:

We made a quiet leisurely departure down the main-stream of Amanamki. The rowers placed little effort behind their strokes, allowing the outflowing tide to carry the prows easily along. Or perhaps this was only my imagination due to the beautiful ease that always seems to follow from once having lived a particular moment for a lifetime. . . . I only wish I could have somehow recorded the twittering mass of sparrows that we disturbed in the trees along the ocean shores. Hundreds and hundreds of the small birds flew madly from one tree to another, succeeding in accomplishing glory knows what. Obscure objects darted among the branches, and first one tree and then the next would bend from the weight of the myriad flying creatures. . . . The air was filled with the whir of wings and the scream of a thousand birds twittering at once.

He also recorded details of business transactions with the natives, for he was collecting their art—to bring back to New York at a later date:

We made an arrangement with the chiefs that we would buy the Bis as we had done in Omadasep. As we had agreed with the Omadasep people, they would also transport the poles in their own dugout canoes to Agats where I would pay for them with axes, knives, and tobacco. However, they had left their larger canoes in the upstream village, so before returning to Agats we decided we would first visit one or two other villages in order to give them time to collect their canoes. In three or four days we would meet at a well-known rendezvous point on the east bank of the estuary of the Bets River, and proceed together to Agats. Although we arrived in time at the rendezvous spot, and waited there for two days, for some reason or other nobody from Otsjanep appeared. According to our paddlers from Amanamki, it might have been that they were still afraid of a possible attack from Omadasep in spite of the peace ceremony that had been held, and therefore were unwilling to leave their unprotected wives behind. . . . That afternoon, after the display of the Bis poles, I inquired whether there were any shields in the village they might be willing to barter. . . . After that I shot a few portraits of people who were either the owners of the shields I had selected, or else the artists who had carved them.

Michael's technical development as a photographer is also methodically recorded through trial-and-error experiments:

Sam and I did a series of photographs in the Yeu of
Awok in an attempt to record as completely as possible the decorated bachelors' hearths of Awok.
They were mostly multi-strobe shots to get a sense
of the proportions and the totality of the decorated
Yeu. These are entirely experimental and it will be
most interesting to see if they come out. The com-
plicated nature of our set-up was marvelous. I was
with the camera, usually with wide-angle lens set up
on a tripod. Once the camera was set, I would open
the shutter with the cord release. Then Sam would
dash from doorway to doorway in the Yeu, illuminating the eighteen Bis poles above and below the raft-
ers. In between the set of flashes from each doorway
I covered the lens of the Nikon camera with the
open end of a drum. The villagers present were
astounded at the process as it occurred over and
over again. [The experimental picture did come out
well.]

Art collecting in the Asmat could be depressing,
however, for Michael often encountered the cheapen-
ing influence of the West on native culture: "One after
the other of the objects brought to us showed the
effects of hasty craftsmanship stimulated by white
man's knives and curio interest. Somehow I had been
led to believe that I would only be at the end of a long
line of collectors that had already ravaged the Asmat."

Realizing that the amazing art and culture of the Asmat were doomed by the white man, Michael
wanted to collect and preserve excellent samples of it.
Having made down payments on a wide variety of Asmat objects and having established trade relations with
the people, he planned to return later on an art-col-
lecting expedition of his own.

Michael and Sam returned to the Baliem Valley
after two mind-boggling weeks in the Asmat. There
they rejoined the Peabody expedition. Filming went
on for another few months, and then the group departed for the States (leaving only an anthropologist,
who remained for a few years more).

During a brief visit home in September, the news was broken to Michael that his parents were planning to divorce—after thirty-one years of marriage. Shortly thereafter, Michael returned to New Guinea.

Michael's purpose in returning to the Asmat was to study the people further and to collect their art for the Museum of Primitive Art in New York, of which he was a trustee. If he found enough art objects, he also hoped to set up a museum in New Guinea.

He arrived in late September and wrote home:

What time is it and where am I? It is nighttime with the crickets going berserk all around me and I'm back in Hollandia. I arrived exhausted today and found that tomorrow Rene (my co-collector) and I will fly to Merauke in order to make a boat to the Asmat. I am now surrounded by my little reality for the next ten weeks: a chaos of cameras and recording equipment cluttering up everything including my mind. . . .

Michael joined up with a Dutch anthropologist from the Bureau of Native Affairs in Hollandia, New Guinea, Dr. Rene Wassing. Together they would travel the Asmat, recording their experiences and bartering for native art.

After arriving in the Asmat, Michael and Rene set about preparing for their expedition. They equipped themselves with supplies, a native catamaran called a proa (made by joining two dugout canoes, to which they added an eighteen-horsepower engine), and hired two native boatmen. It was not all smooth going but Michael was undaunted and full of great hopes. He wrote home:

Our living since our arrival has been out of a Marx Brothers movie. The Papuan houseboy who was supposed to bring in wood and tend the fire for our meals showed his face briefly on the first morning, and has vanished into the jungle ever since. I'm not sure what shocked him—perhaps my 6:30 A.M. appearance. But no one seems to have been able to find him. Then you should have seen us attempting to build a fire from the logs that he brought, and when we finally got it lit, it burned so brilliantly that it soon made a magnificent hole in the "kitchen floor." [Fires in the Asmat are always found on the floor.] But nights here are really the most fun. Something like teeth grinding in the Baliem: a rhythm created by the patter of mice feet over the walls and ceiling with crickets chirping and frogs burping in counterpoint. The roosters here are affected by a curious neurosis which causes them to begin crowing at midnight. Last night we had an earthquake to rock us to sleep.

At this point I really have no idea exactly what our trip will be like or how successful it will be. One moment I am depressed, the next I am filled with excitement. The reports about the areas we are going to and the extent of acculturation are so conflicting that one really has no idea what to expect. We are equipped with good cameras and sound-recording equipment, an Asmat interpreter, and plenty of barter goods, so that I hope we will be able to make the most of what we come up with.

Two weeks later the expedition arrived at a small Asmat town in which Dutch anthropologist A. A. Gerbrands and American anthropologist David Eyde were living with the natives. Gerbrands, an expert in Asmat art, had helped Michael on his first trip in purchasing, cataloging, and interpreting the objects. Michael wrote home:

Rene and I decided to make one trip to the village of Amanamki where I had visited Dr. Gerbrands in order to pick up some Bis poles which had been left from our last trip. At 8 P.M. we arrived exhausted and wet, at the mouth of the small tributary whose banks harbor Amanamki. Simon, our Asmat interpreter and "river boat boy," shouted into the still night air, for it was low tide and the tributary was too shallow for our outboard. We needed help in order to get to the village. Simon

shouted again. There was a hollow chantlike answer in the distance. Then we could hear the slap,
slap of paddles in the water. First the chief who
had been with us on our previous canoe trip arrived. He was wild with excitement at our return.
More canoes arrived and then men jumped into
the water and mud about our catamaran in order
to pull it up the tributary to the village. The Asmat
have a special shout which is chanted at once by
many men and used as a form of welcome. All the
village lined the river bank and we heard this again
and again as we made slow progress upstream.

After a brief rest, they set off again—for remote,
upstream villages. They were accompanied by two
missionaries from a local Catholic mission and
Michael's spirits were soaring. He wrote home:

Together with some rather extraordinary objects, I
was able to gather all sorts of fascinating information about this particular corner of the Asmat.
The excitement is not only in a constant discovery
of the variety and genius in the Asmat art forms,
but in an understanding of how this art is interwoven
through and through the entire culture and in the
discovery of how this culture varies from village to
village and river to river and dialect group to dialect group.
    The Asmat is like a huge puzzle with the varia-
tions in ceremony and art style forming the pieces.
My trips are enabling me to comprehend (if only
in a superficial, rudimentary manner) the nature of
this puzzle. I think now that with my trip, with all
the anthropological work that will have been done
here, and after a careful study of the large collections of Asmat things now in three Dutch mu-
seums, it would be possible to organize a mammoth
exhibition which would do justice to the art of these
people: to show the function of the art in the culture, and to indicate by means of the arrangement
of the objects the nature of style variation throughout the entire area. Nothing approaching this has ever

been granted a single primitive people. You can imagine what fun I am having dreaming these wild dreams and creating earth-shattering hypotheses about the nature of Asmat art.

Michael and Rene spent two weeks in the northwest corner of the Asmat. They visited thirteen villages and traveled over two river systems. Despite the hardships of being explorers in bizarre places, they were enjoying the voyage, as Michael wrote home:

For the most part we have been traveling in a catamaran built of two canoes bound together with a roof on top. The only difference between Mark Twain and me is that his characters used poles all the time while we use an outboard engine most of the time and poles part of the time. We have been known to get out and push after propelling ourselves naively onto a mud bank at half tide. The boat has been christened "Chinasapitch," the name of the most brilliant single artist we have come across thus far. Occasionally it is called "Fo-Fo," the name of a hornbill which we obtained in the village of Amanamki. . . . Thus far we have always had with us an Asmat boy who serves both as houseboat boy and interpreter. As interpreter he converses with our conferees in Asmat and then with Rene in Malay. Rene in turn tells me the news in English. . . . I assure you that I by no means enjoy the prospects of a Christmas in Agats. I am told that the tides rise so high that you can paddle a canoe through the streets of Agats. At that time, the jungle rats flee in great numbers from their leafy abodes in the bush and seek refuge with their allies, the house rats. The latter are already excellent acquaintances of mine. . . .

On November 12, Michael and Rene arrived in Agats, a large town (by New Guinea standards) where the missionaries and government officials have their headquarters. They planned to take a brief rest, reorganize, and then set off again. Michael wrote home on November 16:

Rene and I have been spending the last four days recovering from our northwest trip. This amounts to transporting, cataloging, dividing, and organizing the objects which we have collected, and preparing for our next foray to the south. Otherwise it amounts to remaining unconscious behind mosquito netting for a bit longer in the mornings and escaping the monotony of spam, corned beef, and rice by making use of the Sisters' major contribution to modern Agats: a lunch delivery service. At 1:00 every day you get a stack of seven pots, each containing some unusual goody. You can imagine the excitement of returning midday to our "Government Rest House" to find such a thing. . . . The Asmat artist enjoys some real advantage over the artist of the western world. The Asmat culture offers the artist a specific language in form. This is a language which every artist can interpret and use according to his genius, and a language which has symbolic meaning for the entire culture. Our culture offers the artist no such language. The result is that each painter or sculptor must discover his own means of communicating in form. Only the greatest geniuses are able to invent an expression which has meaning for a nation or people. Furthermore, the Asmat is a culture where art is a necessary and integrated element. There can be no war, no feasting without the expenditure of tremendous effort on the part of the sculptor. Thus as long as the culture is intact, the art will flourish.

This was Michael's last letter.

On the morning of November 18, Michael, Rene, and the two Papuan boys, Simon and Leo, took off from Agats: destination, Ats. To reach Ats they would have to travel on the high seas of the Arafura and then up the Bets River. They never made it.

The Arafura Sea is known to be treacherous, especially at the mouths of the Siretsj and Bets rivers, where strong river currents met with heavy ocean swells. Apparently many people warned Michael that his catamaran was not sturdy enough for oceangoing on the Arafura. Dutch trader Verhey Van Wyck said he told him the craft was unsuitable, but Michael seemed to be "headstrong and determined to prove himself." Missionaries warned him that coastal tides swelled twenty feet high, seventy-five miles upriver, and then back again with a forceful current that overpowered even the best of native crafts. And anthropologist David Eyde warned Michael that the boat was not seaworthy. But Michael seemed determined to do it his own way and had confidence in his "riverboat."

At the mouth of the Siretsj River, the catamaran was swamped by a huge wave and the outboard motor died. There was no panic, but when the boat began a steady drift seaward, Simon and Leo decided to swim for help.

Though it was perhaps only a mile to shore at this time, the currents were so strong and the water so choppy that it took the native youths five hours to swim the short distance. And then almost another day to walk the eleven miles of mud and jungle to Agats, where they notified authorities of the accident.

Meanwhile, the boat drifted helplessly out to sea. As the *New York Times* reported the story later:

A large part of the luggage broke loose and floated around in the canoes. Michael put some luggage on the roof. But the water poured in faster than they could bail it out and the canoes began to sink. They tried sitting on the roof but soon the craft started to capsize. Presently the canoes turned over. They managed to straddle the bottoms of the canoes and even retrieve some of the floating luggage.

All of this time the craft was drifting seaward and southward. The two men wrenched two boards from the wall that had supported the roof and tried paddling but the current was too strong.

They spent that night straddling the raft, wet and cold. Twice they started paddling furiously toward the coast but the current prevailed, pushing them inexorably seaward.

At dawn they could still see land on the horizon but continued to drift offshore. Michael was not optimistic about Leo and Simon and decided that their best chance for survival was to swim ashore themselves.

Rene argued that the tide was against them and the current was too powerful, that they were three to four miles from shore, that they had a fifty–fifty chance of being picked up by a boat (although few ships travel the Arafura). Besides, he was not as strong a swimmer as Michael and knew he would never make it.

As reported in *The New York Times*:

> Mike said, "This is our last chance. If we don't take it we'll float farther and farther out to sea." We had a very long discussion and I tried very hard to talk that idea out of his head. He listened to me, but I knew in advance that he would go ahead. It was always very difficult to make him change his mind. He was a brave man but also very unreasonable. . . . His restless nature made it impossible to endure our drifting around.

Michael stripped to shorts. He picked up a red gasoline can, emptied it, then lashed it to another can which he had tied to his body the night before as buoyant protection in case he went overboard.

"I warned him about the crocodiles. I told him I could take no responsibility for him. . . . His last words were, 'I think I can make it. . . . Well, I go.' . . . I followed him for half an hour—he was swimming in a straight line—until I could see only three dots—the two cans and his head."

Michael Rockefeller was never seen again.

Approximately eight hours after Michael began swimming, a Dutch Neptune patrol plane spotted the capsized boat about twenty miles out at sea. By this time a massive search had been mounted by the Dutch government, but the slim hope of finding Michael would fade with every passing hour.

Newsweek reported: "No man could share the grief

of Governor Rockefeller. But every man could and did understand the tragedy of a father searching for his lost son in a far-off jungle."

Nelson Rockefeller chartered a jet and flew to New Guinea with Michael's twin sister, Mary, and Peabody expedition leader Robert Gardner. "I could never forgive myself," he explained, "if I didn't do everything possible to help find my son." Governor Rockefeller, hopeful against all odds, said he felt Michael could make it, remembering his son's recent army training and prowess as a swimmer. "I have complete confidence in Michael's stamina and resourcefulness."

The search took on the scale of a military operation. Dutch and Australian planes, assisted by Australian helicopters, scoured the area by air. Naval and mission boats explored the lagoons. President Kennedy and the U. S. Pacific fleet offered to send an aircraft carrier—but the governor gratefully declined. Over a thousand native canoes crisscrossed the swamps. Any clue would bring a reward beyond their wildest hopes: 250 sticks of tobacco. More than five thousand natives joined the land search, combing the swamps and shoreline. Hundreds of sharks and crocodiles were spotted, but not a trace of Michael.

Dutch officials were pessimistic from the start and Governor P. J. Plateel of New Guinea warned Nelson Rockefeller not to have much hope.

But Nelson Rockefeller did hope: "Mary and I hope that Michael reached shore safely and is somewhere in the area covered by this search. We want to make sure that a search of every village is made. Some of these villages are hard to reach. Michael may be in a remote area where it would be a matter of weeks before word came out. We believe there is hope for some time to come."

For three days father and daughter joined the search, flying across the jungles and coastline in their chartered jet, but with no results. Gardner explored the waters by boat. On the fourth day, as *Newsweek* reported, "Governor Rockefeller returned to Merauke, his face drawn and his shoulders drooping. For the first time his confidence seemed to have been shaken. To a reporter who tactlessly asked: 'Have you any idea how much the search has cost you?' he replied in exasperation: 'No. Have you?' Then, more quietly, he said: 'It's almost over. Things look bad.' "

Michael's only chance by this time would have been if he had made it to shore. But as Dutch resident general Eibrink Jansen observed: "Mike would have had to swim four miles against a strong current where there are sharks and saltwater crocodiles. It would be a miracle if he is found alive."

By November 24, Governor Rockefeller abandoned the search and the Dutch Secretary of the Interior announced: "There is no longer any hope of finding Michael Rockefeller alive. Our people on the spot consider the situation hopeless."

By this time the search had concentrated on finding the red gasoline cans. "If they are found at sea," a Dutch official stated, "we will know that Michael is dead. If we find them on shore we will be encouraged." A red gasoline can was soon picked up in the ocean by a Dutch patrol boat and given a ninety-percent-positive I.D. by Rene Wassing. Governor Rockefeller considered the finding of the can in the ocean near shore a "good omen." And a day later a wisp of smoke was seen in the forest. But nothing came of these clues, and the official consensus was death at sea.

By November 28, the Rockefellers were heading home with heavy hearts. All official hope of finding Michael had ended. Arriving in New York City, the governor expressed his own hope that by some miracle Michael would be found alive in the jungle. But most of what he had to say was a eulogy for his lost son and for the searchers—in the past tense.

In *The New York Times,* Governor Rockefeller said that even as a little boy Michael had been "aware of people, their feelings, their thoughts. He always loved people and was loved by people. He had tremendous enthusiasm and drive. He loved life. He loved the beauty of life, the beauty of people, the beauty of art and nature and sculpture."

He said Michael had never been happier than during his last few months in New Guinea. He expressed gratitude to all who helped and offered help in the search.

As he completed his remarks, the Governor looked at the large group of reporters, photographers, and television cameramen who had remained silent during his ten-minute statement.

"Are there any questions?" he asked.

The newsmen stood in respectful silence as Governor Rockefeller left to enter his car for the trip home.

One year later, the Museum of Primitive Art put on the amazing exhibition of Asmat art that Michael had envisioned. Five years later Michael's journal was published—along with photographs of the people he had studied and the art he had collected—in *The Asmat of New Guinea*.

After Michael's disappearance, theories and rumors abounded—all totally without evidence and highly incredible. One speculation was that he was captured by naval warriors of the Trobriand Islands and carried off as a captive white god. Another asserted that Michael had wanted to escape from the confines of his wealthy heritage and was now living a free life undetected among the "savages." Another claim was that he had brought about his own death by offering murderously high prices for human heads and thus fatally stirred native unrest. None of these rumors held up under even the slightest scrutiny. But one theory has come to be accepted by much of the public as the "true story" of what really happened to Michael. Grisliest of all the speculations, the one in vogue is that he was slain and cannibalized by the Asmat. Or, as a recent article in *Oui* captioned it: "The billion-dollar lunch."

This story began, according to freelance macho-men's-magazine writer and adventurer Milt Machlin, when the *New York Post* published an account of a Dutch missionary in New Guinea, Father Van Kessel, who felt he had uncovered reason to believe that Michael had been slain and eaten by natives in retaliation for the killing of four tribesmen by Dutch officials a few years previously.

Machlin was reached on the phone by *In Search Of* . . . researchers. According to him, Van Kessel said that "the truth was, he reached the shore and he fell into the hands of the village tribesmen who were still full of revenge feelings about those lost people. . . . The most important detail is about the eyeglasses of Mike and his clothes, his underwear only. He was so wise to put off all his clothes except underwear. They [the natives] told about spectacles, and that was practically the most confirming detail that it would be Michael Rockefeller. There is nobody using spectacles but me."

Machlin continued, "There's an odd desire to hush up the story, but I actually have no idea why. I don't think it's a sinister plot. I think it's misapprehension, and somehow a feeling that it's—I don't know—disreputable or something. I mean everybody surrounding the Rockefellers has been careful not to say anything. Or they said things that absolutely didn't make any sense. For instance, one scientist accused Van Kessel of not actually knowing the natives. . . . Van Kessel was an unimpeachable source. Furthermore, I have three or four other priests who said the same thing."

The interviewer asked Machlin whether the political situation in Dutch New Guinea at the time could have been the cause of the alleged silencing of the case. Machlin responded: "Yes, it was clearly the cause. There were two factors. One was that the incident which provoked Michael's death was partially a case of inept management—colonial management by the

Dutch. I mean they had this inexperienced control officer, and the guy panicked one day and killed four Otsjanep natives. The Dutch did not want that story out, and again, you'll find that the Dutch government still will not release any facts even though it's known that this incident occurred. Furthermore, the Dutch were fighting to retain control of what's now known as West Irian [then named Dutch New Guinea] in order to keep from turning it over to the Indonesians. They strongly believed that any evidence of mismanagement would have even greater significance at that time. For instance, they insisted that it would be impossible for Van Kessel's story to have taken place because there were no headhunters and no cannibals. I'd like to tell you that I have film of stacks of heads eight and ten feet high that were taken more than ten years after Michael disappeared. In other words, not only was there still headhunting then but there is now, in some remote areas."

The interviewer then contacted anthropologist David Eyde, who was in the Asmat area doing his Ph.D. and had known Michael. Concerning headhunting, Eyde observed that headhunting "essentially has stopped, but this varies from area to area. It was the case, indeed, that down on the Casuarinen coast where Mike would be most likely to have gone, headhunting was still going on."

Eyde knew of the rumors that Michael had been killed by natives, and he also knew that it couldn't be disproved. But he thought it quite unlikely. "In general, Europeans were sources of tobacco, axes, knives, and that sort of thing, so I don't think that the Asmats were lying in wait to get a European . . . but the rumor can't be discounted. You know I don't want to make the Asmats paragons of virtue, but I never felt that they were scheming for revenge or anything like that. Who knows? Maybe that village [Otsjanep], which I was never in, did harbor some long grudge, or something like that. But, as I say, I think it unlikely, though I can't disprove it."

Adventurer-writer Lorne Blair went to New Guinea in 1975 with a documentary-film team. They retraced Michael's travels in the Asmat and investigated the cannibalism theory. According to Blair, a number of missionaries had received information that linked the death of Michael Rockefeller to the Asmat tribe living at Otsjanep—which never confessed to the alleged deed. The film team went to live in Otsjanep, to investigate the story.

According to Blair, "As we gained the confidence of the villagers, we worked our conversations around to Michael Rockefeller. At first they were evasive about Tesmaipits (his Asmat name), but after a while their denials of any complicity became more and more ambiguous."

Kukoi, a young government-appointed chief who was a child at the time of Michael's disappearance, said he remembered it well: "The people of the other villages—Omanasep, Ats, Baliem—all say that we killed him. They want to get us into trouble. There were many airplanes and boats everywhere. We were afraid and blocked our river with trees so that all those people could not come up here. . . . Later, when the father from Baliem came and asked us what had happened to Tesmaipits, the old people were afraid to tell him, but I shall tell you what the old people told me—the ones who did it, Ajam and the others. They were fishing and they saw this white man floating in the water. He was floating there and he floated away to sea and that's the truth. But everything was all right, because a long time afterward, when the village split up, we killed Ajam and the others. So it's all finished."

Blair spoke with another Asmat, who is not from Ostjanep. "Ah, yes, I have killed many men and I ate them all. Delicious! Omanasep didn't do it, Amanamki didn't do it—it was Otsjanep and only Otsjanep. The villagers killed him in the water and they brought him back to the longhouse and cut him up. You use a bamboo knife that is used only on people. You cut off the head like this, his arms and his legs like this, and then you cut up here. Then you pull his body back and throw him into the fire. Everyone eats—but only the important men get to eat the brain. The government won't allow us to do this anymore."

Later, Blair reported, he reinterviewed Kukoi, who then told him that Ari, an enemy of his, had been one of the killers. "You know," Blair quoted Kukoi, "Ari was one of the ones who killed Tesmaipits."

"What? And did they eat him?"

"It's true."

Blair went upstream to interview Ari: " 'Did Tesmaipits taste good?' My rash question took him momentarily off guard and then he started to laugh; it was a laugh from the belly and a laugh from the heart, so infectious a laugh that I too began to laugh, and we clung to each other laughing until we could laugh no more. That laugh was a more convincing confession than any words he could have spoken. At last I knew for certain what had happened to Michael Rockefeller."

Whether one can believe the "confessions" that adventurer Blair extracted from the natives is debatable. But certainly one person not likely to agree would be Sam Putnam, Michael's companion to New Guinea on the first expedition and best friend in college. When interviewed by *In Search Of . . .* , Dr. Putnam, who now practices medicine in North Carolina, said he thought the cannibalism theory was very unlikely because he doesn't believe Mike ever made it to shore. He said, "Mike was about twelve miles offshore when he began to swim. Swimming in that sun, it's unlikely he could have made it. Furthermore, if he did make it, it's unlikely any harm would have come to him. The natives knew him. Mike was associated with Gerbrands, a very respected man in the villages."

The interviewer asked, "But why would Father Van Kessel tell such a story?"

"I don't know," he said. "But I do know that headhunting had been stopped. The tribes knew what the reprisals would be if they went back to savage customs."

Dr. Putnam continued: "The people of the Asmat tribe were humans who didn't fall into the patterns or stereotypes that the press attributed to them. You know, the reason I agreed to speak to you was to clarify the real purpose of the expedition. The tragedy and irony of the expedition was that it cast an entirely different tone on Mike's purpose in that it dramatized the might of the white man—an arrogant, strong family and country—in a way which was not true. The press missed the point of the expedition. It was to portray the natives as very human, warm people. But it had the opposite effect. It made people feel that those areas were farther removed from Western civilization than was the case. It portrayed the people as savages with no humanness to them."

My feeling is that the most probable fate of Michael Rockefeller was death at sea. Whether he died of exposure and drowned, whether he was killed by a shark or a crocodile—of this there is no way of knowing, and most likely there never will be. But I doubt that he made it to shore.

Approaching the question logically, since there is no physical evidence, we can look only at known facts and likely possibilities.

Immediately after swamping and only about a mile out, the two strong young Papuans began to swim to shore. It took them over five hours to swim the short distance. The water was rough and the current was extremely strong.

Michael remained on the boat, which drifted at least three miles from shore. During the following afternoon and night, he was exposed to the hardships of sun, emotional stress, cold, salt water—possibly hunger and thirst. The next morning he set out to swim the much longer distance—under a hot sun and against the same choppy water and heavy current that had taken two fresh native youths five hours to swim a mile. Even if Michael traveled with the same speed and stamina, it would have taken him at least fifteen hours to swim three miles. The odds were against him.

The Arafura Sea is teeming with sharks, sea serpents, and saltwater crocodiles. It is possible Michael met his fate in the jaws of one of these creatures.

The red gasoline can was found floating at sea. It is possible that Michael reached land, left the can on the beach, and that it was floated back out to sea by the tide. It seems more likely, though, that the can never made it to shore.

If Michael Rockefeller had been killed and eaten, news would have traveled through the Asmat. Especially with the high reward, at least one native mouth would have unsealed if there had been any information to give.

Overall, then, it seems most likely that Michael Rockefeller died at sea. However, since there is no conclusive, physical evidence, his fate does remain a mystery.

PART II
THE FUGITIVES

Prologue

As I began to examine the mysteries surrounding disappearances of famous persons, I realized I would ultimately be dealing with a category called *fugitives*. In some cases they would be fugitives wanted by the authorities. In others, they might be social outsiders who had set themselves apart from the rest of society by virtue of the goals they had established. They have in common the fact that their disappearances were deliberate.

Each of the four stories presented in Part II are studies of people, power, and corruption. The fugitives are either outlaws or runaways (i.e., émigrés or displaced persons). Sometimes they are hunted because of a specific act or acts they committed, or because of the power they have had or can potentially wield. Strangely enough, despite massive search efforts by professionals, none of the fugitives has been found. They all remain, today, at large.

Professional "skip tracers" have explained to me that it is very hard for a person to remain missing: the existence of written records, handwriting samples, photographs, and medical and dental records make it difficult for an individual to go underground. The traces left by the normal aspects of life, according to the experts, usually yield the person desired quite easily. However, the four stories present herein have defied both the experts and the odds.

If all cultures have their myths, their heroes, then fugitives hold an extraordinary grasp on popular fancy.

The legendary stories of escape become part of national and regional folklore. Desperadoes, aristocratic émigrés, and notorious public enemies gain currency as part of treasured myth. They remain part of that folklore only as long as their whereabouts are cloaked in mystery.

It always amuses me when I find law-abiding citizens hailing fugitives as courageous renegades. I wonder what specific quality in the fugitive inspires such widespread admiration. It seems to me that heroic figures should be made of sterner stuff. Of all the fugitives I sought, only one breed was held in general contempt: war criminals, murderers guilty of gruesome atrocities. In recent fiction from *The Odessa File* to *Marathon Man,* their presence continues to be a source of fascination. Clearly, they are villains. Clearly, they intrigue us.

I began to wonder if fugitives remain at large because their mysterious fate allows us to fill in the missing data with our own fantasy.

I have tried in each case to present both the myths concerning the fugitive and his fate as well as the factual background of the person in question. In all the cases the myths that cropped up over the course of time seemed to strike a familiar chord. I noted a little of my own fantasies nestled in among the speculations about the final fate of the lone fugitive. Perhaps this fantasy reflected a bit of my own image of the hero— the outsider—one man against the system. Perhaps the myths we create fulfill the fleeting fantasies of ourselves within society; for maybe we are all participating in the Great Escape.

5
The Romanovs

Anastasia, princess of czarist Russia, is perhaps the most romantic fugitive of the twentieth century. Her only crime was being born to royalty as the proletarian revolution racked the Soviet Union. Was she executed with her family or did she escape?

Part of the story is clearly known. In 1917 the Bolshevik uprising deposed her father, the czar, and the royal family was taken into custody and hidden away in a mountain redoubt. In July 1918, White Russian and Czechoslovakian armies loyal to the czar counterattacked. One contingent marched toward the town of Ekaterinburg in the Ural Mountains, where the royal family was being held captive. Czar Nicholas II and his family were crucial symbols of the old imperial order. Loyalist soldiers were determined to free them. Ironically, only a handful of Soviet guards stood watch over Nicholas the czar, Alexandra the czarina, his hemophiliac son, Alexis, and his four daughters— Olga, Tatiana, Maria, and Anastasia.

On the night of July 16, 1918, Yurovsky, commander of the Soviet Guard, awoke Nicholas and his family, the czar's physician, and three loyal retainers, and instructed them to dress. They were then led to a small room in the basement and told to wait for further instructions. Suddenly a cheka squad (the secret police) carrying revolvers burst into the room. A fusillade erupted, killing the entire Romanov party. The blood-drenched corpses were then carted away and thrown into the shaft of the Four Brothers Mine, a few miles away. . . . At least that was one "official" story.

While some accounts may vary in minor detail, most conclude that the Romanovs were murdered. One fact that has consistently been ignored is that no bodies were ever found. Also ignored is a little-known incident that occurred nineteen months after the purported executions:

In Berlin an unidentified young woman threw herself into the River Spree; after she was rescued and taken to the Elizabeth Hospital, she refused to identify herself, and after spending two years in a mental institution she finally claimed she was the czar's youngest daughter.

These two disparate episodes are the opening events in what has become for me one of the most romantic and baffling controversies of our time. Who was that girl who leaped into the River Spree? Was she Anastasia? And what really happened at Ekaterinburg that prevented the discovery of the corpses of the royal family?

The more I read about the Romanov story, the more I realized that this was not merely prime missing-person material but indeed missing-*family* material. Even though the historical versions of the last of the Romanovs depicted a mass murder in a cellar at Ekaterinburg, all texts acknowledged that none of the eleven bodies was ever found. Moreover, one of the more orthodox accounts, *The End of the Romanovs* by Victor Alexandrov, stated that, "as for all the evidence collected by the examining magistrats of the White Army, we have to admit that, accurate though it is, it does never-the-less leave a remote possibility that one of the Grand Duchesses could have escaped the slaughter and fled to the West."

In order to fully appreciate why a multitude of theories surround the gruesome episode, it is necessary to understand Russia's royal family. The Romanov dynasty has intrigued and perplexed the world for more than three centuries. Awesome monarchs who wielded absolute power over Russia from 1613 to 1917, their reign was characterized by the extremes of dazzling opulence and ruthless savagery. In the Romanov realm, deep-seated religiosity bordering on the mystical sometimes existed simultaneously with maniacal cruelty. The dynasty included some of the most bizarre, scandalous, violent, and tragic figures in the annals of royalty. The personal characteristics of each generation afford a study in widely varying contrasts. From Peter the Great, renowned for his ferocious cruelty, the Romanov line descended to the reluctant, weak-willed Nicholas II, the last czar to rule Russia.

Despite the personal frailties of the Romanovs, they commanded the loyalty and obedience of their subjects. Glorified by the mystique of autocratic power, they played the major role in shaping three centuries of Russian history.

Russian historian Ian Grey stated in *The Romanovs*:

> For all Russians, the Tsar-autocrat was the nation; it could not exist without him. They looked to him to rule and defend the nation, and since he was appointed by God, they expected of him both magnificence and magic. They retained until the twentieth century this exalted conception of the position and power of their Autocrats. The Romanov Autocrats thus played a far more dominant role in the internal and external affairs of the Russian nation than their Western contemporaries. . . . The History of Russia in the seventeenth, eighteenth, and nineteenth centuries is, in fact, inseparable from the history of the Romanov dynasty.

Nicholas II, the last Romanov to bear the title Czar, was one of the least prepossessing rulers in Russian history. Historians say that he was a gentle man, unhappily endowed with little strength of will. He did not relish ruling the vast and violent Russian wilderness, and when his father, Alexander III, died in 1894, Nicholas II seemed totally unprepared to take over the

throne. To the Russian people he became known somewhat contemptuously as the Little Father. While the
czar had long symbolized national unity, as Nicholas
II took the throne, the Russian people were beginning
to smart from the shackles of anachronistic, feudal institutions.

There were three critical factors that paved the
way for the destruction of the Romanov regime: the
political unrest of the time; Nicholas II's distaste for
governmental functions; and finally, his insistence,
however admirable, on marrying for love rather than
for political considerations. The German princess Alix
of Hesse-Darmstadt became his bride amid loud pro-
testations from his staunchly anti-German parents. The
marriage was one of fierce devotion, and this romantic
union may have been one of the main reasons for the
ultimate extinction of the Romanovs.

The new German empress, Alexandra Feodorovna
(the name she assumed when she was rebaptized in the
Orthodox Church), was a dedicated wife and mother.
She embraced Russian Orthodox religion with near-
fanatic fervor. She thoroughly believed that Nicholas
had been appointed by God to rule the Russian people
and counseled him against falling prey to the popular
demands of a constitutional monarchy. She believed it
her duty to make sure that Czar Nicholas II continued
the autocratic rule of his ancestors—notwithstanding the
advice of wise and devoted government ministers.

Inside the palace walls, protected from the unrest
of the populace, Nicholas and Alexandra had little
inkling of the turbulence that was buffeting Russian
tradition. They were the very center of the storm, yet
they could not see beyond the intrigues of their court.
The controversy was often centered on Alexandra.
Virginia Cowles, in *The Romanovs,* wrote:

If Alexandra disappointed Court circles, she, in
turn, viewed the Establishment with deepest suspicion. "I feel that all who surround my husband

are insincere," she wrote during the first years of her marriage, "and no one is doing his duty for Russia. They are all serving him for their career and personal advantage, and I worry myself and cry for days on end as I feel that my husband is very young and inexperienced, of which they are all taking advantage."

Urged by Alexandra, Nicholas's initial declaration of autocracy antagonized the nation. Demonstrations against the czar were sudden, violent, and widespread. Terrorism increased. Fearful of the growing threat of revolution, Nicholas allowed himself to approve a policy of expansion, which in turn led to an unpopular and unnecessary war with Japan. He hoped that the prospect of war would distract the revolutionary agitators. He was sorrowfully disappointed.

Amid impending war with Japan, Alexandra, who had presented Nicholas with four daughters, finally bore a son, an heir to the royal family. Six weeks after this joyful event, the disease of European royalty became evident—hemophilia. The czarina was desperate. She began seeking a miracle that would save the life of her son, the heir apparent. She had already displayed a leaning toward the mystical and was now ripe prey for the babble of charlatans who claimed to provide miracles.

Enter Rasputin.

Rasputin had roamed Russia as a penitent searching for truth and salvation. A *stranniki,* he lived off the charity of the populace. Grey recorded: "They [*strannikis*] were revered as holy men . . . and were accorded a certain freedom and authority so that they spoke to all, even, on occasions, to Tsars, with simple bluntness. He [Rasputin] was reputed to have great powers of healing and prophesy. . . ."

Upon learning of Rasputin's powers, the empress sought his help. Soon, however, Rasputin was not only healing the czar's son but also attempting, or so he claimed, to heal the wounds of the Russian nation, which he believed the revolutionaries were causing.

Rasputin's reactionary advice inflamed the unrest raging throughout Russia. Despite warnings from loyal ministers, Nicholas and Alexandra continued to listen to Rasputin's counsel.

The massacre of workers by the czar's guards on famous "Bloody Sunday" early in 1905 dimmed the prestige of the royal family. Strikes plagued the country, paralyzing industry. By the middle of October the entire country was in the midst of a crippling general strike: factories shut down; trains screeched to a halt; electric lights dimmed in St. Petersburg; food deliveries ceased. Peasants were raiding opulent estates and the nation's workers were clamoring for a constitution. Finally, at the eleventh hour, Nicholas obliged.

The Imperial Manifesto of October 1905 transformed Russia from an autocracy to a semiconstitutional monarchy. It granted and elected the Duma (Parliament). But Nicholas was unhappy with the demands of the new government. He soon urged Prime Minister Peter A. Stolypin to shut down the Duma. In comic-opera fashion, the Duma opened and closed not once but twice. Under the calming leadership of Stolypin, Russia flourished once more. Industry was enjoying a boom, production was increasing, and foreign trade was growing. The final solidification was prompted by forces operating outside Russia.

On August 1, 1914, the Germans' declaration of war united the Russian multitudes under the czar. The impending war against Germany and Austro-Hungary had complete, unswerving popular support. Nicholas's role resembled that of the Romanovs of old—the czar once more with his people. Despite Rasputin's warnings against war, Nicholas forged on with military preparations. In fact, he was so elated that he decided to go to the front along with his troops, leaving the nation in the hands of Rasputin and Alexandra.

Rumors began to circulate. Some accused Alexan-

dra and Rasputin of being German agents. Certainly
Rasputin's activities did not help. He secured government posts for his reactionary friends. He made a great
show of his influence on the czarina. Then, in December 1916, Loyalists murdered Rasputin.

It was too late for Rasputin's death to cause radical
changes. Still at war on the front, the Russian armies
had lost two and a half million men—almost as many
as all the other allies put together. On the home front,
bread shops were empty. A hundred thousand workers were either on strike or unemployed. The Putilev
works, the biggest metallurgical combine in the capital, had shut down. Virginia Cowles in *The Romanovs*
reported: "On March 9, 1917, the long silent food
queues suddenly ignited. People smashed their way
into shops and helped themselves. The revolution had
begun."

Petrograd went on strike. But Nicholas was still at
the front. His ministers telegraphed him, imploring
him to return home to appoint a government acceptable to the Duma. Nicholas not only refused, he ordered the army to put down the unrest. The army
mutinied.

The Constituent Assembly formed its own provisional government under Alexander Kerensky, but the
Revolution was already in full swing. On March 15,
1917, Nicholas II abdicated. The three-hundred-year
reign of the Romanovs had ended.

The imperial family was under house arrest at Tsar-
skoye Selo. In July 1917, an unsuccessful Bolshevik
uprising caused Alexander Kerensky, leader of the
provisional government, to move the royal family to
Tobolsk in Siberia. And finally, so the story goes, the
Ekaterinburg massacre. They were—all of them, supposedly—executed in front of a firing squad in the
basement of the house on the night of July 16–17,
1918. No one survived, not even the corpses. Nothing survived of the Romanovs except two distinctly
different reports concerning what happened to them.
Both reports were products of so-called official inves-

tigations generated by the White Russian government, which was struggling to maintain control over the Bolsheviks. Yet, the findings reported were diametrically opposed.

The "accepted" report on the alleged cellar murder of Nicholas II and the imperial family was written by Nicholas A. Sokolov. Sokolov was appointed to investigate the case in February 1919 by the White government, which at that time controlled the city of Ekaterinburg.

According to John F. O'Conor in *The Sokolov Investigation,* Sokolov was the last appointed investigator in the case, and it is for that reason that the Sokolov report has always been regarded as the official account. However, O'Conor noted:

> Other accounts describing evidence collected in the course of the investigation would appear to have an equally "official" character. They were written by persons who had an official part in the conduct of the investigation, or who acted as witnesses, or who obviously had more or less complete copies of the record in their possession.

These pre-Sokolov accounts are more intriguing in light of evidence that has recently been uncovered.

The pre-Sokolov reports did not find any evidence of mass murder. In fact, the criminal-investigation division of Ekaterinburg upheld the proposition maintained by the Soviet (Red Russians) regime—only the czar had been killed.

Indeed, according to an account (included in O'Conor's book) by General Dietrichs, the supervisor of the Romonov investigation, the members of the various investigative commissions went off in different directions: "Those who continued to believe firmly in the accomplishment of the foul deed became silent, holding themselves aloof from discussion and questioning. Others, unwilling to accept it, attached themselves to the legend prompted by Yankel Sverdlov; the Tsar

In Search of
Missing Persons

Where did they go?
Why did they leave?

Richard Halliburton

In 1939, Halliburton set sail from Hong Kong in a
lavishly decorated Chinese sailing junk. He never returned.
(The John "Bruce" Potter Collection)

Richard Halliburton was America's greatest swashbuckling hero of the '20s and '30s. Some of his exploits included climbing the Matterhorn, hiking across the Pyrenees, swimming the Nile, scaling Mt. Fujiyama, following Ulysses' trail across Greece, swimming the Panama Canal, leaping into the Mayan Well of Death and living in a cave in Tobago. *(Princeton University Library)*

Percy Fawcett

In 1925, Colonel Percy Fawcett set out on an expedition to Brazil to search for the lost city of "Z." He never returned. No conclusive evidence concerning his ultimate fate has even been uncovered in the dense jungle wilderness. *(Alan Landsburg Productions)*

Amelia Earhart

Amelia Earhart, the queen of aviation,
was the first woman to fly a trans-Atlantic solo.
She was welcomed back to New York with a ticker tape
parade. *(Sherman Grinberg Library)*

Top: On a round-the-world flight, en route to Howland Island in the Pacific, Earhart and her navigator Fred Noonan were lost at sea without a trace. *(Sherman Grinberg Library)* *Bottom:* Joe Gervais has devoted 20 years of research to the Amelia Earhart mystery. He believes President Roosevelt sent her on a military flight to photograph evidence that Japan was fortifying Pacific Islands. According to Gervais, the Japanese forced her to make a crash landing on Hull Island and she was held captive in Japan. *(Joe Gervais)*

Top: America could not accept the account of Earhart's death. Fred Goerner uncovered suspicious material in the National Archives which led him to believe that the flight was an espionage mission staged by the White House. (*Alan Landsburg Productions*)

Bottom: Captain Elgen Long has carefully studied information about the last leg of Earhart's flight. By reconstructing a navigational model, Long's theory is that Earhart was forced to ditch the plane near Howland Island. He believes the plane may be totally intact but submerged under 16,000 feet of water. (*Alan Landsburg Productions*)

<u>Michael Rockefeller</u>

Michael Rockefeller, photographer and adventurer, disappeared on his last expedition to New Guinea in the fall of 1961. One theory of his disappearance, that he was slain and cannibalized, has never been proven. (*UPI*)

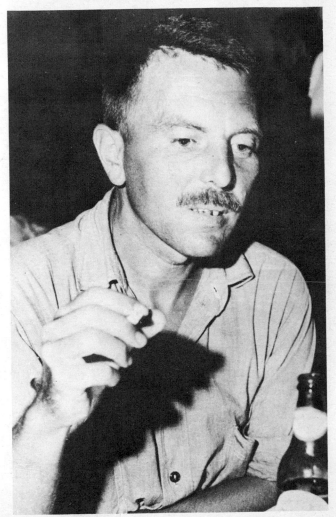

Rockefeller's companion, anthropologist
Dr. Rene Wassing, survived the expedition. (*UPI*)

Anastasia

Was Anastasia, princess of czarist Russia,
executed with her family or did she
escape in 1918? *(Library of Congress Collection)*

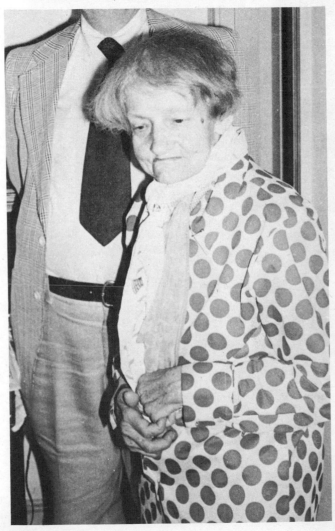

Anna Anderson Manahan, the most famous claimant to the title of the Grand Duchess Anastasia Romanov. So far her claim cannot be disproven. *(Bill Sublette, The Daily Progress)*

Amy Semple Macpherson

In 1926, evangelist Amy Semple Macpherson swam out into the Pacific and, when she didn't return, was presumed drowned at sea. After 36 days, she walked out of the Mexican desert and claimed she had been kidnapped. Or was it a voluntary disappearance? *(Sherman Grinberg Library)*

Top: Amy's return. Was her disappearance a flair for the dramatic or the gratification of seeing thousands mourn her. *(Sherman Grinberg Library)*
Bottom: Amy could draw a crowd anywhere she went. She became a religio-commercial entrepreneur. *(Sherman Grinberg Library)*

"Robert Rich"

A Hollywood blacklist followed the Red Conspirator
hunt of the McCarthy years. During this time Dalton Trumbo
scripted nearly 30 movies under assorted pseudonyms.
In 1956 he won an Academy Award for best screenplay
under the name Robert Rich. Here Trumbo expresses
his outrage at the affront the Committee on Unamerican
Activities was committing on the American character.
He was cited for contempt of Congress and sentenced
to one year in jail. *(Sherman Grinberg Library)*

"D. B. Cooper"

"D. B. Cooper" performed the most famous skyjacking
in the history of air piracy. In 1971, Cooper extorted
$200,000 from Nórhwest Airlines and parachuted to
fame over the rugged country of southwest Washington state.
His identity and whereabouts have never been
discovered. (*Alan Landsburg Productions*)

The Great Gods

The Incas, Mayas and Aztecs had an identical culture
hero/god: Viracocha, Kukulcan and Quetzalcoatl. Legend
had it that a fair-skinned man/god appeared as a stranger and
lingered among the people imparting knowledge of
civilization. Then disappeared never to return.
Could this be what the bearded god looked like?

perished, but the whole family had been spared and removed by the Bolsheviks to a safe place. . . ."

The *Saturday Evening Post* of July 31, 1920, reported that the czar's valet, Tchemodroff, did not believe that the family had been killed. Tchemodroff claimed that Botkin, physician to the czar, and other retainers had been killed, but that the family had been taken away. By killing Botkin and the others, the murder of the royal family was simulated. The house was subsequently ransacked for the same reason.

Thus, the "official" investigative commissions were divided into two camps: pro-assassination and antiassassination.

And yet, only one party line emerged to cover the pages in the history texts. Why? Why was one theory more convenient than the other? There was no evidence in support of the historically official theory. The proassassination theory evoked strong criticism in the form of reliable witness testimony. Moreover, there was never any physical evidence found. The bodies had "disappeared."

John O'Conor, author of *The Sokolov Investigation*, had translated the Sokolov document and was, plainly, suspicious of its conclusions.

I knew from his book that he had concluded that there was no more evidence supporting Sokolov's conclusion of mass murder than there was supporting that of his predecessors, who found no evidence of mass murder.

O'Conor explained to me during a phone conversation that he had originally intended to translate only certain sections of the investigation. "However," he said, "I got into reading and it just sounded to me like it didn't have a ring of truth, so I began to analyze it. I've come across a lot of curious things. But, basically and briefly, I'd say that Sokolov's evidence was insufficient. He tried to make too much out of it. He was too positive. Then there were other things. . . . Sokolov had predecessors who had investigated the murder. And he tried to run them down as being Jewish and too leftish, and this didn't seem to have anything to do with the facts. From what I could see, the previous investigators had done a pretty good job."

Part of the conclusion drawn by the Sokolov report was based on items of clothing found in the basement along with a grisly assortment of supposedly human remains. Sokolov did turn up evidence, but, said O'Conor, "Nothing, really, that couldn't have been planted. There was just clothing and items of decoration or possessions. The finger they found couldn't be identified. And the few bones they found could have been animal bones."

He paused for a moment, then continued: "You know, if the Reds did it and had wanted to conceal their crime, they wouldn't leave all that stuff around. There were too many places where they could have hidden the stuff. The clothing could have been brought back to the house, not spread around in the area to be found by someone."

And: "There were no eyewitnesses really. I mean, the only eyewitness was somebody who said he saw the czarevitch give his last gasp. The witnesses were untrustworthy. And secondly, there was a conflict between what they saw and what other people saw."

O'Conor pointed out that the Sokolov report favored the White Russian causes. O'Conor believes that the White Russians upheld the pro-assassination theory because the public's belief that the czar was dead would make it easier for the Whites to take over the government of Russia. It could also, as Tom Mangold and Tony Summers later suggested in their book *The File on the Tsar,* be used to portray the Bolsheviks as bloodthirsty bullies, thereby rallying the populace to the White cause. But what about the Reds' motivation for maintaining that same theory? Why did it behoove them not to change the official historical version?

"Ultimately," O'Conor said, "the Reds adopted what the Whites had said. I reasoned that the Reds' rationale was to erase any possibility of a Romanov suddenly emerging as a rallying cry against Red Soviet rule."

O'Conor then added a tantalizing tidbit: "Some people say they saw the whole family being taken away." Explaining one way in which this execution could have been fabricated, O'Conor pointed out the possibility that "doubles" of the royal family were murdered. "I think that's very much a possibility. There's an enormous disparity in what historians can find out about what happened in Ekaterinburg [renamed Sverdlovsk in 1924] in the weeks prior to its capture."

O'Conor went on to explain that the revolutionaries had started uprisings in many of the cities along the Volga River—the longest river in Europe—at the point where the Volga is not very far from the Ekaterinburg vicinity of the Ural Mountains. If Ekaterinburg had had such an uprising, the czar and his family could easily have been taken out of the house.

At this point, it became evident to me that my search was just beginning.

Peter Bessell was a British member of Parliament when he first became interested in and then began his investigation into the Romanov mystery. During a visit to New York he read Guy Richards's book *The Hunt for the Czar;* extremely impressed with how Richards had demolished the Sokolov report, Bessell telephoned Richards and suggested that he might be able to come up with additional evidence by raising the matter in the House of Commons. (Britain would have been deeply involved in any rescue mission, for King George V was Czar Nicholas's cousin.) But Bessell had no luck. His Parliamentary questions were rejected on technicalities that Bessell, an experienced Parliamentarian, thought suspicious. He did not campaign in the general election of 1970, having announced two years earlier that he intended to retire from politics. He moved to America, where he continued following the trail, using as guides some rather influential friends in Washington. (Henry Kissinger's name figured among Mr. Bessell's contacts.) Bessell uncovered a group of documents now titled the Chivers Papers.

The Chivers Papers is the day-to-day account of a man named Lange, who, allegedly, was the American agent responsible for organizing the escape of the Romanov family from Ekaterinburg. The Chivers Papers claim that the murder plot, or the assassination story, was really a cover-up for an escape.

Bessell commented during an interview: "What I think did *not* happen to the imperial family is that they were assassinated at Ekaterinburg in the way that history has always assumed.

"I think there are a number of reasons [for that belief]. The first one, of course, is Tony Summers and Tom Mangold's book, *The File on the Tsar,* and the earlier book by Guy Richards, *The Hunt for the Czar.* Both point out that the main evidence on which the assumption of an assassination had always been based was a cover-up. And once you demolish the Sokolov report, you're left without a scrap of evidence to support the assassination theory, and a good deal of circumstantial evidence to suggest an escape.

"The Chivers Papers say that the escape was organized jointly by the United States, the United Kingdom, and Japan, with some participation by the French government. They map out a route from Ekaterinburg to a trade mission, or a house rented by a trade mission, at a town about fifteen miles northwest of Ekaterinburg. It appears from the papers that the imperial family were housed there for several months while plans were completed for their escape along a quite treacherous route which eventually took them to Odessa, to the Black Sea, where we lose track of them."

But are the papers authentic?

"This is a very difficult question for me to answer," he said. "The problem is that although when I saw the papers they appeared to me to be absolutely genuine documents, I am not an expert on such matters. It was evident that they were old. They used phraseology and terminology of the period. They were on official State Department notepaper, and so on. I had no reason to doubt their authenticity as original government documents about the period in question. But then again, I'm not an expert."

He paused for a moment, then continued: "But as to the content of the papers—it appears to be a very logical story. The main bulk of the papers consists of a very long memorandum written by Robert Lansing [Secretary of State at that time] to President Wilson. It's very hard to believe that the Secretary of State would have wasted his time writing a story which had no foundation; that he would have submitted it to President Wilson, who was then in poor health and deeply involved in a battle with Congress over American participation in the League of Nations. Taking those factors into account, I was bound to reach the conclusion that the papers were probably genuine and that the story they told was probably correct.

"There are many aspects of the research done by Anthony Summers and Tom Mangold in their book which would lead to a possible contradiction, but on the other hand they point out some factors that might support an escape such as that described in the Chivers Papers."

Bessell concluded with this statement: "I still think that on the balance of probability, there is a good chance, at any rate, that the story in essence—as it is told in the Chivers Papers—may be correct."

Anthony Summers is a television journalist for the British Broadcasting Corporation in London. He has been working on the Romanov case for the last five years with his colleague, Tom Mangold.

Summers explained how he became involved in the Romanov odyssey. "We had read in the correspondence columns of the *London Times* that people who apparently were qualified to know what they were talking about were claiming to know locations of the burials of the so-called Romanov remains. Tom and I thought that this would be a short television-magazine item on which we could work for a couple of weeks before going on vacation. So we started digging, and instead of two weeks, the digging took us five years."

Summers went on to explain that his findings were based on material he had gathered in the British Foreign Ministry Archives, as well as from interviews with a large number of people who claimed to have witnessed the events of 1918–19. "But," he said, "the key breakthrough was the finding of the original dossiers [at Harvard University] of the judicial officials who had investigated the case for the anti-Bolshevik side in 1918 and 1919. This is the full set of material which Sokolov had to work with, including vast amounts of material which he did not use but had suppressed.

"The conclusion, from looking at all this material taken together, shows that the czar may have been killed around the time and place that he's supposed to have been killed, although not in the famous cellar." Summers, however, believes that "the czarina and her four daughters were taken, alive, from Ekaterinburg by the Communists in a sealed train to a town called Perm, about two hundred miles northwest of Ekaterinburg. They were held alive there for six or seven months after the orthodox date of their deaths, while Lenin bargained with the kaiser about what was to become of them."

If Summers and Mangold were right, then the bodily remains purportedly found by Sokolov could not have been those of the imperial family. Sokolov accounted for the scanty remains by "logically" reconstructing the aftermath of the cellar murder. He claimed that the bodies of eleven people had been chopped up and burned with fire and acid in a clearing in a nearby forest.

However, Mangold and Summers found that theory highly implausible. They requested the help of Professor Francis Camps, a reputable and highly experienced pathologist. Camps told the journalists that in order to destroy bodies as completely as the Communists supposedly had, a crematorium would be necessary. Moreover, Camps claimed that it was nonsensical to use fire and acid together in an open-air environment; these two agents would have acted against each other, burning the remains so completely that they would have been unrecognizable as human bodies.

Summers stopped to light a cigarette, settled back in his chair, and began to explain that because the czarina was a German princess, the Germans were very eager that she would be well treated. Moreover, by the time the family disappeared in July 1918, the Germans were asking not only for the Romanovs' safekeeping but also for their release to Germany. Thus, it would have been political folly for Lenin to have murdered the czarina and her daughters.

Summers said, "It seems, from all the evidence, that Lenin didn't have them murdered—he kept them alive; and, working from the documents we have found, we do not lose trace of them until early 1919, when they are being taken under escort on a train in the direction of Moscow.

"They never appear again, on the evidence we have so far uncovered. But Germany was, by that time, out of the war and the German kaiser Wilhelm was off his own throne, making Germany no longer a threat. I think one has to use one's common sense and assume that sometime in early 1919 they were finally liquidated. But we have no proof of this.

"The most interesting part, though, about the end of the trail is that we find that it was only the czarina and three daughters, not four, who were taken away in the direction of Moscow. One daughter was missing, and that daughter was Anastasia."

Summers further told me that sometime in the period between July 1918 and the end of the year, the authentic Anastasia did escape but was recaptured. "The key thing here is that she was separated from the rest of her family. Once you have any of the family out of the cellar, and then you find that one of the family escaped, and that member of the family is Anastasia, then you have to look at stories about the escape of Anastasia in a brand-new light."

That was just what I intended to do. I made contact with representatives of Mrs. Anna Anderson Manahan —the most famous claimant to the title Grand Duchess Anastasia Romanov. She and her husband live in Charlottesville, Virginia. An aging woman, she has only recently begun to speak publicly and pointedly about her past.

Anna's ghost-written autobiography, *I Am Anastasia,* was used more or less as the basis for the 1956 Hollywood film starring Ingrid Bergman. The film strays from Anna's story recorded in the book.

Anna Anderson first turned up in Berlin after she had jumped into the River Spree in a suicide attempt. For more than fifty years she has said she is Anastasia. She has been the subject of the longest court case of the century. Living today with her husband, John Manahan, she still steadfastly maintains that she is Anastasia.

Summers and Mangold have gathered all the available evidence pertinent to her claim. Surprisingly enough—to me—it does point in her favor. Identification experts have studied photographs of the czar's family and young Anastasia, and they support her contention that she is the grand duchess. Comparison of various parts of the body—ears, nose, bone structure—all suggest that she is the czar's youngest daughter.

I next talked with Peter Kurth, an American expert on the Anastasia case. I wanted to know why he was so convinced that Anna's claim was real. He began by explaining: "For a starter, there's a very strong facial resemblance which, when pictures are put together in the right way, is immediately apparent. Photographic experts base their conclusions on measurements of the face, the distance between the parts, etcetera."

Kurth told me that handwriting analyses have confirmed that there are too many similarities between the handwriting samples for them to have been made by two separate people. And no other contender to the title of Anastasia has met with such sinister opposition. Relatives who denied that she could be Anastasia even went so far as to pay certain people to testify that she was a Polish peasant. Luckily, the attempt to defraud Ms. Anderson was found out. Conclusive evidence, however, that would stand in court is still lacking. The historical Anastasia's fingerprints aren't available. Dental records were judged by the courts as being far too vague for convincing identification.

Kurth continued: "She has told stories and has given information about what it was like as a child; a substantial number of these stories have been proved true. None has been disproved. You know," he added, "she's never been caught out in anything. She's never made a statement that's been proved false. Never once."

Bill Sublette of the *Daily Progress,* a newspaper in Charlottesville, has covered the Anastasia/Anderson story for a few years. According to Sublette, Ms. Anderson disputes some of the new evidence that Summers and Mangold have turned up. Her main complaint against *The File on the Tsar* focuses on what she considers an unflattering photograph of her in younger years. That complaint in itself seems to me to be in line with one who no longer feels a need to prove her identity to the world.

More seriously, however, Ms. Anderson claims that all the members of the royal family survived, including the czar and czarina. Sublette reported: "The person killed at Ekaterinburg was not her father, but 'a double,' said the short, frail-looking claimant. . . . She would not disclose how she and the rest of the family escaped death."

Sublette told me privately that Ms. Anderson does

not agree with *The File on the Tsar* in that she states that she and her sisters and the czarina were *not* taken to Perm.

Ms. Anderson's reaction to and comments about the events at Ekaterinburg add credence to the theory that the murder was simulated, as was claimed by the czar's valet, Tchemodroff.

There are many plausible theories and conclusions as to what really happened to the Romanovs. Did the entire family escape? Were they rescued by the great world powers of the day? Did any survive? Is Ms. Anna Anderson Manahan really Anastasia?

Most of the eywitnesses are dead. The evidence is tattered fragments, well thumbed by a multitude of researchers. Proof of Ms. Anderson's claim seems impossible. But the quest itself remains one of the most enticing challenges I have ever encountered. I wonder if somewhere, in a long-forgotten government archive in Germany or Russia, Poland, Austria or Hungary, or even in the United States, there is a report, a document, a secret file, which holds the key to the identity of Anastasia. I am enough of a romantic to believe that the evidence does in fact exist.

6

Martin Bormann

Martin Bormann is accused of having committed crimes against the peace, war crimes, and crimes against humanity, as charged in a bill of indictment submitted to this Court.

The bill of indictment is on display and can be examined in the Court Building in Nuremberg.

In the event that Martin Bormann appears, he has the rights to defend himself either in person or by counsel.

In the event that he does not present himself, it is possible to proceed against him in his absence. The trial will begin on November 20, 1945, in the Court building in Nuremberg, Germany. Should he be found guilty, his sentence will be carried out without any further proceedings and according to the decisions of the Control Council for Germany, as soon as he is apprehended.

—INTERNATIONAL MILITARY TRIBUNAL

Martin Bormann, in absentia, is convicted of two of the four counts against him. The court sentences him to *"Tod durch den Strang"*—death by hanging.

Never hang a man you don't hold.
Medieval Nuremberg burgher adage

Martin Bormann, *Reichsleiter,* personal secretary, and general controller of Adolf Hitler's life, was the only one of the top Nazi brass to be convicted of war crimes in absentia. His absence from the Nuremberg cell blocks was conspicuous. However, Bormann was not the only Nazi war criminal to escape justice. The Ludwigsburg Center for the Investigation of Nazi War Crimes estimates that nearly 100,000 Germans were involved in various executions. But only 50,000 were arrested, and only a little over 5,000 were ever tried and convicted. Of that, 818 were sentenced to death and only 489 were executed. The record of bringing to justice those who have committed crimes against humanity is very poor.

It is generally agreed, however, that of all the members in Hitler's inner circle, Martin Bormann was the most likely to slip away after the war and live a life of anonymity and wealth. Alfred Rosenberg, Party philosopher, wrote of him, "Nobody could identify his name with a concept, an idea, an accomplishment, a personality." Martin Bormann had successfully created a profession of being Hitler's constant shadow. While he appeared in many group portraits, his name was rarely captioned and his position never defined. Some described him as a "molelike man who preferred to burrow in the dark recesses of Party life." Ladislas Farago, in *Aftermath, Martin Bormann and the Fourth Reich,* wrote: "Bormann was universally disliked as a subterranean worker." But, he preferred his background role, personally, as well. On October 9, 1943, Bormann wrote his wife, Gerda:

"I am sending you a book on orders and medals which I received today. It may well be that a Fuehrer forced to reckon with the vanity of his fellow-countrymen and so to slap orders and the like all over them. As for me, I have all my life been content with my own inner satisfaction and that of the Fuehrer."

Martin Bormann's later life was marked by his dedication to Adolf Hitler, the Third Reich, and his almost fanatical devotion to Nazi precepts. Unlike other believers in the Hitler Reich destiny, I believe he was not ready, as some have claimed, to commit suicide when the end of the Reich was at hand. In fact, the last entry in Bormann's calendar book was: *"Ausbruchsversuch"* ("breakout attempt").

"Breakout" launched the Bormann legend. Rumors about his whereabouts began as soon as Berlin fell to the advancing Russians. On May 4, 1944, four days before the formal surrender, he was reported in Czechoslovakia. Two days later a Prague radio station still in German hands tried to obscure his fate by declaring that he had been killed, during the assault on the Reich Chancellery, along with Propaganda Minister Goebbels and Werner Naumann, Goebbels's deputy.

By May 10, the Allied War Crimes Commission said, the Russians were fairly certain that a body they had found was that of Martin Bormann. On June 12 the *New York Times* carried a dispatch saying that Bormann had been arrested, probably by the Russians. The possibility of suicide was put forth by aviatrix Hanna Reitsch, who had volunteered to fly Hitler out of Berlin on April 30, at dawn. According to Farago, in his book on Bormann, Reitsch said that there had been a suicide pact made but she wasn't sure that the Reischsleiter had abided by it. "When I last saw him," Farago quoted Reitsch, "he was sitting at his desk recording the momentous events in the bunker for posterity, while Hitler raved."

There were conflicting reports about Bormann's state of mind during the final days of the Third Reich. Some say that communiqués he issued from the bunker were nearly hysterical; that because of his methodical, organized nature, he did not handle well the sudden, critical turn of events. A bit of hard evidence contradicts that assumption. The letters to his wife, Gerda, which he wrote nearly every day, indicate that he remained both optimistic and realistic and, above all, that he had a very strong desire to live.

By September 5, 1944, he had written to his wife:

The future looks frighteningly dark. . . . True I would not like to fall into the hands of the Russians now. . . . Anyone who gets caught by the

Bolshevists must know what he is in for. It is a great comfort for me to know that through my absence you have become so self-confident, independent, resolute, and capable of quick decision. . . . I know beyond any doubt that you will cope with things even if something happens to me. . . .

Bormann began yearning for peace. In October of the same year he wrote: "My beloved girl, you cannot imagine how much I am looking forward to life, after I'm pensioned off. . . . As soon as our Fuehrer no longer needs me," and, interestingly enough, he added, "or as soon as there is a new Fuehrer, I shall retire."

On February 2, 1945, in one of the last letters that Gerda Bormann still had in her possession when she died, he said: "As I have often emphasized, I have no premonitions of death; on the contrary, my burning desire is to live—and by that I mean to be with you and our children. I would like to muddle on through life, together with you, as many years as possible, and in peace. And enjoying ourselves! oh, wouldn't it be lovely."

What really happened in the last moments of Hitler's Reich? It would have been entirely in keeping with Bormann's character for him to have assisted Hitler as the Nazi leader swallowed the poison that took his life. Bormann would have faithfully carried out the task of burning the bodies of Hitler and his mistress, Eva Braun. Then what? I believe he set out on his own escape.

With a party of fugitives from the Nazi inner circle, Bormann crept out of the bunker. In West Berlin I interviewed an SS officer who had been part of that group. He told me that the escapees entered Berlin's subway system and emerged at the Friedrichstrasse station, about a mile away, as the Russians were blasting block by block into the remnants of the capital of what Hitler believed would be the Thousand-Year Reich. At the station they spotted a group of German tanks attempting to cross the Wiedendammer Bridge. The fighting was horrendous. Shells were screaming everywhere, and bazooka blasts exploded continuously. Suddenly there was a flash as a bazooka blast exploded near one of the tanks; Bormann was at the side of one of the tanks. Members of the group thought that he had been killed.

One of those who are thoroughly convinced that Bormann died in that blast is Dr. Reidar Sognnaes, who is a professor at the U.C.L.A. School of Dentistry and a specialist in oral biology and anatomy. He discovered, in the National Archives in Washington, D.C., a set of five X rays of Adolf Hitler made in July 1944. These dental X rays, coupled with dental charts, enabled Dr. Sognnaes to resolve any doubt that the charred body found in the Reich Chancellery's courtyard was that of the Fuehrer. He set about on a similar mission to prove or disprove Martin Bormann's death. On December 7, 1972, workers excavating near Berlin's Lehrter Railway Station found the remains of two bodies. The taller of the two bodies appeared to be that of Dr. Ludwig Stumpfegger, the last of Hitler's physicians. The other might be that of Martin Bormann.

In the British publication *The Criminologist,* Dr. Sognnaes wrote:

The mystery of Martin Bormann's postwar whereabouts has been the subject of considerable controversy ever since Hitler's right-hand man was condemned to death in absentia at the Nuremberg trials. However, dental evidence presented . . . now indicates that Bormann's body has been unearthed and identified. Bormann, it now appears, actually committed suicide—more than a year before being sentenced to die on the gallows—by biting into a potassium cyanide poison vial, when he became trapped between enemy crossfire during his attempt to escape from Berlin on May 2, 1945.

Many of Dr. Sognnaes's conclusions were based on the dental diagrams drawn by Dr. Hugo Blaschke, the dentist who attended both Hitler and Bormann. (Blaschke, a German, had graduated from the University

of Pennsylvania in 1911.) Dr. Sognnaes cited a conversation he had had with Albert Speer, a German
architect who was personally close to Hitler and who
served time in prison for his involvement with the
Nazi Party (Speer was among those who were tried at
Nuremberg). Albert Speer told Dr. Sognnaes that Dr.
Blaschke had had a poor relationship with Bormann,
"so that he could have no interest in making his
[Bormann's] identification difficult." This less than
cordial relationship with Dr. Blaschke would be in
keeping with Bormann's relationships with other medical personnel who attended either Hitler or himself.

However, Dr. Blaschke had died shortly after the
war, and Sognnaes's further research was confined to
the recollections of Blaschke's assistants.

Sognnaes based his analysis and identification of the
skull that had been dug up near Lehrter Station on
these primary dental problems: 1) the right side of the
lower jaw in the back was badly decayed and there
was an incompletely erupted wisdom tooth; 2) there
were two open spaces, both upper and lower jaw, where
teeth had not been replaced; 3) there was a three-unit
bridge in the lower right part of the mouth; 4) there was
another three-unit bridge on the upper right portion of
the mouth.

With the aid of extremely sophisticated tools, Dr.
Sognnaes examined the mouth and discovered tiny
glass slivers that had scratched the surfaces of some of
the teeth; these glass slivers corresponded directly to
the vials of poison that Hitler had presented to those
still with him in the bunker. Sognnaes said that the
ante-mortem diagrams drawn by Dr. Blaschke coincided
almost perfectly with the findings of the post mortem
examination. But there was one initial hitch in the investigation. When the skull was unearthed, there were
no front incisor teeth, and according to Blaschke's assistants' recollections, Bormann's incisors had been
replaced by a bridge. Three months after the skull discovery, however, workmen hosing down the site found
the bridge.

"As far as I'm concerned, Martin Bormann died on May 2, 1945, and that's the end of that," Dr. Sognnaes told me adamantly. "I know it is not a very romantic end—people like to believe all sorts of wild stories. But my conclusions lay all those ideas to rest." Dr. Sognnaes is irritated at those who try to keep alive what he calls "the Bormann myth." "In fact, I don't even want to be associated with a publication that in any way says Martin Bormann is alive—what purpose would my theory have?" I explained to Dr. Sognnaes that I was looking into *all* the possibilities, and that his theory seemed as valid as anyone else's and had as much right to be aired, but he seemed unconvinced. Three days later, however, he mailed me most of his published articles. In one of them, *Scanodont,* a Swedish dental publication, even Sognnaes admitted that there were some what he called "explainable" inconsistencies between Blaschke's diagrams and the findings of the postmortem examination. He wrote:

> The question then arises whether any features of the skull which Blaschke had not recorded could have been overlooked as he was recording the situation. The answer to this question is yes. For example, I found individual silver filings in the skull. . . . One wisdom tooth in the skull's upper right jaw, for which Blaschke did not recall the color, in fact happened to be covered with a gold crown. In the lower jaw there is a bridge replacing the two central anterior teeth by abutments through window crowns on the two lateral incisors. Blaschke does not indicate any vacant or replaced area in this part of the jaw or whether or not he had placed a bridge in this area. . . . One would think that if Dr. Blaschke were involved with a planted fraud, then it would seem that this lower incisor bridge would have been a must on his charting of the ante-mortem record.

But a number of other Bormann trackers, including Ladislas Farago and Simon Wiesenthal, the Nazi hunter who has probably done more than anyone else to bring the problem to the attention of the authorities, still believe that Bormann made good his escape from Berlin and secreted himself in South America.

There is a plethora of information indicating that Bormann did not die. For example, in March 1947 a strange article appeared in the *Aargauer Tageblatt,* a Swiss newspaper. The article had all the ring of a new Nazi manifesto proclaiming that there would be a war between the United States and Russia and that Germany would be the only strong nation to take the reins of world leadership. Written long before Germany clawed its way out of the last holocaust, the article went on to say that Germany would then march in war against the present allies and that the "head of the German government will be Martin Bormann who presently is reportedly hiding in the Swiss Alps." The report may not have been as farfetched as it initially appeared.

On July 26, 1945, three months after fighting had ceased, anti-Nazi journalist Heinrich Lienau, who had been released from Sachsenhausen concentration camp, was on a train heading for Flensburg, his native city. He was stunned to see Martin Bormann sitting across from him. When the train arrived in Flensburg, the border crossing between Germany and Denmark, Bormann hurriedly got off the train. Lienau notified two British soldiers, but they were too late. Bormann had disappeared into the crowd; his trail was lost.

And then there was an interesting coincidence. Farago, while researching his book, accidentally stumbled upon the first clue indicating a Nazi underground railroad. In Buenos Aires, he found that dictator Juan Perón had an Argentine national, Carlos Pinegro, posing as a diplomat in Denmark while aiding Nazis to escape to South American havens. The Danes' reaction was to expel the culprit on December 6, 1947. Farago said: "The evidence on which the Danes acted was conclusive. Prominent on a list found in the bogus diplomat's dossier of the Nazis he allegedly had aided was the name of Martin Bormann."

There seems to be some evidence that before the

war's end at least some of the top Nazis made plans
for escape to South America. These plans were not
commonplace among those closest to Hitler. In fact,
historians have often commented, it is nearly inconceivable that men of so high a rank would be left to
scurry like rats on a sinking ship when the end came.
It seemed as if no escape plans, no matter how rough,
had been laid. Bormann seemingly did not differ from
the others. However, when his date book/diary was
found, in addition to his famous *Ausbruchsversuch*,
was a hand-drawn map of an escape route. Additionally, there are other clues. All of Hitler's property and
valuables were in Bormann's name. Even before the
war's end, Bormann had salted away substantial portions of Nazi plunder and riches in banks throughout
South America. Nowhere, not even in his letters to
his wife, did he betray any knowledge of an underground railway or other means of escape. However, in
a return letter Gerda slightly alludes to the possibility.
Gerda, perhaps an even more vehement Nazi than was
her husband, wrote on February 7, 1944, less than
three months before her husband would be running for
his life: "Without absolute faith in our Reich, which God
has given us, that we may build it up for our children
and our children's children, we could not carry on.
But the Reich will emerge victorious, even if we no
longer survive. The Fuehrer has given us our idea of
the Reich which has spread—and *in secret* is still
spreading—throughout the world." How mysterious.
How tantalizing.

I sat back at this point and reflected. The uppermost
questions in my mind were whether Martin Bormann
would have the character to leave behind his wife and
family and start a new life, and whether he believed
thoroughly enough in the Reich to try to start all over
again. Attempting to determine his character was almost as difficult as trying to track him. However,
particularly after scanning the book *The Bormann Let-*
ters—those that he and his wife wrote to each other
from January 1943 to April 1945—a number of char-

acteristics emerged. First, while it was obvious that he cared a great deal about his wife, he rarely mentioned the children, except in the collective, "the children." I found it intriguing, however, that he wrote to his wife extensively about a woman named Manya Behrens, an actress with whom he was having an affair. He even forwarded his lover's letters to his wife. Gerda's reaction was equally puzzling to me. It was incomprehensible that anyone could be so endowed with the national socialist spirit as to actually encourage the situation, but Gerda did, if only superficially. She knew the woman, referred to as "Miss M," and thought that it would be nice if Manya Behrens had a child by Bormann. Gerda's idea was that Hitler should legalize polygamy so that more women could have children (particularly since the women so outnumbered men, as a result of the war). Additionally, she advocated that she, Bormann, and the "Fraulein M" should buy a house and all live together. Each year one woman would produce a baby for the good of the country. Bormann supported this idea. In the end, however, each renounced this stand, at least to some degree. Bormann said that living together with "M" was impossible, and that he had in some ways soured on "M." Gerda, for her part, admitted some jealousy.

There seemed no conclusive evidence that Bormann would make up his mind to leave Gerda to start a Fourth Reich in South America. As I researched further, however, I found the problem solved. Bormann did not have to make a decision. Gerda Bormann died of abdominal cancer in 1946.

What of Bormann's belief in Hitler, in the Reich? What was it that made Bormann so powerful in his own right? Some experts claim that Bormann helped found the secret organizations that would keep Naziism alive should the Third Reich falter. Bormann, they say, encouraged groups like Die Spinne (The Spider), and Organisation der Ehemaligen SS-Angehoerigen (Organization of Former SS Members), sometimes known as ODESSA, made famous in John Forsythe's *The Odessa File*. These groups aided Nazi criminals in sustaining themselves in exile. Again, according to Farago, "Only The Spider attained importance after the war, mainly in South America. Thanks to its access to Martin Bormann's treasure, it had substantial funds, which at first were husbanded judiciously by meager disbursements to the needy and then built into enormous assets through wise investments."

Such organizations would aid Bormann later. While the Third Reich was still functioning, Bormann exercised almost complete control over Hitler's life, particularly in the final months. After Germany's defeat at Stalingrad, Hitler began to shun all demands for speeches and personal appearances. Bormann screened everyone who wanted to see Hitler and was the only man who saw the Fuehrer at will. William Stevenson, in *The Bormann Brotherhood,* quoted Walter Schellenberg, chief of the Nazi SS:

> I studied Bormann's technique with Hitler and realized he controlled the Fuehrer. He did this by making himself indispensable. . . . He remembered everything. He knew exactly what to say and when to say it, but only in regard to Hitler. He was like a devoted and intelligent wife, removing from the Fuehrer any responsibility for small daily worries. . . . You see, Bormann had a cast-iron memory and the constitution of an ox. . . . He looked like an ox. . . .

There is no doubt that Bormann did take care of Hitler's day-to-day chores. But there may be an even bigger reason why Bormann controlled Hitler and simultaneously showed complete devotion to the man. Freely circulated in Nazi circles was the rumor that the Bormanns' eldest son, Martin Adolf, was actually Hitler's son by a previous mistress. No one will ever know. But, there is little doubt that Hitler was dependent on Bormann and Bormann stood in awe of Hitler. Later U. S. intelligence reports hinting that Bormann was a

Soviet double agent in Hitler's inner circle and then escaped to the Soviet Union are not only laughable but absurd.

Accurately tracing Nazi escape routes is nearly impossible. There are a number of pipelines that have been identified. The one that Bormann probably used was from Denmark, back down through Germany, Austria, Italy, and then perhaps Spain, from where he, like other Nazi fugitives, was shipped to South America. *Die Tat,* a German-language newspaper published in Zurich, said that one of the escape routes led across the Austrian border to Switzerland, Italy, and then Spain. The report explained that along the way fugitives would be met by Nazi sympathizers offering overnight shelters in "safe houses," similar both to the slave underground railway in America preceding the Civil War and to the type of hide-and-seek practices employed by the covert groups that hid Patty Hearst and company.

It is known that a small band of mercenaries operating under the guise of the Red Cross was aiding Nazis to slip into Denmark. Once in Denmark, there were a number of wealthy Danes who put them up in rather grand style. Bormann apparently was able to move about quite freely until October 17, when the International Military Tribunal plastered his indictment, his picture, and his description on as many walls and signposts as possible. His obscurity ended, Bormann was forced to burrow deeply underground.

In *The Murderers Among Us,* Simon Wiesenthal recounts the testimony of Peter Franz Kubainsky. Apprehended in Innsbruck, Kubainsky admitted that on December 12, 1945 he drove Martin Bormann from Bavaria to Salzburg and farther south to Nauders, near the Italian border. Kubainsky's confession seems confirmed by Bormann's instructions to his family to move to the southern Tirol, that part of Italy that the Italians and the Austrians have been scrapping over for years. The Tirolians, a hardy, independent bunch who never took kindly to Italian rule, have a culture different from that of the rest of Italy. Their architecture is distinctly Austrian, and their dress and food are also Germanic. And they don't readily speak Italian. A few words are thrown in here or there, but otherwise the operative language is barely intelligible southern German dialect. In other words, the Tirol provides a likely spot for a German on the run to settle peacefully and not be noticed. That is precisely what Gerda Bormann did. Although there were British occupation troops in the area, the residents did nothing to notify them of her presence. In any case, Frau Bormann was critically ill. Whether Bormann knew that is questionable. But he did know where his family was and he did have a strong desire to see his wife.

According to Kubainsky's testimony, he then drove Bormann south to Merano, Italy, in the Dolomites, and to the very city where Gerda was. There, he said, he arranged for Bormann to be hidden in a house for one night. At the Merano railroad station Kubainsky bought a ticket for Bormann. His destination was Rome. According to the late Fritz Bauer, former Prosecutor for Frankfurt and director of West Germany's manhunt for war criminals still at large, the Merano train station was the last confirmable stop in the Bormann escape.

Merano raises more questions about Bormann's plans. Why would he use Merano as a waystop to Rome? It would be easier and more logical to travel from Bolzano, a larger town, which would have a direct route and a faster train to Rome. The longer Bormann spent on a train, the more likely he was to be recognized. Also, it is nearly inconceivable that Bormann would leave without attempting to visit his wife. More logical is the premise that Farago outlines in his book. He says that once Frau Bormann admitted her identity, the British commandant in the area graciously offered her medical assistance. With a little encouragement, she accepted. Simultaneously, according to Farago's scenario, Bormann was making his way over the Austrian-Italian border with the help of Hanno Bernhard, a mountain guide.

On the Italian side of the Resia Pass, approximately five thousand feet up, there was a monastary where Farago believes Bormann holed up. He was supposedly kept abreast of his wife's worsening condition, but he never dared visit her. At first when she had been admitted to the hospital, a twenty-four-hour guard kept watch around the hospital entrances until George S. Patton, Jr., then commanding the Fifteenth U. S. Army in Bad Tölz, heard of the situation and called off the guards, saying, "Let the poor woman die in peace." Most people in the area concede it would have been relatively easy for Bormann to visit his wife. The hospital was German-staffed. There was an overwhelming number of German prisoners of war who were helping clean up northern Italy but who had the run of the place. There were few occupation troops. Still, Bormann did not try. It is interesting to note that Gerda Bormann, who was as adamantly anti-Catholic as was her husband, entrusted her children to the care of a priest. She maintained that she never heard from her husband and assumed him dead. Perhaps so. But Farago claims that Bormann moved to Bolzano under the name of Luigi Bogliolo. In the larger city he submerged into the daily routine. He would stay there for two years.

Questions arise as to how the Nazis who escaped got to South America. No doubt some got there by strange means. Rumors held that Bormann was delivered to the South American shores via submarine. It is possible. Equally possible, and more likely, is that a number of Third Reich survivors got there on forged passports. Still others might have gotten there on Vatican passports, arranged by Bishop Alois Hudal, a Nazi friend inside the "Eternal City." An Austrian paper in Graz reported on April 17, 1963: "After the collapse of the Third Reich, [Bishop] Hudal played a prominent role in organizing the escape of Nazi leaders overseas, mainly to Argentina. Hudal thus aided the flight of Eichmann, of Martin Bormann, Hitler's deputy. . . ."

The Germans wanted to believe that Bormann was dead. In 1954, a court in Berchtesgaden, where Hitler had had his "Eagles Nest," declared him legally dead. But by 1961 so much new evidence was emerging that Fritz Bauer reopened the case. In November 1964, the Bonn government posted a twenty-five-thousand-dollar reward for Bormann's capture.

Exactly how Bormann escaped and where he might have gone is, according to Simon Wiesenthal, "the biggest unsolved Nazi mystery of our time." In 1956 a woman who had known Bormann personally in Berlin claimed that she saw the Reichsleiter on a bus in São Paulo, Brazil.

So the hunt moved to South America. Investigators looked to cities like São Paulo, where a large, prosperous German immigrant population can be found, and to countries dominated by governments sympathetic to ex-Nazis. One such country is Paraguay, long ruled by a dictator who bore the Germanic surname Strasser.

Farago claims to have pictures of Bormann's home in Paraguay and further contends that Bormann is living under the alias of Ricardo Bauer; he backs his claims with a series of impressively official-looking documents supposedly removed surreptitiously from a number of Argentine and Paraguayan files. Perhaps the best testament to Farago's belief that Bormann, along with other top Nazis, was long shielded by Juan Perón, and later other South American governments when Perón was exiled, has nothing to do with official documents. Colonel Hans Rudel, one of Germany's top air aces and a favorite of Hitler's, became the champion of Nazi fugitives. He almost single-handedly created the Kameradenwerk, an organization that was what the ODESSA was supposed to be: a highly sophisticated network of ex-Nazis loaded with money. Rudel, although not a war criminal himself, decided on self-imposed exile in Argentina. When Perón was deposed,

Rudel hopped back to Europe. When Perón triumphantly returned, one of the first persons to visit him
was one Hans Ulrich Rudel. The Nazi ties were never
broken.

No events unnerved ex-Nazis as much as the Israeli
capture of Adolf Eichmann, in Argentina, and their
sub-rosa extradition of the former Third Reich officer
to Tel Aviv. The news of this drove the one-time Hit-
lerites deep into the South American jungles.

The Mato Grosso, the region that swallowed Percy
Fawcett, spreads over three South American nations.
Inhabited for centuries by a few Indian tribes, this
dense, swampy jungle has become a refuge for men
who have fled society. Rumors persist that hiding in
prosperous German colonies like El Dorado are Nazi
war criminals.

Walon Green, a journalist filmmaker with whom I
worked on a revival of *The March of Time,* ventured
into the Mato Grosso in search of Martin Bormann.
Wally speaks German and Portuguese with some flu-
ency. What carried Wally to El Dorado was the knowledge that it was the home of Aloisus Mengele, brother
of the infamous Josef Mengele, chief doctor of Auschwitz. Wally described the dangers in a TV special
we produced called *Search for Vengeance.* He said,
"As a one-time visitor to El Dorado, I was partially
accepted because I spoke German. I found that to the
three thousand people who live in this area, fugitive
Nazi war criminals are not rumors or vague shadows.
Men like Martin Bormann are spoken of in present
tense and known to some by their first names or by
their aliases. My own search for Martin Bormann in
1965 convinced me that the final refuge for the most-
wanted man in history is in the jungles of South
America."

Wally followed Bormann's trail into the Mato Grosso and reported an attempt to throw all searchers off
the track. Here's how he put it: "It was in Ita that
plans were developed to get searchers permanently off
Bormann's trail. In 1959 a story was circulated that

Martin Bormann had died and was buried in a small village cemetery. It might have worked, except that I found the gravedigger who witnessed the ceremony and later came back to rob the grave of jewelry. In so doing, he discovered that the body was that of a village Indian.

"The people of Ita," he continued, "have become accustomed to reporters and police agents. They call visitors aside to whisper information about the famous German, yet most of the natives have not heard of Nazis and know nothing of Bormann's crimes!"

Wally carried the hunt deep inland. The Paranah River winds through the jungle and forms the boundary between three nations: Argentina, Brazil, and Paraguay. The river is truly open water with few check points. Wally figured that if Bormann was forced to leave Ita when searchers had too closely tracked his trail, he and any other fugitives most likely came to the Paranah River. In some places the Paranah is the only passageway through the jungle, and the natives use it to come and go as they please, ignoring political boundaries. In the midst of this river region, on the Argentine side of the river, is an isolated German community known as El Dorado.

"El Dorado has become a proud, prosperous community," Wally told me. "It was here that I encountered the persistent rumors that Bormann and Josef Mengele, the notorious chief doctor at Auschwitz, were living. I talked to a man named Osmond Kahn, a Dutch engineer who has worked in the Paranah River region for fifteen years. He knows much about the area's history but refuses to speak about his own past. He said to me, 'They say that Josef Mengele and Martin Bormann are here, living along this river. If you come here and you make friends, then be sure that nobody will harm you. You live here quite well and it would be very difficult to get you out of here against your will.'

"There are people in El Dorado who claim that 'They say that Josef Mengele and Martin Bormann When I went there, I said that I was filming a documentary about German settlers in the Paranah River region. My inquiries about Nazi fugitives, however, aroused suspicion and hostility. I was eventually warned against asking further questions. It soon became quite clear that I best leave El Dorado."

On the foreboding Paranah River, El Dorado is far from modern civilization. It would be difficult if not impossible for a commando raid to successfully extract either Bormann or Mengele from the Mato Grosso redoubt. The trail for Green ended in El Dorado with a glimpse of the man he is convinced is Mengele and a threat to leave town. He did.

Other searchers believe that they have located Bormann himself in South America, but because of South American laws against extradition they were never able to bring him to justice. We can guess that Eichmann's abduction from South America to Israel for trial must have shaken Bormann. For one thing, it laid bare the escape route Eichmann had used, providing investigators with possible clues to Bormann's trail. The abduction of Eichmann and his subsequent trial served notice to the likes of Bormann that they had not been forgotten. The Eichmann trial was staged amid an international furor. Argentina protested Eichmann's abduction while some jurors condemned the trial as one of vengeance. But the majority of people admitted that sometimes there are considerations other than the laws of men.

Lawyers like James Donovan, assistant to the U. S. chief prosecutor, said: "I think that in the trial of Eichmann the usual theorists could very well take exception to the steps that were employed, except for the pragmatic approach, which was that if you commence with the premise that this man should have been brought before some bar of justice, where was the bar of justice if not in Israel?"

In the wake of the Eichmann trial, Israel abandoned any plans of again bringing a Nazi criminal to justice in her courts. The Bormann story seemed to end, except for the activity of Simon Wiesenthal, the man who helped to bring Eichmann to trial. After Eichmann's trial Wiesenthal became interested in following up the sporadic stories of Bormann sightings throughout South America. Eichmann's son wrote an open letter imploring Bormann to come out of hiding and take responsibility for his own crimes. Wiesenthal has good reason to believe that Bormann is most likely living near the Argentine and Chilean frontier.

In *The Murderers Among Us,* Wiesenthal explained: "It has been my experience that whenever we are on Bormann's trail, he is reported at an entirely different place, thousands of miles away. This has convinced me that he has a double, who is brought into play by Bormann's friends as soon as they have reason to believe that Bormann's real hiding place has been betrayed."

Even though Simon Wiesenthal has collected many substantial leads pinpointing Bormann's present location, he is not encouraged by the prospects of ever bringing him to justice. In fact, Wiesenthal states, "The mystery of Martin Bormann . . . will degenerate into a simply biological equation. He is well protected. No country will want to attempt a second Eichmann case."

In retrospect, I think Wiesenthal is right. My search for Martin Bormann impressed me with, above all, the meaning of justice. It has been said that the whole process of justice, whether it's international or domestic, is designed to reenforce moral standards. Justice was designed to make us remember.

A thought came to me as I was concluding this chapter. Perhaps Martin Bormann has not been found because in reality we do not want to remember. We would like to forget.

7

James Hoffa

Jimmy Hoffa. As a labor leader his name inspired fear and respect and conjured images of raw power. His Teamsters exhibited a loyalty toward him matched by few union rank and files. State and federal government officials took endless potshots at him. He was constantly hounded by Senate committees, district attorneys' offices, grand juries, and plagued by accusations that he was a willing partner of organized crime. However tarnished his reputation, his hold over the Teamsters remained. On July 30, 1975, the barrel-chested, tough-talking Teamster boss disappeared. Forces beyond the law succeeded in doing what no indictment, no conviction, no jail cell could do. They extricated Jimmy Hoffa from his dominion over the International Brotherhood of Teamsters.

Hoffa's last known day began uneventfully. Hoffa had told Josephine, his quiet, demure wife, that he had a business meeting with some associates at the Machus Red Fox Restaurant, about thirty miles north of Detroit, not far from his Lake Orion home. She did not question him. Jimmy Hoffa had always shielded his family from his business. During the various investigations that blighted his life, he often remarked that he was most fearful of the news-coverage effects upon his family. But Josephine Hoffa did later report that Jimmy had appeared agitated that morning. She also recalled that he kissed her twice before leaving—unusual behavior for Jimmy Hoffa.

Before arriving at the restaurant rendezvous, Hoffa stopped at the office of an airport limousine business to chat with Louis "The Pope" Linteau, an old friend. But Linteau, a former head of Teamster Local 614, was out to lunch, so Hoffa stopped to talk with other employees. He made mention of his meeting with Anthony "Tony Jack" Giacalone, Anthony "Tony Pro" Provenzano, both identified in news stories as Mafiosi, and Leonard Schulz, labor consultant and reportedly key associate of Giacalone.

Hoffa drove to the restaurant, one of his favorites. Witnesses say that he was greeted by two acquaintances. At two-thirty he called his wife, asking: "Has Tony Giacalone called?" He then told her specifically where he was. At three-thirty he called Linteau and said: "Tony Jack didn't show, goddamn it. I'm coming over there." Then James Riddle Hoffa disappeared. He never even walked into the restaurant. The restaurant manager was sure of that James Hoffa was well known there—after all, his son's wedding reception had been held at the Red Fox.

The search was on. Police scoured a nearby cornfield. Nothing. Police informants were pressured. There seemed to be few, if any, leaks. The Hoffa family tried on their own. Josephine contacted Jeane Dixon, the famous psychic who predicted John Kennedy's assassination. Dixon told Josephine that Hoffa was still alive. Then, five days after the kidnapping, Josephine awoke clutching her heart. Jerry Stanecki, investigative reporter for WXYZ radio in Detroit, reported that Josephine had said: "I knew then, and only then, that Jimmy was dead." Dixon called later the same morning and told Josephine the exact same thing. Even more strange was that after an appearance on a morning news show, Stanecki received a call from a woman who said that Jimmy Hoffa was in a boat with a very wealthy organized-crime figure and they were headed for Harsan's Island in Lake Saint Clair (not far from Detroit). Stanecki claims that he told no one of the call, yet one week later a woman calling herself a psychic claimed that she "saw" Jimmy's naked body under water, near Harsan's Island. He had been shot twice in the head.

Even before Dixon's predictions, Barbara Crancer, Hoffa's daughter, called Edward Levi, U. S. Attorney General, and Clarence Kelley, FBI director. She was her father's daughter. In typical Jimmy Hoffa style she reportedly screamed over the phone: "You used two thousand agents to put my father in jail. How about using a couple of agents to find him."

The FBI finally entered the case, citing extortion demands received by the Hoffa family. A Detroit newscaster cynically commented: "The FBI, which has yet to solve the Patricia Hearst case, has finally entered the Jimmy Hoffa case."

Then a mob informant contacted the Senate Permanent Subcommittee on Investigations. He claimed that Hoffa was buried somewhere in a Waterford Township field about fifteen miles from the Machus Red Fox Restaurant. Some said that the Mafia wanted Hoffa's body found, in order to eliminate the federal heat. Police investigators armed with a variety of digging paraphernalia including bulldozers turned the field inside out for three days. No body.

The search led to New Jersey, reported stronghold of Tony Provenzano. Again, nothing. Each of the three men with whom Hoffa was to have had lunch had perfect alibis: Giacalone was getting a haircut and manicure at the Travelers Tower Building in Southfield, ten minutes from the restaurant (the posh complex is operated by Leonard Schulz's two sons); Provenzano made sure everyone saw him at a union hall in New Jersey; Schulz was at home, tending his petunias. Jimmy Hoffa, Jr., sarcastically noted, "It's damn funny. Everybody involved in this damn thing was either getting his nails done or was someplace with ten thousand witnesses when Dad disappeared."

The attention began focusing on Chuckie O'Brien, a man Hoffa had raised as a foster son from age three. O'Brien admitted he was in the area at the time, but he denied any knowledge of the Hoffa abduction. Police later found that O'Brien had borrowed a car from one of Giacalone's sons and that there were bloodstains on the back seat. O'Brien claimed they were from a fish that he had been delivering. The police confirmed that the blood was not of human origin. Back to square one.

Nearly five months after his disappearance, CBS admitted to being suckered into a ten-thousand-dollar payment to a supposed informant who absconded with the money, leaving CBS red-faced and holding an empty bag. Every aspect of the search, including this one, was dogged by the specter of the mob. Richard Salant, president of CBS news, commented that he was sure that the informant was gone for good, and added: "I hope so; he's the most terrifying guy I've ever seen. He's got everyone scared that he might come back."

Jimmy Hoffa was presumed dead. The victim of a Mafia hit. But why?

Newspapers speculated that Hoffa had been killed because he wanted to retake the Teamsters presidency. Why did that so threaten whoever killed him? Was Jimmy Hoffa killed not for what he knew but rather for what he didn't know?

In order to understand Jimmy Hoffa, one of the most powerful labor leaders in American history, one must understand first Hoffa the man, and then Hoffa the Boss.

Jimmy Hoffa was born in Brazil, Indiana, on Valentine's Day, 1913. His Dutch-German father died when Jimmy was seven. Hoffa's mother moved a number of times, attempting to earn a living by taking in laundry and later by working in a small manufacturing plant. Jimmy graduated from grammar school to a life on the streets in order to help the family financially. He saw firsthand the hideous injustices imposed upon the working men and women. By age eighteen he had successfully concluded his first collective-bargaining package when he encouraged other employees of Krogers, a large midwestern food chain, not to unload a highly perishable strawberry load until management agreed to higher wages and better working conditions —two years later, in 1932, he was an official with the Teamsters and had begun his rise to power in Detroit.

The union that Hoffa joined had neither strength nor management respect. Deftly Hoffa carved out a serfdom for himself; winning a reputation as a tough-minded negotiator, Hoffa rose through the varied levels of local union ranks.

The Central States Drivers Council (CSDC), established in 1937 by the Marxist-influenced Minneapolis Teamsters, became the bargaining representative and organizing group for all mideastern over-the-road drivers. Hoffa insinuated himself into the CSDC and by 1940 held sway as the council's negotiations chairman and as its vice-president. The CSDC extended its influence beyond the handful of central states and insidiously Hoffa's influence and power spread. The CSDC ultimately propelled Hoffa into the nation's labor scene. By 1955, as head of the Central Conference of Teamsters, he was negotiating contracts for all midwestern and southern over-the-road and local-cartage drivers.

Hoffa personified the tough-as-nails-on-the-outside, soft-as-jelly-on-the-inside character. On one hand he was a remorseless negotiator; on the other hand, he was a zealous father and devoted husband. Ralph James, a professor of economics at the University of California at Davis, received a rare opportunity to travel with Hoffa, which gave him a closer view of Hoffa than anyone outside his family or the Teamsters organization. After intensive observation of Hoffa and those around him James wrote *Hoffa and the Teamsters*. In his book he stated: "I have twice heard him regretfully explain that had he not expected a violent early death, he would gladly have acceded to his wife's desire for a larger family."

Hoffa doted on his two natural children, particularly Barbara, who he thought was "more like her father." When she announced her upcoming marriage to Robert Crancer—son of the owner of the St. Louis Steel Company—more suddenly than Hoffa had expected, his fatherly ego was hurt. However, with style and grace he put on a lavish wedding for her.

He often criticized "egghead intellectuals," yet both of his children attended college. When Jimmy Jr. went to Michigan State, which was anxious to use his football talents, Hoffa demanded to know if he was going there to learn or to play games. It pleased his father greatly when Jimmy Jr. replied that he intended the former, and when he later became a lawyer. Hoffa bragged openly that Barbara had graduated Phi Beta Kappa from Michigan's prestigious Albion College.

Hoffa's personal life was a study in contradictions. He was almost a prude. He disliked seeing erotically suggestive, nude performances either on stage or on film. Sexually promiscuous aides had prematurely short careers. Yet, Hoffa helped finance, through the powerful pension fund, an opulent Texas hotel that featured a dazzling mural of Romans in various stages of sexual orgies.

He was a physical-fitness freak who encouraged subordinates to exercise rigorously. He added a gym to the Teamsters Washington headquarters, "The Marble Palace," and even attempted to start an exercise class for secretaries, but abandoned the idea when only one showed up.

Unlike most of the truck drivers that Hoffa represented, he abstained from alcohol and cigarettes. Often, following long, grueling negotiating sessions, he would open all the windows to refresh the smoke-clogged room.

Hoffa, the moralistic "purist" in his personal life, operated the Teamsters in a style that was altogether brutish. Violence was an integral element in achieving what he wanted. Professor James wrote: "Fist fights, picketline brawls, and internecine, inter-union squabbles were standard operating procedure in Detroit in the 1930s." Not only was violence an integral part of union life then, but it is now. A local Teamster once snickered to me: "Hell, beatings, bombings, that's just business as usual in an organizing fight."

Hoffa was an "old boy" with "old boy" values that he either could not or would not adapt to the 1970s. These values may have blinded him to the realization of his fate.

But in the 1930s and '40s Hoffa was a man suited to his times. James wrote: "Hoffa ran his local . . . the way old-time sheriffs kept law and order. . . . The job was done, but by no formal rules. . . . The system worked well."

Since the Teamsters inception it had been closely associated with underworld activities. Union men legally organized where mob bag-men were illegally shaking down. Often they became one and the same. Many of the union organizers had police records for one reason or another. They seemed to use the same methods for recruiting members and for encouraging compliance with their way of conducting business.

Hoffa's attitude toward the mob was one of "you scratch my back and I'll scratch yours, but otherwise leave us alone." There was no doubt that Hoffa controlled his locals; he knew what was going on. He did not allow the mobsters to run the union.

In 1955–57 Hoffa became involved with a major mob-related scandal. He was accused of chartering seven "paper locals" in New York in order to swing votes toward the election of his own man as head of the New York Teamsters. These so-called paper locals were controlled by "friends" (reportedly with underworld connections). That was just the beginning of Hoffa's legal problems.

He succeeded to the presidency of the union because of Senator John McClellan's Senate investigation of the "vice and corruption" of David Beck's associates in the Pacific Northwest. Beck had left the country but he returned to take the Fifth in front of the committee. He was a broken man. Hoffa was elected president, and the committee investigating the union—and, most notably, an energetic lawyer named Bob Kennedy—turned its attention to him. Hoffa would later call Kennedy "that little monster."

Esquire, March 1975, said: "From the time Hoffa took over the presidency of the Teamsters from 'disgraced' Dave Beck in 1957 until the day he entered Lewisburg Prison ten years later, he was a god under attack."

The Senate Select Committee on Improper Activities ultimately accused James Hoffa of more than eighty-two specific acts of betrayal of his union obligations in the labor and management field. These charges included granting union charters to men who had long criminal records, keeping jailed Teamster officials on the union payroll, manipulating hundreds of thousands of union dollars for personal benefits, making enormous amounts of union money available to his friends without union approval, and profiting from conflict-of-interest business arrangements between management and labor. The charges were endless, but none stuck.

Finally, in 1962, the government returned an indictment against Hoffa on a million-dollar kickback. The proceedings resulted in a mistrial. The case led obligingly to his downfall. He was accused of jury tampering and ultimately convicted for it. Four months later Hoffa was convicted for mail and wire fraud and misuse of union pension funds. Hoffa received a thirteen-year sentence, but after he spent almost five years in Lewisburg Prison, his sentence was commuted in 1971 by former President Nixon.

When Hoffa was convicted he stated emphatically that he was innocent. "Whatever may happen, nobody can say that I have betrayed my trust, because the record speaks for itself regarding the wages, hours, and conditions, and the fringe benefits, the pensions, welfare, that has never before been attained in the history of this country." Hoffa's critics say that he missed the point. The means was called to question, not the end.

Interestingly enough, Edward Grady Partin, a government witness who fingered Hoffa for jury tampering, repeatedly admitted that he had been assisted by the prosecution regarding what to say in order to finally secure Hoffa's conviction.

At least two separate seeds for Jimmy Hoffa's ultimate downfall were planted while he was in prison. The first seemed relatively minor. While there, he became more closely acquainted with Tony Provenzano, who had been convicted of extortion. Provenzano wanted Hoffa to secure a union pension for him. Hoffa refused, citing his felony record. The rift between the two deepened. The second seed was planted when Hoffa entered prison after naming Frank Fitzsimmons to be president of the union. Hoffa claimed that he gave Fitzsimmons that post only with the understanding that Hoffa would regain power after his release.

The core power structure of the Teamsters union that Hoffa left behind was interesting. First, Hoffa was extremely popular with the rank and file. Yet, wrote Professor James in his book *Hoffa and the Teamsters:* "Hoffa's frequent explosions made it difficult, if not impossible, for deep personal loyalties to develop." Countless times Hoffa called down Harold Gibbons, his executive vice-president, in front of others, growling out insulting comments. Gibbons was one of the few who remained fairly loyal. Curiously, Hoffa could never bring himself to fire anyone. A fantastic amount of disloyalty was evidenced, yet Hoffa never did anything about it. Those he liked he simply gave more power and more prestige. Those whom he didn't like stagnated in dead-end jobs.

Jim Drinkhall, former investigative editor for *Overdrive* magazine, a national publication for independent truckers, talked with Hoffa before his death. He was also an astute student of Hoffa and the Teamsters. Now working in San Francisco for the *Wall Street*

Journal, Drinkhall took a moment to reflect on the differences between the Hoffa Teamsters union and the one run by Fitzsimmons. "Hoffa," he said, "had a close relationship with the people out in the field. If a local had trouble, it could come to him." Hoffa often used "as close as the telephone" as his motto. "Hoffa," continued Drinkhall, "would go see how the locals were being run. Sometimes he would just pop into town and go see the local unannounced. He kept abreast of what was happening and in effect he ran the locals. Fitzsimmons doesn't really know what's going on. His regional vice-presidents do what they want. Besides, Fitzsimmons doesn't really run the union. Roy Williams and Bill Presser do."

Bill Presser was a former union trustee from Ohio. Williams at one time was a top Hoffa lieutenant from Kansas. Both were instrumental in getting union pension funds to underwrite various local projects before the recent government-inspired pension-fund shakeup. Prior to the shakeup the fund was controlled by Presser, Williams, and Fitzsimmons.

One of the keys to the Teamsters power was and is the pension plan. When Hoffa joined his local in Detroit it had four hundred members and a four-hundred-dollar pension fund. Today, Teamsters number 2.2 million and the fund is in the billions. Nothing was more slipshoddily handled than the money held in trust for the old age of the union membership. Loans from a half a million dollars to fifty million were granted apparently on whim. Often they were not repaid. The losses accrued against the future security of drivers pounding out, on tough hourly wage, on American highways. It is a tribute to Hoffa that all the revelations of corruption in the misuse of pension funds caused little or no visible stir inside the union. Hoffa and his lieutenants remained the supreme powers.

For Hoffa, his release from prison was flawed. He claimed that he never knew of the provision preventing him from regaining the Teamsters presidency and that his very release was the result of a mishandled cloak-and-dagger routine between the government and Teamsters president Fitzsimmons.

In one of the last in-depth interviews before his disappearance, he spoke extensively with Jerry Stanecki, the WXYZ reporter who was requested by *Playboy* to interview Hoffa. In the interview, Hoffa said:

"During the whole time I was in prison, Fitzsimmons kept telling everybody, my son, my lawyers, all the union representatives—'Now don't do anything, you'll rock the boat. I'm taking care of it with Mitchell.' Well, when Mitchell later gave his deposition, he said the first time Fitzsimmons ever talked to him about me was in June 1971. I'd been in jail five years. . . . Then I found out that he's fired Edward Bennett Williams as Teamsters counsel and replaced him with Charles Colson. And when I found out there was a restriction on my parole until 1980, it didn't take a ton of bricks to fall on me to put two and two together—that he's been lying all along."

Hoffa said that Fitzsimmons told him that he was working on Mitchell so that influence could be used in obtaining executive action to get Hoffa out of jail. Hoffa continued:

"John Dean testified that he and Colson had discussed the 1980 restriction and what with Colson already having the offer from the Teamsters to become general counsel, it all adds up to . . . it leads me to believe that Fitzsimmons deliberately double-crossed the membership, the convention, my lawyers, and myself. And that's it. So I don't wanna do business with a double-crosser . . . or a liar."

If Fitzsimmons did not intervene on Hoffa's behalf, how was he sprung by executive pardon? Hoffa claims that it was the petition, which had over one million signatures, plus the heat applied to congressmen by their constituents, which convinced the Nixon administration that a pardon was a smart political move.

Hoffa contended that no one, not even his lawyers, knew of the stipulation preventing him from involving himself in union activities: that the clause had been inserted before the President signed the pardon, unbeknownst to him.

Hoffa blamed presidential advisors John Dean, Clark Mollenhoff, and Charles Colson, and the Teamsters own Frank Fitzsimmons. *It is true* that Fitzsimmons hired Colson on at the lucrative post although he had limited previous labor dealings.

Hoffa's assessment of the union's condition upon his release was not far different from that of many reporters who covered the labor scene. Hoffa said:

"There are (were) no master contracts, other than the ones I left them. The organization campaigns and the joint councils of the local unions have deteriorated. And the morale of the local officers, the organizers, is at an all-time low, from what I hear. Even the members feel uncomfortable, they don't have someone steering the ship. The leaders are too busy on the golf course, flying around in seven jet airplanes they own. Why the hell do they own seven? Most corporations don't own that many."

Hoffa was not taking the matter lying down. He began challenging, in the courts, the restraint on his parole. Some observers thought he would have a fairly good chance of winning. Hoffa seemed confident. He even went so far as to begin outlining changes he would make when he returned to power. Hoffa wanted to restructure the union back to the way it was before he went to jail, and to reinstate the trade divisions. He also wanted to add some additional organizers, for the purpose of having master contracts. "We need," said Hoffa in the *Playboy* interview, "a common expiration date for the contracts of all unions." Stanecki pointed out that that could give Hoffa a virtual stranglehold on the American economy. Hoffa replied: "Corporations have it. . . ."

It was fairly well known, however, that Hoffa did

not favor massive strikes. He felt that in the long run they were detrimental to the union and that they only drained the union's strike-benefits fund. Instead, Hoffa outlined a number of key cities that, if struck, would paralyze the entire country. Some people in business did not like the way Hoffa was talking.

As I evaluated what Hoffa had said to Stanecki, I mused over what others had said about Hoffa's philosophy of the world being basically divided into power camps. I thought of all the clues that pointed to a Mafia hit on Hoffa and thought how ironic it would be if Hoffa had been a victim of a force fictionalized in *The Parallax View* . . . how corporations could hire people to kill those who endangered their turf. Hoffa, I knew, often said with a snap of his fingers how easy it was to hire a killer. I'd read where he'd said that all you needed was two thousand dollars for a contract and it could be done. Perhaps it wasn't union officials and the Mafia that knocked off Hoffa . . . perhaps it was something or someone much more "legitimate."

Hoffa didn't expect to be knocked off by Fitzsimmons, that's for sure. He didn't think that "Fitzsimmons had the guts." The union members themselves seemed divided on the question. Some in the Detroit area had bumper stickers reading: FITZ—WHERE IS JIMMY? Those further away from the action were less inclined to think that union leaders had anything to do with Hoffa's disappearance. One Teamster commented to me: "They'll fight [Teamsters] . . . hit you in the jaw, kick you in the ass, but they wouldn't go this way. Now, some of the members do strange things. They'll blow up a car, a boat, or something. It's just part of the business. But it doesn't mean a hell of a lot."

The stakes could have been much higher than just a little union wrangling. Some speculated that Hoffa had been eliminated in order to keep him from interfering with kickbacks allegedly being passed along to underworld brokers of loans from the Central States' pension fund, long accused of continually loaning money to the mob for its pet projects.

Investigators in the Hoffa case reportedly uncovered what they believed may have been on the lunch agenda of Giacalone, Provenzano, Schulz, and Hoffa: A three-million-dollar loan from the central fund that the Mafia was trying to arrange for a "recreation center" in Detroit. Investigators knew that other Mafia figures had gotten as much as a ten-percent kickback from borrowers. On this particular loan they were reportedly demanding an additional ten percent from the union officials.

But Jim Drinkhall doesn't buy the assumption that Hoffa was snuffed out because of this particular deal. "I just don't think they'd kill him for that," he said. But before Hoffa's disappearance Drinkhall discovered an interesting subplot that may somehow have figured in the case. Drinkhall said that Hoffa told him he had put large sums of money into a Pennsylvania holding company called Great American Coal Company. The ownership of the company, which was being reorganized at the time of Hoffa's disappearance, was curiously silent. Hoffa wouldn't say how much money he had put into the operation but he hinted that it was near $1.5 million.

It is known that following his release from prison Hoffa withdrew an estimated $1.7 million from a pension fund established for Teamsters officials. After taxes he was left with approximately $1.2 million. It was known that the people involved with the holding company had previously borrowed large sums of money from the Central Teamster Pension Fund. Investigators also established that James Durkin borrowed money from the union pension fund in 1973 to get the company started. He claimed, when Hoffa disappeared, that the company had passed into the hands of New York/Florida businessman Hyman Green, who had also borrowed extensively from the pension fund.

Drinkhall did not find any direct relationship between the incident and Hoffa's presupposed death: "For example, I don't think that Hoffa would have been pressuring them for his money."

If none of these business dealings had a direct effect upon Hoffa's demise, what did? Drinkhall commented: "It probably wasn't one specific deal. They just all added up to Hoffa regaining control of the union. The Mafia had been having a good time of it since Fitzsimmons took over. They could do more of what they wanted without Hoffa than with him. Then, too, for some of the union people it was proving much more lucrative when Hoffa was out of the picture."

Who would have benefited most? This point is difficult to determine, because no one, for sure, knows specifically what was at stake.

There *had* been a power split between Chuckie O'Brien (Hoffa's "adopted" son) and Hoffa in 1974, according both to Hoffa's son and to Linteau. O'Brien had wanted to take over the presidency of Detroit's Local 299, headed by Dave Johnson. Johnson was being challenged by Richard Fitzsimmons, Frank's son. But Hoffa wouldn't back O'Brien; instead, he kept his loyalties with Johnson.

Investigators also knew that O'Brien had become close to the Giacalone family—so close that on August 1, one day after Hoffa disappeared, O'Brien had dinner with the Giacalones at a restaurant in Port Huron, and the next day he met Tony Jack in the barbershop where Giacalone had been getting a haircut when Hoffa disappeared. By August 4, O'Brien had flown to Washington, D.C., apparently to consult with Fitzsimmons. Some said that O'Brien had thrown his support to Fitzsimmons. Hoffa's son and daughter demanded that O'Brien take a lie-detector test. He refused.

Papers and magazines reasoned that perhaps Hoffa had been lured to the meeting in hopes of burning the hatchet with Tony Provenzano, or, as others said, perhaps both Giacalone and Provenzano were going to attempt to persuade Hoffa away from his goal of regaining the Teamsters presidency.

The Hoffa family maintained that Hoffa would have

had to trust whoever enticed him out of the Machus Red Fox Restaurant parking lot. He would have put up a fight if he hadn't trusted them.

Street talk around Detroit, however, was that Tony Giacalone, allegedly one of the mob's most feared enforcers in that city, had gotten the contract. Journalists tapping their sources as far west as Las Vegas heard stories that Eugene Mayday and Robert Maheu, a consultant to Mayday's Leisure Industries since leaving Howard Hughes, were being investigated. Supposedly Mayday went to Las Vegas on Hoffa's orders to revive the ailing Checker Cab there. None of this was ever proved.

The tangle of events was mind-boggling. By August a grand jury had been called in order to investigate all the various charges. The star witnesses: Anthony Giacalone, Tony Provenzano, Chuckie O'Brien, Louis Linteau, Leonard Schulz. Linteau was, of course, interested in giving whatever information he could. He spent hours before the grand jury. Chuckie O'Brien pleaded the Fifth. The others, for various reasons cited by their attorneys, would not talk.

But then investigators thought they had a break. A loan shark associated with Anthony Provenzano was found dead. This was, perhaps, the wedge that investigators had been looking for to break the case. Shortly thereafter two witnesses supposedly came forward, claiming that they had seen all or a portion of Hoffa's abduction. The situation began heating up. Salvatore Briguglio and his brother Gabriel, both allegedly attached to the Vito Genovese family and both prominent in New Jersey Local 560, former stronghold of Tony Pro, along with Thomas Andretta, were called before a police lineup. The results of the lineup were kept quiet. Later the results were admitted as evidence to the grand jury.

Investigators then focused on the Gateway Transportation Company in Detroit. Hundred-gallon barrels filled with chemicals were regularly shipped out of its trucking docks. They reasoned that Hoffa's body may have been removed from Detroit in this manner. For all the investigators' efforts, Jimmy Hoffa's body was never found. No one was ever indicted for his death.

There had been rising incidents of violence around Detroit prior to Hoffa's disappearance, and that had bothered Hoffa. Local 299, the union that Chuckie O'Brien had wanted to take over, had been plagued by beatings and bombings. Dave Johnson, still president of the local, had his boat blown out of the water; Richard Fitzsimmons's car had been blown up; Ralph Proctor, an official of the local, had been viciously stomped in broad daylight. There had been warnings of impending danger. Hoffa preferred to ignore those warnings. He often had said, "If you ignore a problem long enough it will simply go away." He also denied, at least publicly, the existence of any "organized crime."

In a speech before some union members he said: "All this hocus-pocus about racketeers and crooks is a smokescreen to carry you back to the days when they could drop you in a scrap heap like they do a worn-out truck. You know me since I'm seventeen: the 'kid' you called me. They say I've got a police record. Sure I've got a record and you know where I got it. It's no secret. There's not one thing there outside the labor movement. And I'll tell you, I will have it again if they start kicking the truck drivers around. . . ."

Even in one of his final interviews with Stanecki he said: "I don't believe there is any organized crime, period. Don't believe it. Never believed it . . ."

Hoffa never had a bodyguard, always drove his own car, and before he disappeared he almost never carried a gun.

Who killed Jimmy Hoffa? That question probably will never be answered. Why did Jimmy Hoffa die? Again, pure speculation. But perhaps part of the reason was due to the realities of life that Hoffa either didn't know or didn't want to know.

8

D. B. Cooper

A cold, wet, mid-fall afternoon descended on Portland International Airport. Passengers waited in the boarding lounge at gate 49 for the last leg of Northwest Airlines flight 305, bound for Seattle. It was Thanksgiving eve, November 24, 1971.

Flight 305 had begun as the most ordinary of commuter flights. It was a milk run, originating in Washington, D.C., at 8:30 A.M., with scheduled stops at Minneapolis, Great Falls, Missoula, Portland, Spokane, and finally Seattle. Flight 305 arrived in Portland without misadventure and was about to be boarded by a flurry of new passengers.

Holiday cheer was in the air. Thoughts of succulent roast-turkey dinners and family reunions occupied the passengers' minds. Larry Feingold, assistant U. S. attorney, had rushed to Portland to catch the plane, having told his family he would arrive in Seattle at three-thirty. Here's how he remembers the end of the flight:

"As we came to Seattle I noticed that we circled not just once for an approach but twice. At that point the pilot came on—and this was only thirty-five minutes after we took off—and said that there were certain difficulties. I assumed that it may have been because there were a lot of flights coming in for Thanksgiving, that things may have been stacked up. What seemed like an eternity later, the pilot came back on and said they were continuing to have difficulties. None of us

165

knew that there was a skyjacking, except the crew members, and the crew ought to be complimented because they handled themselves extremely well during the entire ordeal. About three hours after takeoff—about two and a half hours after we should have landed—we were informed that finally the difficulties had been ironed out. We landed, and my assumption was that there was engine difficulty (so they should get us off the plane very quickly). Instead, some gas trucks drove up, and I thought, The nerve of Northwest Airlines—more interested in the fuel on the aircraft than they are in the passengers! We sat there patiently for about five minutes and then had to all get up and quietly walk out of the plane. We were out on a runway about six or seven hundred yards from the terminal. The only individual out there was one man in an unmarked car. As an assistant U. S. attorney at the time, I'm not sure I was ready to go out personally and arrest him, but I certainly was ready to prosecute him. I walked over to see him and said, 'What the hell is going on?' and he said to me, 'There's a skyjacker on the plane, just keep going.' "

The taking of flight 305 was to become the most famous skyjacking in the history or air piracy. The criminal was an inconspicuous traveler identified on the Portland passenger manifest as Dan Cooper. He extorted $200,000 from Northwest Airlines. He took the money and parachuted to fame over southwest Washington State.

Dan Cooper vanished, leaving behind a string of baffling entries in the annals of crime. He was the first man ever to parachute from a plane that he had commandeered, carrying with him the largest ransom ever extorted from an American airline. All attempts to identify and capture Dan Cooper have failed—he is still at large.

After five years of intensive search efforts, the FBI admits that they are no closer to solving the crime than they were on the night it took place. Cooper, erroneously described in the press as "D.B." Cooper, has not been heard from since he strapped twenty-one pounds of twenty-dollar bills onto his person and bailed out of the Boeing 727 jet on that fateful Thanksgiving eve. The seven-year statute of limitations will not protect Dan Cooper, because a federal grand jury indicted him for skyjacking just before the five-year period ran out. If he is caught, a bevy of lawyers will spend years untangling that indictment.

According to FBI special agent Ralph Himmelsbach, "We're going ahead on the assumption that the statute doesn't apply because when he did what he did, capital punishment was a possibility. There's no statute on capital crimes. We're continuing to process suspects. Of course," he added, "it has slowed down a great deal."

I spent a great deal of time talking to Ralph Himmelsbach about Dan Cooper. Taciturn and businesslike, Ralph rarely volunteered more information than was specifically asked for. His answers were clear and measured, and I felt that everything he said was absolutely accurate. He told me that other than Cooper, he —Himmelsbach—probably knows more about the skyjacking than any other person. He studied the story from the inside out, and much of his free time is still spent covering old ground to be sure no critical item slipped past his attention. I wondered why Cooper was still missing. To demonstrate one of the reasons, Ralph took me into the area where Cooper is believed to have landed. It's rugged country marked by a reservoir, steep hills, a dense thicket of forest and pine trees, and a swampy area of rain forest. Experienced hunters are known to have vanished in this trackless, green, lush labyrinth. If Cooper had been killed in the jump, what would it take to find Cooper's remains? FBI agent Himmelsbach said, "It might take five thousand men five years. I mean, how do you search a blackberry thicket higher than your head? . . . We have to accept the possibility that we may never know. I guess we can live with that if we have to."

The FBI has checked more than one thousand reports, as well as a long list of missing persons. And after five long years of scrupulous sleuthing, they still don't know if there ever was a Dan Cooper.

Bit by bit, a portrait of Dan Cooper has emerged. He is a male Caucasian; mid-forties; height 5 feet 10 inches to 6 feet; weight, 170 to 180 pounds; average build; olive complexion, with dark brown or black hair parted on the left; low-voiced, no particular accent; intelligent vocabulary; heavy chain smoker. The story of Dan Cooper's crime is short and the clues to his identity are few. As Ralph Himmelsbach put it, "We still don't know who he was, where he came from, or where he went. We know he had to be somebody. We know he had to have a beginning. We know he had to have had friends, associates, perhaps a job, a family, and he's missing from somewhere. We just don't know where, yet. The one thing we *do* have going for us— we have the list of the bills that we used in paying the ransom. There were ten thousand twenty-dollar bills. We have a photograph and the recorded serial number of every bill."

As best I could piece it together, this is how the skyjacking was carried out:

Dan Cooper, wearing a plain business suit and dark glasses, purchased a ticket, with cash, for flight 305. About 2:30 P.M. he boarded the 727 Boeing in Portland and took a seat at the rear starboard side of the plane. He did nothing out of the ordinary, nothing to distinguish himself from the rest of the passengers. Nothing, at least, until he handed a stewardess a note.

Cooper's note demanded that upon arrival at the airport in Seattle, $200,000 ransom and four parachutes (two backpack type and two front-pack) be delivered to him, minus any funny stuff. Cooper then showed a stewardess his briefcase, which contained two red cylinders and a mass of wires—the implication being that if his requests were not granted, the makeshift bomb would explode. The stewardess acknowledged the threat and immediately relayed the skyjacker's demands to the captain, who in turn radioed Seattle ground control.

Orders were quickly issued to cooperate fully with the skyjacker. Ground control sent the following message to the plane: FBI AND POLICE HAVE ADVISED NO ACTION BE TAKEN. REPEAT NO ACTION TO BE TAKEN. WE ARE AWAITING HIS CONCURRENCE THAT YOU SHOULD LAND.

As the plane neared and then passed Seattle, passengers began to wonder why there was a delay in arrival. They were reassured that because of slight mechanical problems the plane would have to circle Seattle for a while in order to burn up excess fuel.

Shortly before 6:00 P.M., the plane touched down. The passengers remained on board until the money and parachutes arrived. When Cooper's boodle was finally delivered, he agreed to allow all the passengers to disembark except for the flight crew and one stewardess. The minutes dragged by. Cooper was getting nervous. At one point in the negotiations, an official of the Federal Aviation Administration boarded the plane and tried to talk the hijacker into surrendering, only to hear Cooper snap, "Let's get this show on the road."

As the plane was readied for takeoff, Cooper said that he wanted to fly to Mexico City, but the crew protested that Mexico was outside the jet's maximum range. Cooper quickly agreed to stop for refueling in Reno.

Although he did not specify the route, Cooper did make rather specific requirements for the takeoff and flight to Reno. He ordered that the altitude be maintained below ten thousand feet, that the flaps be kept down and that the rear exit door be kept open, thus forcing the plane to coast at near its minimum cruising speed of two hundred miles per hour.

At 7:30 P.M. the tower cleared flight 305 for takeoff from Seattle and advised the captain that he would have an Air Force company escort all the way down to Reno.

According to the *Seattle Times Magazine,* Oct. 3, 1976: "When the 727 lifted off to become a tiny dot in the sky, radar operators tracked a total of eight additional planes shadowing the three-engine jet. Six jet fighters, one jet trainer, and an H-130 rescue plane with emergency gear and jumpers were launched from bases in Washington, Idaho, and California. No one was able to maintain constant visual contact."

Then, slightly more than half an hour after flight 305 took off from Seattle, the captain noticed that instruments in the cockpit indicated that the steps from the rear exit had been lowered during the flight. The gauges flip-flopped, indicating a change in cabin pressure.

John Doe, alias Dan Cooper, had bailed out of flight 305 somewhere over southwestern Washington State.

I traveled there in the late fall to see for myself the area in which Dan Cooper's story took place. I found a skydiving school and talked to an experienced parachutist about the possibility of Dan Cooper surviving his leap from flight 305.

"I imagine he wouldn't have had too much trouble surviving it," he told me. "The only thing he might have had a problem with is coming down in the trees. The temperature wouldn't be that big a factor. I know I've jumped from airplanes when the temperature was four degrees below zero. As we exit the aircraft we're going about ninety miles an hour, which would put the windchill factor at around sixty, seventy below. But you really don't feel it when you're up there. As far as speed, I know paratroopers come out of airplanes going about two hundred fifty miles an hour. This one was only going about two hundred, so I don't think it would have been any problem at all for him to survive the exit from the aircraft.

"He would have had problems with his landing, though. The terrain is pretty rugged and he would almost surely have come down in trees. There are a lot of pine trees around here, and those are the worst things. Hardwoods aren't so bad, because they'll catch your parachute, but in pine trees the canopy will hit the side of the tree and slide right off the branches. If he hit a tall one it could have killed him, because his canopy would have collapsed right at the top of the tree, and down he would have come, seventy or eighty feet. The jump sure wouldn't have been a factor and speed wouldn't have been a factor. The only problem would have been in his landing, and if he survived that, he wouldn't have had any trouble at all coming out."

As I listened to the parachutist, I realized why many officials feel that Cooper's skeleton is hanging from the shreds of a tattered parachute somewhere near Ariel Dam. It seems to be the only plausible explanation for the complete disappearance of Dan Cooper. In the five hours during which the skyjacker and his intentions became known, his very existence left clues to his identity. For example, a reasonable portrait of his face and body had been drawn. The manner in which he chose to exit the plane gave still another indication of his background: apparently he knew "something" of airplanes and of bailing out of them.

However, one informed person suggested that Cooper was not terribly familiar with leaping out of planes. Lev Richards, the so-called Bald Eagle, aviation editor of the *Portland Oregonian,* explained to me why he believed Dan Cooper was not an experienced parachutist:

"They gave him four parachutes. He cut the risers on the best one and tied the money to his belt with those strips of risers. He chose the two worst parachutes to use. One of them was a twenty-eight-foot canopy, which would cause him to fall too fast for safety, and he also took a chest pack, a chute that you use for training purposes in which the panels are sewed together. It couldn't have opened if he had tried to use it. He couldn't have used it anyway. The harness on his backpack could not have been used with a chest-type, because there were no rings there to attach the chest pack. They say that anyone who knew anything about parachutes would never have made that many mistakes."

Lev Richards pointed out another very important point: "He didn't know where he was. He didn't know for sure what route they were taking. He'd asked them to fly at ten thousand feet. The temperature in the cabin was seven below zero at that altitude, and there was a terrific storm blowing that night."

The FBI, with the aid of Northwest Airlines, reconstructed the whole skyjacking the next night, using the same plane, crew, and fuel load, and flying at the same speed and altitude. FBI agent Himmelsbach described to me the re-creation process:

"We flew the same aircraft at the same altitude, ten thousand feet, one hundred seventy knots, with the same approximate loading, with the same power settings, the same flaps and landing-gear configuration, and with the air-stair-door down. We had a two-hundred-thirty-pound sandbag on a sled lowered by a line down the stairway to the bottom step, and then when this sled was dropped off the bottom step, the stairs retracted to within a few inches of closing—causing a pressure change in the cabin that we have since learned announces the time that the jump occurred. The course of the aircraft was plotted on radar by air traffic control the entire time, with markings to show where the plane was at any given moment. The engineers from Northwest Airlines computed, from the variable factors such as the specific wind direction and velocity, how long the hijacker waited before he pulled the chute and how long it took him to go to the ground."

The re-creation test helped discern the probable drop zone. On a map the outline formed a trapezoid covering about twenty-five square miles. It centered in the Merwin Dam region, about twenty miles southeast of Kelso. Low hills covered with dense underbrush and some first- and second-growth timber make the terrain ideal for efficient vanishing acts. FBI man Himmelsbach has attempted to "psychoanalyze" Cooper's reasoning for jumping when and where he did. As we talked, Himmelsbach described what it must have been like for Cooper on the night of the jump.

"If he had looked for the worst possible place to land, he couldn't have selected one along the entire route. The area has some very steep, wooded hillsides and rocky country. It has a very deep, cold lake, a number of rivers and streams, and much thick underbrush. On a dark night, with no visual reference to the ground, he had to have been landing blind. There are no known portable navigation systems that he could have used to calculate or determine where he was from inside an airplane. There was no visual reference to the ground, and in my judgment it would have been impossible for him to know within perhaps a dozen miles precisely where he was at the time he left the aircraft. I feel that he intended to get out of the aircraft just about as quickly as he could after it departed Seattle, heading south. His request to fly to Mexico City or someplace south was just a ruse to get the aircraft on its way and give him an opportunity to make the jump whenever he wanted."

The twenty-five-square-mile area was searched many times, in vain, in the days and years afterward. Nothing, however—not even the remains of a parachute—has ever been found.

In mid-March 1972, police called in the National Guard to search the area. With the aid of five helicopters, three hundred soldiers from Fort Lewis, Washington, spent eighteen days in the area, to no avail. Dan Cooper had disappeared.

Almost every detail of the Cooper skyjacking has been subjected to careful analysis. Much was made of the fact that of all U. S. commercial aircraft, Cooper had chosen the only one equipped with a rear exit positioned to permit safe parachuting. As a result, some newswriters credited Cooper with extensive knowledge of aircraft and parachuting. All his requests caused much speculation. Why, for example, had he asked for four parachutes? He might have reasoned that the authorities would think he was going to ask a stewardess or other crew member to parachute with him—obviously, they would be sure to provide parachutes that opened. Cooper explicitly ordered sport parachutes rather than the military type. The significant difference is that the military models open automatically after about two hundred feet, whereas sport chutes allow the user to free-fall as long as he likes before pulling the ripcord.

FBI man Himmelsbach disagreed with those who credited Cooper with being smart:

"I don't think he was well prepared at all. He set about it without really planning very far ahead. He didn't ask for the things that he should have asked for, the things that, logically, he would have needed beyond the parachutes. He could have requested a hard helmet, goggles, gloves, a flight suit, a flight jacket, jump boots, small hand tools to aid in his escape from a tree or a barbed-wire fence when he landed. He asked for none of these things."

The inclement weather and dense terrain were perfectly suited to the deed. In fact, or so it seemed at the time, Cooper had planned everything just right. He left no fingerprints, paid for his ticket with cash, and in general was totally unremembered and undistinguished. Stepping out of obscurity one November day to board a 727 jet, Dan Cooper has seemingly managed to return to the shadows of routine life totally unscathed by the massive search efforts undertaken in his name. And it was just this lack of information about him that stimulated a rash of provocative conjecture. What kind of man could conceive of such a crime?

Psychologist Dr. David Hubbard has interviewed almost every captured American skyjacker. To my surprise, Dr. Hubbard had drawn a highly detailed psychological portrait of Cooper which was far beyond anything I had ever before heard or read. "He's being billed as a Robin Hood, when in truth Cooper was, as an individual, a failure. He was an early-middle-aged ex-aircraft pilot who had deteriorated mentally. He was impulsive in the sense that his capability to plan was very limited and he was subject to the power of suggestion. You see, he did not create this crime—skyjacking—he imitated it. A man in Canada created the crime two weeks before this so-called Cooper ever acted. Now, the act—to jump out the rear end of a plane—in itself requires a high level of exhibitionism and a great deal of compulsivity. The man was not a parachute jumper; indeed, he knew very little about it and jumped in a pair of shoes that were totally inadequate. He was extremely nicotine-addicted, which was evidenced by the fact that he smoked nearly three packs of cigarettes in the very short period of time that he was on board that aircraft. Clearly, he had flown in the Far East and in the Vietnamese War, and undoubtedly he had taken part in the airdrops in which the tailgates of 727s were used for dropping material."

And there Dr. Hubbard's portrait ended. After the interview was finished, I began to wonder if the skyjacker might have had an accomplice waiting for him on the ground. At the beginning of the search, countless rumors unfolded concerning unidentified aircraft landing and taking off in the skyjack area. All these leads were checked out and proved to be dead ends. Cooper had had no accomplices.

Perhaps Cooper managed to land without injury and successfully made his way through the woods, and is now walking the streets a free man. If this is so, then why haven't any of the ten thousand twenty-dollar bills—all of which were meticulously recorded by the FBI—shown up?

If Cooper is dead, why hasn't his body been found by now? Have the searchers been looking in the wrong place? There are still no answers. Yet, the prospect of all that money—both ransom and reward—has sent fortune hunters scurrying into the woods ever since Thanksgiving 1971.

The social reverberations in the aftermath of the Cooper heist are fascinating. The name D. B. Cooper has been eulogized. The same public fancy that made folk heroes out of Bonnie and Clyde has transformed Cooper into a highly commercial legend. In short order, a Portland manufacturer had a T-shirt on the market with the slogan D. B. COOPER, WHERE ARE YOU? and a picture of a parachute floating down with a suitcase marked "$".

The initials D. B. separate Cooper the folk hero from Dan Cooper the criminal. He's D. B. to the reporters who want an easy "sell" for their stories, and he's D. B. to the people who would make of him a daring rogue. At a party in Ariel, Washington, I heard troubadours singing original folksongs in honor of the skyjacker. They were celebrating the man who had, in their words, "gotten away with it." It was Germaine Tricola, owner of the Ariel Store and Tavern, who best explained the Cooper legend. She told me, "It was just like giving the finger to the big guys, you know, and the big companies. The people see themselves as being squeezed dry by the big people. They just think it's time."

As the party went on and I watched the group toast "Ol' D. B.," I began to sense the frustration that Ralph Himmelsbach was feeling. I recalled his musing over the folk-hero aspect of the Cooper case: "I think people worldwide get a little bit of satisfaction out of seeing the mighty humbled. When you talk to people who say they admire what he did, they're talking about admiring a man with the spunk to undertake a bold challenge like that, and they don't realize they're saying hooray for a guy who jeopardized the lives of forty-three people."

Good fortune prevented the loss of lives and thereby placed a tough veneer on the Cooper case. The public felt that Cooper had done little harm. Anyone who chose to prosecute him was, by extension, "picking on the little guy." The attitude of the public tended to make the prickly case even more difficult. The flash and fury of the Cooper case tended to obscure a fact that Lev Richards, aviation editor of the *Portland Oregonian*, underlined in very straightforward terms.

We were in the airport in Portland when he said, "Now all of it seems like a lot of fun, but if you stop and think, you realize that everybody in this terminal is paying for that crime. The cost of the security system is added to your ticket. It doesn't show on the face of it, but it's there."

It's there, and we're saddled with the results of the five hours in which Dan Cooper skyjacked that plane. Cooper's possible success caused a rash of imitations of his crime. Not one of his successors, however, escaped a prison sentence. Nevertheless, the rash of skyjackings caused airlines to institute elaborate security measures in terminals the world over. In five years the cost of policing the airlines and the airports has exceeded the total spent by the United States in World War I. So much for Cooper heroics.

Is Cooper alive? I posed the question at all the stops I made in Washington. Ralph Himmelsbach allowed himself a few minutes of speculative consideration concerning Cooper's potential for survival before he replied:

"At a hundred-ninety-six miles an hour, the force of air is something like having a fire hose stuck in your face full blast. The eyelids get puffed out and the little blood vessels around the eyes rupture. He probably got a couple of nice black eyes out of it and impaired vision as well. So I picture the guy coming down in an absolutely dark night, coming down very fast, half blind, and sock-footed, and he had to land in who knows what."

Les Nelson is now sheriff of Cowlitz County, Washington. A sandy-haired, straight-talking lawman, he was chief of security for Weyerhaeuser Paper when Cooper hijacked flight 305. His company's helicopter launched the first search over the suspected drop zone, the region around Ariel Dam. Sheriff Nelson's view of Cooper's potential for survival is as granite-tough as is Nelson himself. As we talked, we were standing at the edge of the icy, blue Lake Merwin.

"It's possible," he said, "that he went into the lake.

We've lost fishermen here who we've never recovered due to the depth of this thing. On the other hand, if he was unfortunate enough not to get his chute open, why he would have just made a hole in the ground and pulled the hole in after him, money and all. I kinda think, though, that one day some hunter somewhere, someplace in this area, may come across a lot of tattered money, a few bones, and this will be D. B. Cooper."

In general, FBI man Himmelsbach agrees. When I asked him if he thought Cooper was alive, he said, "I feel the greatest likelihood is that he is still lying right where he fell. I don't know where. It had to have been in the zone somewhere, perhaps in the lake, perhaps in the woods, but my feeling is that he probably is still there. If somebody ever stumbles across him, I suspect they'll find the larger bones of the skull, and perhaps the pelvis or a thigh bone. Perhaps even some of his gear will have survived. The small animals will have dispatched most of him unless he went into the water. If he went into the deep, cold water, it is very possible that he may remain pretty much intact."

I couldn't resist one question: "If somebody finds the money, can they keep it?"

Himmelsbach thought for a moment, then said, "Well of course the money is stolen property. Turn it in. The story would be much more valuable than the money itself, plus the fact that the finder would be able to sleep nights."

I realized that I had been accorded a rather rare glimpse behind the scenes of an FBI investigator. I asked agent Himmelsbach if he thought his appearance on our TV show would be helpful to the investigation. He replied, "I would hope that the interest generated by this presentation would stir some individuals who may have an idea who Cooper was or is to tell us about it. He had to have had some connections, some past, some life, some loose ends dangling. I would hope that someone might tell us about it, give us the benefit of their knowledge, give us an idea, a place to start."

Somewhere, someone has a piece of information about a dark-haired, chain-smoking ex-pilot, medium height, desperate, a bit of an extrovert, who dropped from flight 305 during Thanksgiving week, 1971. The need for that information remains. D. B. Cooper is *still at large.*

PART III

STRANGE DISAPPEARANCES

Prologue

Part III of *In Search of Missing Persons* deals with strange, bizarre disappearances of a variety of legendary, historical, and contemporary people. I have assembled four accounts of men and women who vanished under extremely interesting circumstances. No one as yet has been able to determine where the subjects sojourned. All of them, however, without exception, seem to have disappeared voluntarily during the prime of their life. Some reappeared with strange explanations regarding their temporary absence. Others promised to return but as yet have not fulfilled their pledge. Each of the reports presents significant facts and a multitude of plausible and popular theories.

These disappearances have several similarities. Despite the variety of incidents, settings, and costumes, a number of latter-day culture heroes offered similar responses to life's questions. In the course of my research I discovered that in each age a few persons have appeared whose words and actions seem to demonstrate that they were denizens of an order different from the rest of society. Their wisdom and their teachings were said to have guided humanity over critical periods in the development of civilization. But perhaps, as in the case of Jesus Christ and later the Middle-American man-gods, the historical accuracy with which their labors have been described may be called to question. They left behind enduring mysteries. Where did these great men and women go? Why did they leave?

Christians all over the world still await the Second Coming of the Savior. In the hot, inhospitable forests of Central America, the myths of the bearded, fair-skinned gods (the bringers of civilization who suddenly disappeared, with a promise to return) are recorded in picture and symbol upon the remnants of lost civilizations they reputedly established many aeons ago.

In the course of my travels for Part III of this book, I found that in each case the missing god-figure, by virtue of a strange and abrupt disappearance, entered the world of myth. In all times and under every circumstance the myths have flourished. The tales have become the living inspirations for mankind's giant leaps forward. As more time passes, however, the accuracy with which the lives of great personages have been depicted becomes clouded by the popular legends that surround them. Sorting out fact from legend becomes increasingly difficult, and the more time that has passed, the more blurred is the boundary between truth and fancy. In the case of the ancients, the game of search moves uneasily back and forth across the line.

Modern-day figures such as Aimee Semple Macpherson and Robert Rich became famous for the act of setting themselves against the accepted order of their time, thereby introducing a new perspective to social customs and mores. By virtue of their deeds and mysterious disappearances, they were able to insure themselves a unique place in our memories. Their captivating stories are told in the following pages.

9

Jesus Christ

"Jesus Christ, Jesus Christ, who are you, what did you sacrifice?" Into the clear night a chorus raised the question against the backdrop of a million lights twinkling like a spray of diamonds. It was a performance of *Jesus Christ Superstar* in an outdoor theater—enough to send a tingle down my spine. Even in the early 1970s, when the rock opera and then the movie were produced, the question was still being asked. Who was that man who had more effect on Western civilization than anyone else in recorded time? *Was* he a man? Was he divine? Was he both?

The questions are intriguing for a number of reasons, and the few answers that can be found are complex. What we do know is that between the time Christ was born and the time he was crucified, only the last three years—those that he devoted to preaching—were recorded with any detail and accuracy. Why would a man who was supposedly hailed as the Messiah upon his birth, a man supposedly the Son of God, by divine conception, a man of Davidic lineage (descending from David)—why were the years of his maturation so ignored?

Ronald Hock, a professor of religion at the University of Southern California's School of Religion and a specialist in the New Testament, offered this explanation: "The idea that Jesus was the Messiah was not really thought about until he was crucified. Then he was declared the 'King of the Jews.' The Messiah. Then you have to say that the stories of Jesus's birth couldn't possibly have been written until after the crucifixion, some thirty-odd years after. The Gospels of Matthew and Luke, for example, originated independently of each other. They say entirely different things [in regard to the Nativity]. In either case, we don't have anything historical about [the early life of] Jesus. It's all imagination as far as we can tell."

Professor Hock's thoughts may raise the ire of some traditionalists, yet his point of view has been derived from a study of historical documentation. Certainly thousands of manuscripts have been written comparing the Gospels and searching for the accuracy of their statements. Some may protest that "these are the words of the Apostles." If only it were that easy . . .

Scholars point out that many of the stories about Jesus were aimed at spreading "the Word," at attracting and persuading people to join the faith. The First Gospel according to Mark, was written nearly thirty years after Jesus's death, and in the intervening years was subject to much alteration. Tales of Christ's life, it must be remembered, were told, not written.

According to *Life* magazine reporter Robert Coughlan, oral teaching of tradition was a part of Jewish custom. Moreover, most of Christ's disciples were illiterate, and the written word was not at all the common way of teaching. Of the manuscripts that were written, some were authored by the Apostles, while other parts were written by people in the Apostles' name. In attempts to legitimize the works, the Apostles' names were often tacked on without their knowledge. The question of accuracy arises from the fact that there were a number of Christian or Christian/Jewish communities and manuscripts supposedly documenting Christ's life and teachings were written in nearly every conceivable language of the area. The manuscripts as well as the fledgling Christian organizations were vying for the "most authenticity."

By the fourth century A.D. the Roman Church had

consolidated its power and held the upper hand. Twenty-seven writings were then "canonized," and these became the New Testament, the Gospels, the "true teachings of Christ." But what determined those twenty-seven writings? Professor Hock explained: "The first criterion was that the book had to be apostolic in origin. How that was determined was another matter. Secondly, and most importantly, the book had to be orthodox in content. In other words, those people who were in power decided what was orthodox and what wasn't."

Jesus's life and his teachings are interpreted differently according to the era in which they are studied. In today's more secularized society it is quite easy to deduce that if Mary was really a "holy" woman, if Jesus was given life by means of "Immaculate Conception," and if as a child he performed miracles, then in fact every aspect of his life would have been carefully documented. As I have said, this is not the case. But in the period following Jesus's crucifixion there was a rush to fill in the gaps, the unrecorded years of his life. The emphasis, no doubt, was to write "gospels" that agreed with ancient prophecy. There are two series of so-called Infancy Gospels, which supposedly trace the early part of Jesus's life, and which tend to emphasize his paranormal powers. The Gospels according to James and to Thomas both appear in the New Testament Apocrypha, but the writings were not canonized in the fourth century. James, most scholars agree, is much more straightforward; Thomas, blatantly, tends to glorify. For example, in the Protevangel of James:14, "And Joseph feared greatly and parted from her [Mary] pondering what he should do with her. And Joseph said: 'If I conceal her sin [her pregnancy] I shall be found opposing the law of the Lord. If I expose her to the children of Israel, I fear lest that which is in her may have sprung from the angels, and I should be found delivering up innocent blood to the judgment of death. What then shall I do with her? I will put her away secretly.' And the night came upon

him. And behold, an angel of the Lord appeared to
him in a dream, saying: 'Do not fear because of this
child. For that which is in her is of the Holy Spirit.
She shall bear a son, and you shall call his name Jesus;
for he shall save his people from their sins.' And Joseph arose from sleep and glorified the God of Israel
who had bestowed his grace upon him, and he watched
over her." In other versions, the angel came to Mary,
but, as I've said, interpretations vary.

While James is dignified, even restrained, in his approach, Thomas waxed highly poetic in the Infancy
Gospels: A sample: "When this boy Jesus was five
years old he was playing at the ford of a brook and
he gathered together into pools the water that flowed
by, and made it once clean, and commanded it by his
word alone. He made soft clay and fashioned from it
twelve sparrows. And it was the sabbath when he did
this. And there were also many other children playing
with him. Now when a certain Jew saw what Jesus
was doing in his play on the sabbath he at once went
and told his father Joseph, 'See your child is at the
brook, and he has taken clay and fashioned twelve
birds and has profaned the sabbath.' And when Joseph came to the place and saw [it], he cried out to
him, saying: 'Why do you do on the sabbath what
ought not to be done?' But Jesus clapped his hands
and cried to the sparrows: 'Off with you!' And the
sparrows took flight and went away chirping. . . ."

Thomas portrays the child Jesus not only as savior
but as avenger. With regularity he strikes people down,
makes them suffer with diseases, blinds them, and pro-
claims any number of other retributions for their mis-
deeds: For example: ". . . the son of Annas the scribe
was standing there with Joseph; and he took a branch
of a willow and [with it] dispersed the water which
Jesus had gathered together. . . . When Jesus saw
what he had done he was enraged and said to him:
'You insolent godless dunderhead, what harm did the
pools and the water do to you? See, now you also shall
wither like a tree and shall bear neither leaves nor

root nor fruit.' And immediately that lad withered up completely; and Jesus departed and went into Joseph's house." When Joseph later admonished him, Jesus supposedly said: "I know that these words are not yours; nevertheless for your sake I will be silent. But they shall bear their punishment."

Today, through musicals such as *Jesus Christ, Superstar, Godspell,* and a number of less notable and even sometimes pornographic pieces, Jesus Christ has been examined as a man rather than as the Messiah.

In the days preceding the crucifixion such examination was not possible. The mores of the time were much in evidence in the Gospels. "Asceticism was gaining strength when they were written," explained Professor Hock. "Monks would stand on poles in the desert for hours, days, punishing their bodies, trying to escape their bodies. In order to have a sinless Jesus you had to have a sinless mother. This movement had a very strong effect. But there has always been this dualism of the spiritual and the flesh." This trend, and the usual religious emphasis of a fantasy flight from earthly things, colored the Gospels as they were being written.

For example, in many of the Gospels we see a list of Jesus's brothers and sisters. But the sisters' names, in particular, change, according to which Gospel is read. Additionally, certain parts of the New Testament Apocrypha give reason to believe that some of the children belonged to Joseph by an earlier marriage. The idea of a previous marriage was introduced as part of the rationale behind the assertion that Mary was a virgin. Virginity and pureness became major factors as asceticism grew stronger. Some stories say that Joseph took Mary as his wife; others say that he never did. Some questioned that if James was Jesus's full brother, did he too carry some holiness with him, or was he just an ordinary human being? Questions regarding whether Jesus was part of the Davidic line through Joseph, through Mary, through both of them, have not been satisfactorily answered. Today's biblical

scholars question whether Mary and Joseph traveled
from Nazareth to Bethlehem, where Jesus was born,
or whether they lived in Bethlehem and later moved
to Nazareth. This question arises because, according
to ancient Roman writings and other calculations,
there couldn't possibly have been a census at the time
indicated in Luke which would have forced Mary and
Joseph to travel from Nazareth to Bethlehem.

Almost with exasperation, Professor Hock declared:
"Now we don't even know if Jesus was a carpenter."

Attempting to create a "whole" Jesus, a complete
picture of what Jesus was like, is not a new quest.
We can see that it began with the Gospels, but efforts toward humanizing Jesus began only a few hundred years ago. Nineteenth-century philosophers, such
as David Friedrich Strauss in *The Life of Jesus,* began to attack the miraculous or supernatural element
in the Gospels. For his efforts, Strauss's career was
blighted until he died.

However, the Life of Jesus movement in the nineteenth century encouraged such writings. In France,
Joseph Ernest Renan's *La Vie de Jésus* sparked a great
deal of furor, for he portrayed Jesus as a living human being, albeit a fictional one.

In 1906 Albert Schweitzer—philosopher, theologian,
musicologist, and physician—published *The Quest of
the Historical Jesus.* While Schweitzer portrayed Jesus
as a man, replete with fears and obsessions, who died
due to his incontrovertible conviction of and preoccupa-
tion with impending doom and a new world order,
Schweitzer made an even more significant point by
claiming that Jesus should have been allowed to stand
in his own time against his own peculiar environment.

Biblical scholars now argue that the best way, and
perhaps the only way, to determine anything about
Jesus is first to thoroughly examine all the literature
about him and then to draw as accurate as possible a
picture of Galilee.

The Roman historian Tacitus, writing in the second
century A.D., made a brief reference to Jesus. In his

Annals of the year 116 Tacitus refers to the fire in
Rome in 64: "A persistent rumor associated Nero with
the starting of this fire. To combat this, he decided
to provide culprits and inflicted the most atrocious
tortures upon that sect, popularly detested for their
practices, who are known as Christians. This name
comes to them from one Christ, who was condemned
to be crucified by the procurator Pontius Pilate in the
reign of Tiberius."

Pliny the Younger, governor in Asia Minor, wrote
a letter to the emperor Trajan in approximately 112
A.D. in which he made a terse reference to Christus,
a man honored as God by a certain sect.

Suetonius, another Roman historian, a contemporary of Tacitus and the biographer of the Caesars,
mentioned reprisals against the Christians. In one passage he confirmed Nero's persecutions. He wrote that
Claudius "expelled the Jews from Rome because under the influence of Christ they had become a permanent source of disorder."

The Talmud—a combination of the religious laws
of Judaism and scholarly commentaries about them
—and the writings of Jewish historian Flavius Josephus are the two primary sources of information about
the Jews. The Talmud contains some references to a
disciple called Yeshu the Nazarene. Josephus's *An-
tiquities of the Jews* appeared in 93 A.D. Although
Josephus must have known about Christianity, he
made no direct mention of Jesus. The famous "silence
of Josephus" is itself a much debated topic. He mentioned only one contemporary of Jesus, stating: ". . .
the brother of Jesus, called Christ, whose name was
James and some others . . ." James, immediately after
Christ's death, became the first bishop of Jerusalem.

Another view of Jesus's life was put forth by *Life*
reporter Robert Coughlan:

Through the millennia of wars, rumors of wars, op-
pressions, occupations, afflictions, injustices, frustra-
tions and indignities that comprised most of Jewish

history up to the time of the birth of Jesus, a few
strands run with significant consistency. One of these
was the belief embedded in the words of the proph-
ets, that miraculous deliverance was just around
the corner. The agent of deliverance, the proph-
ets had written, would be a messiah, a king. He
would come in human form and from among the
ranks of the common people as Saul and David. He
would be a descendant of David and would be born
in Bethlehem, the home city of David . . . he would
not be known at first, for no one, not even the Messiah himself, would realize his true identity until he
had fulfilled or was definitely fulfilling the task for
which God had selected him. But the Messiah would
surely come. . . .

It is entirely possible that no one—not even Jesus
himself—truly understood his significance until he was
nailed in agony upon the cross.

Geza Vermes, in *Jesus the Jew* wrote:

First, to reanimate Jesus, his natural background, first-
century Galilee, must be filled in. Second, to perceive
the truth and purpose of his mission as an exorcist
and healer, it must be reinstated in the place to
which it belongs: that is, in the charismatic stream
of post-biblical Judaism. . . . The real inspiration of
rabbinic Judaism was of Judean provenance. More
precisely, its source was Jerusalem. Galilee's regional
identity was deeply affected by the influx of leading
Judean rabbis who managed to survive the Bar
Cocheba rebellion against the Roman empire of Ha-
drian (A.D. 132–5) and its aftermath, and were compelled by imperial legislation to settle in the North.

Flavius Josephus provided an even greater indication that Galilee was distinguished by its political,
social, and economic organizations, which were in large
part different from the rest of Palestine. . . . The prov-
ince was basically an autonomous, self-contained polit-
ico-ethnic unit. Galilee was not ruled by Roman hand
throughout the time of Christ, although Judea was.

Vermes wrote:

Rome did not appear on the scene except between
AD. 44 and 66. Then Galilee, in the time of Jesus, was
relatively free. From the middle of that last century
before Christ, the Maccabean revolution (167–42
B.C.) had been launched from this area, and had
succeeded in winning one of the few intervals of
Jewish National independence, until Judea began ca-
pitulating and gave control over to puppet king
Herod the Great.

This area seemed a likely place for a rebel, or perhaps a messiah, to be born.

The Galilean countryside was economically ripe to
support political revolt. Unlike Jerusalem, which was
suffering, Galilee was relatively well off. Nazareth specifically depended upon grain fields, cultivation of
vineyards, and various groves. Galilee exported fish,
wine, wheat, and olive oil throughout the Middle
East (it was a crime, however, to export oil and wine
to non-Jewish neighbors). There was an abundance of
flax that was made into linen of unusually fine quality
and beauty. The fisheries on the Sea of Galilee, particularly the southern portions, during the time of
Christ, produced some of the choicest fishes in the
world. Contrary to popular belief, Galilee was not an
impoverished land.

Galilee, however, was not heavily populated. Nazareth, it has been estimated, during Jesus's lifetime
could support only one family per trade. It probably
was a logical deduction of the Apostles that if Jesus's
"father" was a carpenter, his eldest "son" would practice the same trade.

The healthy economy, the sparse population, and
even the beautiful countryside would have had an effect upon Jesus's consciousness. From a hill behind
Nazareth, Jesus must have scanned the horizon and
been awed by the view. To a child, indeed even to a
modern-day traveler, it could easily seem as if one
were standing in the middle of the world. To the west
he could see the Mediterranean Sea, and Mount Carmel and the Plain of Sharon to the south. The broad

Plain of Esdraelon with Mount Tabor was on the north; to the east, the Sea of Galilee, the Jordan, and the hills that marked the beginning of Bashan Gilead.

Jesus of the Gospels, wrote Vermes:

> . . . conforms to the specifically Galilean type. He is, to begin with, an appreciative child of the Galilean countryside. The metaphors placed in his mouth are mostly agricultural ones, as would be expected from a man who spent the major part of his life among farmers and peasants. For him, the ultimate beauty is that of the lilies in the field. The city and its life occupy scarcely any place at all in his teaching. It is in fact remarkable that there is no mention whatever in the Gospels of any of the larger Galilean towns. . . .

Josephus portrayed Galileans as fearless fighters and sometimes as unsuppressed rebels. This view contrasts sharply with the rabbinic portrayal of the northerners as fun-loving and stupid. Galileans were often chided by their southern cousins for not speaking correct Aramaic. Jesus himself spoke Galilean Aramaic.

Vermes wrote:

> However, far graver than the criticism provoked by their regional accent were the accusations leveled at the Galileans by the Pharisees and their rabbinical successors concerning matters related to sacrifices and offerings in the Temple of Jerusalem, to levitical cleanness and uncleanness, and to the rabbinic code of proper behavior in general . . . for Pharisees and the rabbis of the first and early second century A.D., the Galileans were on the whole boors.

So Jesus came from an area regarded as religiously unorthodox and politically unstable. Jesus ultimately became a political suspect, but not because of what he said; it was primarily because he came from Galilee and secondarily because he had followers. In the end,

Jesus was crucified not for the actual threat that he was but for what he represented.

A number of writers have fantasized about his more earthly desires. In the writings during the centuries following the crucifixion, for example, there was even discussion whether Jesus ate and drank. According to the *New Testament Apocrypha* edited by Edgar Hennecke and Wilhelm Schneemelcher:

> According to the Gospels, Jesus felt hunger and thirst like men, and assuaged both in the same manner. Later also this was the dominant view. Valentinus [second-century Gnostic Christian theologian] allowed Jesus to consume food, but makes Him absorb it all. Clement of Alexandria, an early Christian theologian, himself denies that Jesus could have required nourishment for the maintenance of His life. Docetists denied drinking, so the Jesus of the Encratites [an extremely ascetic Christian sect] renounces the enjoyment of meat and wine and wants to have no knowledge of any kind of sexual intercourse. On this point there prevailed within Christianity a belief about Jesus from which spirits the more extreme persuasion derived from an injunction for the sexual relationships of His people also.

Speculation on Jesus's sex life is nothing new, but the theories and ideas recently expounded are more blunt and perhaps more tantalizing. David H. Lawrence in his book *The Man Who Died* pictured Jesus as sexually neuter—emotionally paralyzed from the waist down. Supposedly he never desired a lover or sexual companion. According to Lawrence, "touch me not" was Jesus's belief. All through his earthly life Jesus distorted true love with privation and denial. It was only after Jesus's public ministry had ended that he came to see the light, according to Lawrence's reckoning.

Whether Jesus in fact was totally aloof from sexual desire has been much debated. Nikos Kazantzakis, a

Greek novelist, was eager to rescue the image of Jesus as a sexual man. In *The Last Temptation of Christ,* Kazantzakis wrote that Jesus struggled all his life to overcome sexual desire. "Christ passed through all the stages which the man who struggles passes through. . . . If he had not within him this warm human element, he would never be able to touch our hearts with such assurances and tenderness; he would not be able to become a model for our lives."

William E. Phipps, chairman of the Department of Religion and Philosophy at Davis and Elkins College in Elkins, West Virginia, and author of the new book *Was Jesus Married?* explored the possibility that if Jesus did indeed follow the traditional Jewish way, he would have married. He stated that most people are "unable to read the Gospels except through the blurring lenses of ascetic eyeglasses." Phipps argued that Jesus shared the traditional Jewish belief that marriage was a sacred duty, for himself as well as for others. "The time between the twelfth and thirtieth years, on which the New Testament mentions nothing at all, covers the period when betrothal, marriage and reproduction took place in Jesus's society. Since the New Testament says nothing about whether Jesus was or was not married, it is reasonable to assume that he did not go counter to the mores of his time."

Phipps's view is perhaps most popular among those who hold more-secular beliefs. Critics of Phipps cite the Dead Sea Scrolls, which were found in 1947 in caves near the Dead Sea. While the scrolls did not shed any light directly on Jesus's life (much to the disappointment of biblical scholars), they were the first sample of an ancient library containing the sacred literature of the Essenes, a large Jewish sect in Jesus's time.

The Essene-like community which is carefully documented in the scrolls seems to have had its headquarters near the northeast shore of the Dead Sea. The community, which was called the Covenanters of Qumran, was a separatist movement that began during the Maccabean revolt. This sect retreated into seclusion and considered themselves the True Children of God. Their rituals were marked by periods of self-deprivation, and while they were known as "healers" their methods were markedly different from those of Jesus and other Jews. These people dealt heavily in the mysticism of exorcism, whereas Jesus confined most of his healing to the "laying on of hands" and to prayer. However, it is entirely possible that their ascetic lifestyle influenced Jesus. How greatly we probably will never know.

The reason that Jesus's life wasn't better chronicled is no mystery. In fact, Roman rulers of the same era have often unknown birthdates, although their reigns were carefully recorded. It seems, too, that there is no mystery about why much of what Christ did and said was not immediately recorded. Perhaps it was as prophecy told—that even he would not know his role. The mystery that does remain, however, is how such a man, from such an obscure and even unimportant background, could, after his death, have nations marching into war for him, have great stores of wealth created by and for institutions claiming to spread his word—how after all these years such a man could so mark an entire civilization.

10

Aimee Semple Macpherson

During the afternoon of May 18, 1926, an auburn-haired, thirty-five-year-old evangelist who had captured the imagination of a country sat soaking up the sun on Pacific Ocean Park Beach in Los Angeles. Dressed in a conservative green bathing suit of the day, complete with knee-length skirt, she quickly began writing another of her sermons. Genesis lapped as fluidly on her paper as waves did on the shore. She had already taken a vigorous twenty-minute swim. Suddenly she realized that it was too late for her to keep the four-thirty appointment she had made. She told her secretary to make the necessary calls and to return with some orange juice. The secretary returned, complete with orange juice and a box of candy, and settled down on the beach. In the distance she could see the swim-capped head of Aimee Semple Macpherson bobbing in the waves. Aimee swam strongly, almost joyously. It seemed as if her fervor, her zest for the flamboyant, was transmitted into everything she did.

The sun's rays were lowering. It was still too early in the season for prime beach weather in southern California, although the air temperature hovered at a comfortable sixty-eight degrees and the waves were calm. A few minutes later Emma Shaffer, Aimee's longtime secretary, squinted against the sun and scanned the western horizon. She didn't see Aimee. Sister Macpherson had vanished in full view of at least a dozen other swimmers.

Her disappearance was announced too late for the evening newspapers, but by the next morning her picture was featured on the front page of every newspaper in the country. The firebrand of the Holy Rollers and high livers, a woman who had brains and charm, who breathed love and hope into every sermon, and who had turned it all into a million-dollar business, had disappeared.

Not a morsel of information regarding her life or suspected demise escaped the public's scrutiny. Their hunger for tales of "Sister Aimee" or "Sister" was insatiable.

There were many puzzling aspects to the incident. Aimee was a strong swimmer, yet she had disappeared without a cry, without a struggle. The only conclusion that law-enforcement officers proposed was that a cramp had suddenly struck her and she had drowned.

Amazingly, her mother accepted the news more calmly than did many of her followers. As if scripted by Aimee herself, thousands of her followers crowded onto the beach for "The Search." Complete with the theatrics that made her Angelus Temple famous, the hopeful, the tearful, and the prayerful gathered to moan, sing, and beg God on bended knee to return Sister Aimee, while the clatter of roller coasters and the screams of funseekers at the Coney Island–like Lick Amusement Pier plunge provided the background effects. Cecil B. DeMille could not have provided a more fantastic scene.

The chanting, incantations, and pleading did no good. The sea had nothing to give up. Finally, after thirty-six days, Aimee Semple Macpherson wrote the next line to a phenomenal script. She walked out of the Mexican desert and said that she had been kidnapped. What could be a more fantastic explanation for a more fantastic occurrence! The story that had been front-page news for five weeks remained there for eight incredible months. No other missing person except Patty Hearst held the fascination of the media for so long.

Aimee Semple Macpherson's saga was romantic, fantastic, shocking, and bold. Aimee herself was all of these. Unlike Patty Hearst, before her disappearance Aimee had won the hearts of thousands through her Pentecostal religion and the Fundamentalist International Church of the Four-Square Gospel, which she founded in Los Angeles. Her escapades provided a release from the mundane life to which most people relegate themselves. Aimee's fantasies provided an oasis of relief; her slightly bizarre, Horatio Alger–like life gave them hope.

Born in 1890 near Ingersoll, Ontario, her father was a farmer and a devout Methodist; her mother, Minnie, was a hard-headed woman who had been trained as a Salvation Army girl. Minnie was primarily responsible for infusing Aimee with the evangelistic spirit. Later her mother would become the key to Aimee's financial empire.

Aimee's rebellious Irish spirit was not so easily channeled. A rugged tomboy, her athletic prowess and pride extended into her adult life. In addition, Aimee had a penchant for acting and theater. Often as a child she preached to the animals in her parents' barn, pretending to be the "Voice of God." As Aimee matured, so did her audiences grow. She became obsessed with the idea of acting, and dedicating her life to Christ no longer appealed to her. Aimee often told friends that she was planning to head for New York to try her luck in the theater.

But there was to be a change of plans. At seventeen she became a born-again Christian during a Pentecostal revival conducted by a handsome young preacher named Robert Semple. Aimee reportedly later told Ishbel Ross, one of her biographers, that she had had a vision during the days following her conversion. "It seemed that the heavens were brass," she said, "and would fall upon me and I would be lost if I did not immediately repent of unbelief and Christ's rejection. I raised my hands to heaven and cried, 'God, be merciful to me, a sinner.' The light streamed over my soul. . . . My fear was gone and in its place there was a blessed . . . sense of security. . . . I consecrated my life to Christ then and there. I have never done anything halfheartedly."

Aimee's last statement was never more true. But before she embarked upon her own hell-raising road, there were a few more twists of fate. Robert Semple was ushered into her fold, and just as she would charm future followers, she charmed him, and they married. With a touch of the melodramatic that made her so successful, Aimee reportedly later said of her marriage, "My lips whispered 'yes' to Robert and my heart said 'yes' to the Lord."

The newlyweds became missionaries and headed off to China. The first seeds of Sun Yat-sen's revolution were sowed just as the couple arrived on the mainland. The Semples' stay in China would not be long. Robert Semple contracted fever and died in Hong Kong, leaving Aimee no money and a month-old daughter, Roberta Star.

Aimee struggled back to the United States, never once giving up her missionary fervor. Five years after her first husband died, she married a New England wholesale grocer, Harold S. Macpherson. Aimee quickly set about involving her new husband in her fiery preaching. Like roving peddlers, they set up camp whenever they could around Ontario, Canada, preaching to farm families. But the constant nomadic life and Aimee's fanatic devotion to her religion, added to her frightening quest for recognition and control of her flock, drove Macpherson to return to the United States and to the grocery business. The fire of fancy cooled quickly. The two simply were mismatched. Both made repeated attempts at reconciliation, but in 1921 Macpherson sued for and was granted a divorce on grounds of desertion. Aimee Macpherson was alone again, this time with not only a daughter but also a son, Rolf, to take care of.

Aimee criss-crossed New England and Canada, living from hand to mouth, pitching her evangelist tent wherever people would listen. Lately Thomas (pseudonym for Richard Steele), another of her biographers, wrote:

> Often hungry; sleeping in tents, in automobiles, in bars, in wayside shelters; struggling to save her canvas from hurricanes and slashing rain; swinging a maul like a circus roustabout, jeered by unbelievers and despised by decorous churchmen; anathematized by co-religionists for preaching in contravention of Paul's injunction that women should keep silent in the churches, she persisted, and in a few years advanced by dint of grit, incredible labor and incomparable platform gifts to the front rank of evangelists.

Aimee hit strongly on the theme of love and wholesome, comfortable, clean living, but she did it in unusual ways. Vivien Keatley, in *Coronet,* August 1957, wrote: "She knew how to draw a crowd. Once when nobody attended her first meeting in a small town, she stood on a chair on a downtown streetcorner, head upraised, and prayed silently—a crowd of curious onlookers gathered. Then she jumped down shouted, 'Quick, follow me!' and led the bewildered crowd to her tent." Sarah Bernhardt would have been proud. An Oscar was definitely in order.

If the first two significant acts in Aimee's play were a struggle, act 3 would prove to be a piece of cake. By 1918 she had crossed the country and landed in Los Angeles. Perhaps because Hollywood was beginning to make a name for itself, the draw of southern California proved to be irresistible. There never could have been a better match between stage and heroine.

The outlandish sense of style that has always characterized Los Angeles helped bring overflow crowds to

Aimee's pulpit. To be sure, there were reasons other than the "freaky" nature of the locale. Los Angeles was, and would continue to be for nearly another twenty years, riddled with political corruption in the city offices and the police department. Los Angeles could easily have been called "Little Chicago." Prostitution and dope—primarily opium and cocaine—were big business. When Prohibition became a reality, bootlegging was a popular pastime for local hoods when prostitution and pimping got boring. Ordinary citizens were looking for a bit of relief and Sister Aimee obliged. Her mother soon arrived to manage the business affairs and Aimee's rise became meteoric. By 1923 she had built Angelus Temple in Echo Park, an arena-like hall seating fifty-three hundred. It had the majesty and mysticism of a Roman temple. With the grandeur that would mark her later life she decorated the hall with furnishings estimated at one million dollars, all raised by "Sister" from the pocketbooks of her generous, unthinking flock. She preached at least six times a week, with three or four Sunday services. With her style and her mother's tight-fisted money sense, Aimee Semple Macpherson became a religio-commercial entrepreneur who set the model for the likes of successful evangelists for years to come. And the money kept flowing in.

By this time Aimee had created *Bridal Call Four-square*, a publication through which, if she needed, she appealed for money. Sister freely admitted that her anxieties over money matters were never long-lived. "Several times when we were wondering how to meet the expenses, the money came by mail from some Child of God to whom He had telephoned," Aimee once said. People not only believed her, they demanded more.

Sister Aimee was the first woman in the United States to gain an FCC license and her own radio station, with the call letters KFSG for K-Four-Square Gospel.

Yet, according to her detractors, although Aimee

baptized, married, and supposedly faith-healed thousands she was not sponsored by an established church until 1923, when she was ordained by the First Baptist Church of San Jose.

Her weekly production illustrations or religious tableaux, coupled with her sermons, added to her renown. Some called it a sensuous debauch served up in the name of religion. Shelton Bissel, a Los Angeles minister, described a visit to Angelus Temple in *Outlook:* "In her pose, her gesture, her facial expression, her lifted eyebrows, her scintillating smile, her pathetic frown, Aimee is a perfect exponent of the art of how to say a platitude and delude her hearers into thinking that it is a brand-new truth just minted by her." Her religious services were considered vaudeville. Aimee had combined what most church persons had known for years: that pageantry, mysticism, even sex, were integral parts of delighting the crowds. It was just that "Sister Aimee" could do a better acting job than anyone else.

Sarah Comstock of *Harper's Monthly* magazine described Aimee Macpherson's style of religion:

There is a blare of trumpets, and the murmur of more than five thousand people hushes sharply. A baton flickers—"The Stars and Stripes" flings itself in a long red and white streamer of sound. Glances swing abruptly toward a staircase which comes down to the flower-decked platform. A figure descends—plump, tripping, balancing an armload of roses. "There she is. That's her." . . . Mrs. Macpherson (her own) methods. Her Sunday evening service is a complete vaudeville program, entirely new each week. [If not the Academy Award for Best Actress, perhaps Cinematography?]

Heaven and hell, sinner and saint, the fleshpots of Egypt, angels of Paradise and temptations of a bejazzed world are made visual by actors, costumes and theatrical tricks of any and all sorts that may occur to her ingenious mind.

Aimee did what others didn't. She preached about goodness and happy things. If the "good" things were fantasy, then let fantasy be your reality—that seemed to be her message. Her fantasies, her sermons, did become many people's reality, with Aimee as the prime protagonist.

In more concrete terms she outlined in *Sunset* magazine the tenets of the Four-Square Gospel:

> The Four-Square Gospel is a practical, wholesome, work-a-day religion that gets right down to the home. Men today want something that is going to save them from sin; something that is going to heal their sick baby in the night; something that will solve their problems and make the home a happier place in which to live. . . . When we planned the edifice that is now Angelus Temple, we decided to break with the traditions of ancient church architecture, to banish mystic darkness, discomfort and dank corners, to make the temple as bright, as modern, as cheerful, as homey as planning and skill could make it, and to emphasize it is not the torment of hell but the deep abiding joy of salvation, the glory that comes with complete surrender to the love of the Lord.

Aimee promised the moon, but she delivered. With Mary Poppins–like dexterity, she sugar-coated the pill of religion to appeal to the people of both the 1920s and the '30s. She devised a religious sell technique so effective that it would last no matter the economic or political climate.

Perhaps it was this success that made Aimee Semple Macpherson even more daring, almost arrogant in her approach. "If an angel from heaven should come down and tell my people that Sister is not a child of God," she remarked to *The Nation*, "they wouldn't believe it." Amazingly, fifty years after her disappearance, her mission is still being pursued.

She was right. The Reverend Charles Duarte, an

administrator of the Church of the Four-Square Gospel, curator of Aimee Semple Macpherson heritage, settles back in a sparsely furnished office in the United California Bank building in Echo Park, just behind the temple. The Church of the Four-Square Gospel, Inc., shares the floor's suites with the Bank of Tokyo. On the desk, for ready reference along with a few other books, is the Holy Bible. A stack of literature telling the curious "It's Time for 'The Truth' to Be Repeated" is readily available in another room. Duarte seeks earnestly to "set the record straight." "People accuse her of being gaudy," he says. "But Sister would take a simple story and bring it to life. She was trying to get that truth down to the humblest heart. But Sister was never idolized. She made it clear that she was just an instrument of God. . . . People never talk about that she borrowed a quarter of a million dollars on the temple just to feed hungry people during the Depression."

Her people provided her during the 1920s and '30s with enough money to buy property and acquire assets worth millions of dollars. During the early years the church was owned outright by Aimee and her mother in a fifty-fifty partnership. They never had to, nor did they ever, account for any of the money they acquired from church members. Estimates of their wealth could be based only on her overflow crowds, therefore not taking into account the numerous anonymous benefactors that she had. In the heyday of Angelus Temple, at the time when Aimee disappeared, the operation rivaled that of any major movie studio or government agency. A carpenter's shop was established to build sets used in Aimee's services. The lavish productions that Aimee used to reach "the humblest heart" have been discontinued—except for occasional Christmas productions—because of their fantastic cost. The temple housed a commissary with food and clothing for the destitute. Today, in 1977, one hundred families per month still receive help from Aimee's church. The Life Lighthouse Bible College continues to train missionaries, and KFSG, which once broadcast her sermons each evening, still is on the air. When Aimee was in charge, the temple even offered a twenty-four hour call-in service that would give the time. Nothing, it seemed, in public service was overlooked.

By 1926 Sister Aimee, who had forty thousand devout followers, stood at the apogee of her fame. Then she disappeared.

On May 25, 1926, six days after her daughter's disappearance, Minnie Kennedy received a letter signed "Revengers" demanding a ransom of half a million dollars in return for Aimee. On the following day, Kenneth G. Ormiston flashed into the headlines for the first time. Ormiston was the chief radio engineer at Angelus Temple. Handsome and engaging, he walked with a slight limp and had been the subject of gossip. Rumor had it that he had accompanied Sister Aimee on a recent trip to the Holy Land. Now he was missing from Los Angeles, and his wife had turned in a missing-person report, citing a "prominent" woman as the reason for his disappearance. Mrs. Ormiston even warned Mother Kennedy that she would name her daughter in a divorce suit. The search was on.

By May 29, Los Angeles district attorney Asa Keyes told the *Los Angeles Times* that he wanted to speak with Ormiston, that a woman had claimed she had seen a man with a limp talking to Aimee at the beach. News hit the papers that Ormiston's car had been spotted. According to the report, a woman wearing goggles was also seen. Further checking indicated that the same man and woman had checked into hotels in San Francisco, San Luis Obispo, and Sacramento, registering as Mr. and Mrs. Frank Gibson.

Mother Kennedy offered a twenty-five-thousand-dollar reward for the safe return of her daughter. The ante and the stakes were getting lower.

On June 1, R. A. McKinley, a cousin of the twenty-fifth President of the United States whose Long Beach law clientele ran primarily to bootleggers and petty offenders, told police that he was in contact with Mrs. Macpherson's kidnappers. He greeted the Long Beach detective investigating the case with, "You know I get more information from the underworld than any other man in Long Beach." He claimed that two men—a Mr. Miller and a Mr. Wilson—were demanding a twenty-five-thousand-dollar ransom for the safe return of the evangelist. The police cross-checked; McKinley's story held.

Speculation and rumors plagued both the newspapers and the police. Then on June 19 an "Avenger" letter, similar in tone and name to the "Revenger" message, arrived. It was ominous for a number of reasons. First, Mother Kennedy had given McKinley four test questions to be forwarded to the supposed kidnappers. McKinley said that he had complied and that the questions had been mysteriously picked up. The "Avenger" letter, in addition to demanding a half million dollars, enclosed a lock of Aimee's auburn hair and the answers to two of the four questions. The supposed kidnappers also made reference to a small scar on Aimee's right-hand middle finger, the result of gashing her finger on a corn hook as a child. The letter also warned Minnie Kennedy that she had precisely one week to gather the money, and should she need further proof that they had her daughter, they would forward the scarred middle finger. The kidnappers' letter said, according to Lately Thomas, that Aimee was "suffering with hysteria and heat" but had "been taken good care of by a woman who had been with her constantly." If the ransom was not forthcoming, the kidnappers said that their only alternative would be to "sell her to old Felipe of Mexico City. We are sick and tired of her infernal preaching. She spouts scripture to everything."

If Aimee was indeed in the hands of kidnappers, her evangelistic spirit apparently did not waver. To the end she was soliciting converts.

With all the various possibilities—murder, kidnapping, drowning, or even voluntary disappearance—the county coroner refused to sign Aimee's death certificate.

Mother Kennedy, in an attempt to quiet some of the rumors and innuendos, held a memorial service on June 20 for her daughter. Seventeen thousand crowded under the hand-painted, pastel-blue, sky-like dome of the temple. Minnie Kennedy tried to convince the weeping and wailing crowd that the reason that Aimee's body had not been recovered was because Jesus wanted to keep it for himself. Millions more clung to her words over the radio.

Frederick Conrad Shansel, a slaughterhouse custodian; Ramon Gonzales, proprietor of the O.K. Bar; Ernesto Boubion, politician; and Johnny Anderson, taxi driver—all of Agua Prieta, Sonora, Mexico— had no idea that on June 23 their lives would be fodder for the front page of virtually every American newspaper. These men had no idea that when they helped a limping, exhausted woman out of the desert, that woman would end up being one Aimee Semple Macpherson. Her walk out of the desert seemed no more miraculous to them than it would have seemed to her followers if she had strolled out of the waves. After all, they reasoned, lots of American women came over the border during Prohibition, got drunk, and wandered off into the desert.

After being sufficiently revived with water and rubbing alcohol, Anderson took Aimee across the border to Douglas, Arizona, where she called her mother. She babbled about a fantastic story of having been kidnapped and then imprisoned in a desert shack. Aimee claimed she had broken her bonds and struggled across miles of arid, sandy wastes to Agua Prieta.

The press and the police descended upon her like a bunch of starving vultures on a single, lonely corpse in the desert. Her story was simple. While she was swimming, a couple approached her and requested her to attend their sick child, who was "in a car." They led her to a sedan where a man was waiting in the back seat, holding what Aimee assumed was the sick baby. Instead, she was shoved in and smothered with blankets. When she awoke, she was in the desert cabin. There were three captors: Jack, Steve, and Mexicali Rose. Steve, apparently the most sadistic, burned her with cigar butts, and Jack cut a lock of her hair. Otherwise she was left unmolested. One night, left alone with Mexicali Rose, Aimee managed to crawl toward a tin can lying on the wooden floor and used its ragged edge to cut the thongs strapping her hands and feet. She struggled out into the desert and found her way to Agua Prieta. All the people who helped her confirmed the following facts:

There were welts on her wrists, apparently caused by rope, and some blisters on her feet, and she appeared exhausted. She did not, however, seem to be suffering from heat, nor was she very dirty—indeed, her shoes were barely scuffed. She had no sunburn, her lips were not cracked or parched, and her tongue wasn't swollen. A nurse at Calumet Hospital in Douglas, Arizona, noted that her temperature was 98, pulse 72, respiration 20.

Douglas, Arizona, a copper-smelting town with a population of thirteen thousand, never had it so good. The hospital was flooded with flowers and the town reveled in the trade brought by the out-of-towners.

Reports of her condition in the hospital varied. Some said she looked bedraggled and shaken; others said that she was in incredibly good shape for someone who had just trekked across cactus-studded terrain. In order to prove her story, Aimee volunteered to accompany a posse in search of the shack. It was never found, and the natives of Agua Prieta told investigators that a shack with a wooden floor would never have been built in such terrain. However they did find a shoe print, reportedly matching Aimee's, next to fresh tire tracks. Could Aimee have been driven to some convenient place in the desert and then have made her way to the small border town of Agua Prieta?

While police and the press were plainly leery of her story, Aimee accurately predicted that her followers' faith would not be shaken. Testimonials by the thousands deluged the papers. Lately Thomas recalled a number of them in his book. For example:

Dear Sir:
I will not call you brother any more than a skunk is a brother. You are a disgrace to the animal family. You raise Old Ned because a woman becomes so tired with the religious cranks and crippled nuts that surround her that she once and a while wants to get away from them to where she can be natural. Shame on you. Mrs. Macpherson is a human being, isn't she? Mrs. Macpherson has healed me of seventeen diseases already and I am going back to the Temple to be healed again next month.

The testimonies of faith in Aimee poured on.

Meanwhile, the Kenneth Ormiston question came back into focus. Everyone wanted to know where Kenneth Ormiston was during *his* disappearance, if he wasn't with Aimee. Why did he remain so elusive? Ormiston ultimately admitted to spending ten days in Carmel with a "Miss X" whom he declined to further identify. But "Miss X" came forward in the person of one Mrs. Lorraine Wiseman-Seilaff, who remained somewhat a mystery. First she claimed that her twin sister was the woman who had been in Carmel with Ormiston. Then she denied it. Then she "admitted" that she had been bribed by Mother Kennedy to impersonate Aimee. The story became more and more confused.

There were so many loose ends, so many incongruities, that the state of California finally alleged that Aimee had not been kidnapped but had spent ten days at Carmel with Kenneth G. Ormiston. The state claimed that she was goggled and veiled to conceal her identity but that she had incautiously signed charge-account receipts for groceries with her own hand. These receipts, interestingly enough, disappeared while locked in a grand-jury courtroom.

The story should have been carried on the sports

pages instead of the front pages. Each day it was a battle between the forces of evil against God, light, and Aimee Semple Macpherson. Every day one or the other claimed a coup, another point to be added to the score. Aimee claimed, "That's my story and I'll stick with it. If you don't believe it, disprove it." The state and the district attorney tried.

After Mrs. Wiseman-Seilaff confessed that she had been bribed, she then further implicated Mother Kennedy and Aimee by claiming that with the good Sister's money she had in turn bribed a Miss Rachel Wells of Philadelphia to come forward as "Miss X" in order to satisfy the public demand for a confession by the mysterious, "indiscreet Lady of Carmel." Lions 1, Christians nothing—but Aimee was far from done.

Sister Aimee, who preached of love and forgiveness, informed the public that Mrs. Wiseman-Seilaff had been committed to a Salt Lake City insane asylum for several weeks. The reason: incurable lying. Lions 1, Christians 1, and going into the finishing rounds.

Ormiston refused to cooperate. He tantalized the district attorney with possible leads but refused to show himself in Los Angeles. The authorities fumed. Warrants were put out for Aimee's arrest. She preached while out on bail. Deals were made and remade for Ormiston to appear. He demanded immunity and was refused. The case against Aimee was outlined in the press: (1) the kidnapping story was a fabrication; (2) to support the kidnapping story, Mrs. Macpherson conspired to commit acts injurious to public morals and to prevent and obstruct justice; (3) Mrs. Macpherson hid at Carmel with Kenneth Ormiston with the knowledge and consent of her mother; (4) Mrs. Macpherson tried to have another person indicted for the fictitious kidnapping; (5) Mrs. Macpherson hired Mrs. Wiseman-Seilaff to produce a false Miss X; (6) Mrs. Macpherson caused false affidavits to be prepared and signed; (7) Mrs. Macpherson hired McKinley to manufacture false evidence.

The Hall of Justice and the D.A.'s office were turned

into something resembling a three-ring circus. Then, as if to clinch the case, the D.A.'s office claimed they had secured a trunk that had been sent to Ormiston at a New York address, which contained Aimee's clothing. However, the most identifying piece—a blouse with a Carmel, California, dry-cleaner's tag—mysteriously disappeared when the trunk was shipped from New York to Los Angeles.

After all the furor, the accusations on both sides, the case was dismissed. Ultimately a judge was impeached for misconduct on the case, and at least a half dozen public officials came out of the mess ruined professionally. Sister Aimee, although not unscathed, was not so seriously wounded.

But questions remained. If Aimee had engineered her own disappearance, why had she done it in such a fantastic manner? She could just as easily have slipped off unnoticed to spend a few quiet days at the seaside with a friend or lover. Just as Ormiston had allegedly slipped off with Aimee to the Holy Land, they could have done it again. Maybe, as some speculated, it was Aimee's flair for the dramatic. Maybe she thought that life was "too safe" and she wanted to liven up the process. Perhaps she sought the gratification of seeing thousands, perhaps millions, mourn her possible loss. Or perhaps she really had been kidnapped.

Even now, administrators of the Church of the Four-Square Gospel, which her son, Rolf, now heads, staunchly support the kidnapping theory. "Individuals came to Angelus Temple," said Duarte. "Prostitutes, alcoholics, drug addicts. While counseling them, Aimee was told all about who was behind many of these illegal operations. She talked about these things on the radio and threatened to disclose names. She was a threat to these people. They wanted to shut her up. That's why they kidnapped her. They wanted to scare her into being quiet."

While Aimee did reach millions through her radio show, it was doubtful, even if she had revealed the names, that much would have been done. And if she had proved to be such a great threat, those who felt threatened by her would have never left her disposal to the work of three amateur individuals, nor would they even have allowed her to live. The story seemed to have as many holes in it as did all the other stories.

In February 1927, Aimee seemed to draw more logic in a *Sunset* interview when she commented:

> The absurd, insulting insinuations that I, pastor of this mighty church, that I, editor of a Christian magazine—mother of a handsome son and charming daughter—that I, of a Christian family—that I should with a sweep of my hand topple the whole thing over in an insane moment and run away with a former employee to a little seaside village and hide behind goggles and shaded window . . . is too absurd and too patently a plant and ill-concealed forgery of ambitious publicity men to be dignified by a serious answer.

In many ways, after the kidnapping and until the time of her death she behaved much like a chastened child, one who, having played with fire and having had her clothing catch on fire, was saved from serious hurt by her own wits and by the hands of fate. She dutifully sent two million Bibles to servicemen overseas during the war, collected twenty-eight hundred pints of blood for the Red Cross, and sold hundreds of war bonds.

But she wasn't done yet. Aimee, against the precepts of her own church, would marry again, unhappily—this time to David Hutton. Even now, church officials publicly say that that was a mistake.

On September 27, 1944, Aimee died of a barbiturate overdose. Suicide or accident? Church officials claimed that over the previous two years she had been suffering from an incurable intestinal infection that allowed the sleeping pills to be absorbed directly into her bloodstream. The story seems as fantastic as if it had been concocted by Aimee herself.

Her love for fantasy, for flight from reality, was an

integral part of her personality. Aimee needed it in order to survive. Perhaps another unhappy marriage and the mundane reality of collecting of blood and Bibles proved to be too much for the auburn-haired firebrand of the Four-Square Gospel.

11

▼▼▼▼▼▼▼▼▼

Dalton Trumbo

The shiny black limousines pulled up as softly and sleekly as groomed cats. Doormen stepped smartly to open the doors, revealing the furs, gold, and glitter bedecking the bodies of Hollywood's "beautiful." The crowds straining at the barricades oohed and ahhed. Two searchlights crossed like luminous fingers in the sky. Academy Awards night for 1956 promised to be not much different from any other. But it was.

The fanfare of the moment belied a more serious blight not only on Hollywood but on America. The nation had just seen the last of the Army-McCarthy hearings that had brought about the downfall of the vitriolic Joe McCarthy. While McCarthy's methods had cost him his political career, the seeds of unease he had sown had rooted and were in full bloom. Hollywood had long been a target for "Red Conspirator" hunting. The McCarthy years solidified the posture originally set in moviedom by the House Committee on Un-American Activities. Over 250 artists—writers, directors, actors, technicians had been blacklisted, refused work because of their political associations. Some had served jail time for refusing to name so-called fellow travelers. And in 1956 the blacklist was still in operation, preventing loosely identified Communist sympathizers from working in the film industry.

The Academy Awards show of 1956 seemingly paid no attention to the blacklist. It tripped along with the

216

usual number of faux pas, missed lines, mechanical failures, and endless thankings of "the little people who made it all possible." One of the screenplays up for a nomination was *The Brave One*. The story revolved around Mexican bullfights and *indulto*, the "show of kindness" that is allowed a bull that fights particularly valiantly. In this case, the bull had been raised as the pet of a young Mexican boy, and, after fighting courageously against the matador, was granted his life by the overwhelming number of handkerchiefs waved at the end of the contest. I had seen a screening of this low-budget film and had been genuinely impressed, as apparently others in the academy had, that the screenplay was superb—obviously the work of a gifted writer. The writer's name: Robert Rich. That intrigued me. I had never heard of Robert Rich.

Deborah Kerr finally slipped graciously up to the mike to read the list of nominees. Then, with the proper dramatic flair, she announced: "The winner for Best Original Motion Picture Screenplay is . . . Robert Rich, for *The Brave One*." The anonymous voice intoned over the loudspeakers: "Due to Mr. Rich's unavoidable absence, Mr. Jesse Lasky, Jr. [the vice-president of the Screenwriters' Guild] will accept the award for Mr. Rich."

Jesse Lasky, Jr., climbed quickly onto the stage, and just as glibly announced that his good friend Robert Rich had been called away to the hospital because his wife was having a baby. How all-American.

The morning after the awards, Lasky was informed that there was no Robert Rich in the Writers' Guild. Lasky, much to his chagrin, informed the academy that no one in the Writers' Guild had the vaguest notion who or where Robert Rich was. Later Lasky would lamely explain in his book, *Whatever Happened to Hollywood*, "The name sounded familiar [Robert Rich], but I couldn't place him; but in a guild of almost two thousand, one couldn't expect to know everybody."

After the papers broke the story, hundreds of men claiming to be Robert Rich called Lasky, demanding the award. The Kings Brothers, who had produced the film, pleaded ignorance; they claimed that no one from their organization had actually ever met Mr. Rich and that they had dealt through an agent, which was an exceedingly common practice that had become all the more popular during the blacklist years. The agent in turn claimed that "Robert Rich" might be a nom de plume. Questions of who had signed the contract and why the agent hadn't met or at least talked with his client remained unanswered. The unsaid conclusion was that Robert Rich was either a front, was a person who sold works for blacklisted artists, or was the artist himself, gone underground. In any case, the nagging question was: Who is Robert Rich?

Robert Rich was alive and well, I would later find out. Not really "Robert Rich," of course—that was a nom de plume. The need, however, for a Robert Rich character started years before the 1956 Academy Awards ceremony—in fact, before World War II.

On June 7, 1938, Representative Martin Dies of Texas introduced a resolution establishing by a vote of 181 to 41 the House Committee on Un-American Activities. Later, Albert Maltz, one of the victims of the committee, commented: "I doubt that at the time those people who voted for it [the committee] knew to what extent it would grow or go."

According to the resolution, the committee's purpose was "to investigate any activities deemed to be un-American." This was the committee that, after investigation, deemed the Ku Klux Klan an "acceptable American institution." However, Maltz commented further, saying that the purpose of the committee was "to investigate primarily the area that, as I understand the Constitution, forbids Congress or anyone else for that matter from investigating, on the basis of the First Amendment. This committee was unconstitutional to begin with."

The committee didn't gain steam until the late 1940s. It used as fuel Winston Churchill's Fulton, Missouri, speech, in which he called for a world crusade to crush Soviet Communism. The speech was the first clear signal of what soon would become the Cold War. A year later, in 1947, Harry S. Truman, President of the United States, issued the Truman Doctrine, which called for America to become the world's keeper against Communism. Essentially, Truman pledged American support to any revolution against Communism anywhere in the world, if it threatened U. S. security. Coupled with Truman's institution of a governmental "loyalty oath," the House Committee felt encouraged to launch a crusade against suspect American Communists. In short order it became a truth of American politics that the surest way to doom was to be labeled "soft on Communism." Congressman vied for platforms from which to condemn "pinkos." None was more dedicated than the chairman of the House Committee, J. Parnell Thomas. "We are going to continue to expose Communists," he declared, "and if you will just sit around here every day this week you will see more exposure and more spotlighting of Communists than you have seen before."

On May 15, 1947, the House Committee on Un-American Activities engaged a hotel suite in Los Angeles to conduct a "secret investigation of Communism in motion pictures." The committee promised that it would purge the industry of subversives in open hearings to be held later in Washington, D.C.

On September 29, 1947, nineteen people of the "Hollywood community" were subpoenaed to appear before the committee. (It is interesting to note that the subpoena power of any congressional committee is supposed to be directed at obtaining information so that specific legislation can be drafted. In its nine years of existence the committee had proposed only one bill that was passed, and it was declared unconstitutional by the Supreme Court.)

The nineteen who were subpoenaed were, as can be expected, a diverse group both in personality and in political views. They were joined by the common thread that all, at one time or another, had been involved with some sort of social movement. A split in the group's philosophy soon became evident. One group, later called the "Bogart group," partially comprised of Bogart and his wife Lauren Bacall Bogart, William Wyler, and John Huston, did not believe that any of the groups should make their stand on First Amendment grounds. Then, people tagged as the "Hollywood Ten" believed the opposite. John Howard Lawson, Dalton Trumbo, Albert Maltz, Edward Dmytryk, Samuel Ornits, Herbert Biberman, Ring Lardner, Jr., Adrian Scott, Lester Cole, and Alvah Bessie had made up their minds to take a stand. "I don't think we would have done it," Maltz said later, "if we would have known that we would have lost or if the prison sentences would have been, say, ten years instead of one." The Hollywood Ten also did not anticipate the blacklist.

When the formal hearings of the committee began on October 20, 1947, the Hollywood studio chiefs, Louis B. Mayer, Jack Warner, and Eric Johnston, president of the Motion Pictures Producers Association, all charged that the committee's agents had urged a blacklist upon the film industry. They hotly denounced the committee as "trying to dictate and control through the device of these hearings what goes on the screens of America." Johnston solemnly declared: "As long as I live I will never be a party to anything as un-American as a blacklist and any statement purporting to quote me as agreeing to a blacklist is a libel on me as a good American. We're not going totalitarian just to please the committee."

Hollywood itself, however, would soon become divided. The Motion Picture Committee for the Preservation of American Ideals, headed by John Wayne, Ward Bond, of *Wagon Train* fame, and Roy Brewer, head of the Stage Hands Association, actively supported the search for Communists. Others, like Bogart, flew to Washington and publicly condemned the proceedings. Bogart, Paul Henried, John Huston, June Havoc, and Danny Kaye, plus others representing the Committee for the First Amendment, presented to Congress a petition for a redress of grievances.

But the House Committee was drawing in more than its share of friendly witnesses. Sam Wood, a director, accused Katherine Hepburn of giving "substantial aid" to the Communist Party. "For example," he said, "at a rally which she attended, they raised eighty-seven-thousand-dollars. It did not go to the Boy Scouts."

Gary Cooper testified that he had rejected many scripts because he felt they were "Communist-tinged." Urged to recall their titles, he replied: "I don't think I could, because most of the scripts I read at night." Lela Rogers, Ginger Rogers' mother, complained to the committee that her daughter had been asked to say in a film: "Share and share alike, that's democracy, which," added Mrs. Rogers, "I think is definitely Communist propaganda." Cedric Belfrage, in *The American Inquisition 1945–1960,* wrote: ". . . evidence of a Russian plot in the movie colony was reinforced by Ronald Reagan . . . Mickey Mouse's progenitor, Walt Disney, Adolphe Menjou (who defined a Communist as one who enjoyed listening to [Paul] Robeson [American screen actor, perhaps most notable for his performance in *Showboat.* He later lived in Russia.]). . ."

Of the Hollywood Ten, perhaps one of the best-known and most highly paid was Dalton Trumbo. Author of a number of books, including *Johnny Got His Gun,* a strong antiwar novel that won him the American Booksellers Award in 1939, he was a tireless writer. *Additional Dialogue,* which covered only twenty years of his life, runs nearly six hundred pages. A flamboyant man with a sense of wit, he sometimes surrounded himself with the necessary writing paraphernalia and retreated to the bathtub. Once, he even wrote a thirty-seven-hundred-word letter, to his college-student son, on the joys of masturbation.

Yet, nothing in Trumbo's life had prepared him for the grueling ordeal that he was undertaking. Trumbo grew up in the small Colorado town of Montrose. His father was variously a shoe salesman and beekeeper, perhaps most notably a failure. But both he and Trumbo's mother, a Christian Scientist who tirelessly waged a battle with the school board to prevent her son from various vaccinations, were free thinkers. The current ran strong in Trumbo's blood. Once, he even remarked that he wanted to be a member of the Ku Klux Klan, because, as he explained, some very strange people were interested in joining. (He later abandoned the idea.)

He did a number of odd jobs to help his family, including hosing down infected corpses, shoveling sugar beets, and laying rails with a section gang. After moving to Los Angeles, his longest work stint was a job in a bakery for eight years, during which he wrote six unpublished novels. He sold his first piece to *Vanity Fair*, urging universities to offer courses in bootlegging (in which he was also involved), and shortly thereafter met Clare Boothe (Luce), their traveling editor. Because he lived in Los Angeles she assumed he was involved with movies. With that kind of inspiration, Trumbo got a job on the *Hollywood Spectator*. By 1934 he was a reader at Warner Brothers and one year later was a writer there.

As a rising young man about Hollywood, Trumbo became a joiner. He enrolled in the American Youth for Democracy and in the Joint Angeles chapter of the Civil Rights Congress. Fifteen years later, both organizations would be condemned as Communist fronts. Trumbo never seemed to be exceedingly impressed with the Communist Party, saying that he joined not out of any real philosophical commitments but because some of his dearest friends were involved. Ring Lardner, Jr., a compatriot of Trumbo's, later wrote in a *Saturday Evening Post* article that he found "thoughtful, witty, and generally stimulating men and women" in the Communist Party, along with "bores and unstable characters." For many in Hollywood, the local Communist Party coffee klatch was more a social than a political gathering.

Trumbo left the party in 1948, because, as he explained, he was living eighty-five miles out of town and he just drifted away.

But that wasn't good enough for the House Committee. And Trumbo, true to his character, proved to be a difficult witness. He used the First Amendment as his defense and expressed his outrage at the affront that the committee was imposing on the character of the American people. For his efforts he was held in contempt of Congress, sentenced to one year in jail, and charged a thousand-dollar fine.

Within one month of the beginning of the hearing, Eric Johnston, who had declared his solidarity with the Hollywood Ten and who had decried the efforts of of the committee, said: "We will forthwith discharge without compensation and we will not reemploy any of the Ten until such time as he [Trumbo] is acquitted, or has purged himself of contempt and declared under oath that he is not a Communist."

At least five of the Hollywood Ten were writers under contract. They sued their studios for breach of contract and in most cases either received small settlements or lost. The reason? Their contracts contained a "morals clause" that dated to the Fatty Arbuckle scandal in the 1920s. A young girl had died, and Arbuckle was charged with murder. As a result, his pictures were condemned. From that time until 1977, most Hollywood contracts had a morals clause that made the terms invalid if the individual brought shame or disgrace upon the studio. The clause held in the case of suspended "Communists."

The Hollywood Ten, including Trumbo, appealed to the Supreme Court. They lost. The court refused to review their appeal and an appellate-court judgment against them stood. Albert Maltz now says that if two of the youngest, most-liberal Supreme Court justices had not died the summer before their appeal (1950), the story would have been different. Maltz said simply: "There would have been no McCarthy era."

While Trumbo had been awaiting the decision of the court he wrote a pamphlet, *Time of the Toad*. In it he said that America was "surrendering its mind," having "become simply against something. Whatever the enemy does," he observed, "we mustn't do. Each morning we observe the drift of the wind out of the Don Basin. At lunchtime we test the temperature of the Siberian wilderness. At night we are canny with the moon, for it shines also upon the domes of Moscow."

Trumbo didn't seem to mind prison as much as one might expect. Later he wrote, "All a writer needed was a paper, a pencil, and a nice clean cell." He never became bitter. Perhaps to underscore his point, Ring Lardner, Jr., would recall how he and Lester Cole, another of the Hollywood Ten, one time spied a large posterior protruding from a chickencoop in the Danbury, Connecticut, penitentiary where they served their year's time. When finally the head emerged, it was that of J. Parnell Thomas, former chairman of the first House Committee on Un-American Activities. He had been convicted of embezzlement. There seemed to be some sort of strange justice.

While Parnell had a specific jail term, those "indicted" by the House Committee would have much longer, indeterminate sentences. When they were released from prison they found the blacklist still in full swing. No one would hire them.

Trumbo, Maltz, and a number of others fled to Mexico. They subsisted on their previous savings, book sales abroad, and sales of scripts bearing the names of "safe" writers, which were sold secretly through Hollywood agents. Bruce Cook, a recent biographer of Trumbo, said that Trumbo during the time of the blacklist did the first script of *The Young Philadelphians,* and when new producers of the project wanted a script change they went to Trumbo, not knowing he had authored the first. He also scripted *Cowboys* and *Roman Holiday,* and once remarked that during the blacklist years, both in Mexico and in Hollywood he wrote nearly thirty movie scripts under assorted pseudonyms.

Actors for the most part suffered more severely than

did writers. At least writers could have other people front for them. An actor's face was what he sold. A few found parts in the New York theater, which was never as severely affected by the blacklisting as was the movie industry. Like Will Geer, who devoted himself to raising flowers, some found strange professions far removed from acting, and others dropped out, never to return even after the blacklist was lifted.

Hollywood went through a variety of contortions in order to satisfy the committee. Bruce Cook, in his book *Dalton Trumbo,* wrote:

> Michael Wilson . . . was awarded an Oscar the year that he was blacklisted (1951) for *A Place in the Sun,* written, produced and released before he was named in testimony before the Committee. As a direct result of that, the Producers Association ruled that no blacklisted writer was to receive screen credit—even for work done earlier. And so when Wilson's pre-blacklist script for *The Friendly Persuasion* was produced the following year, his name was simply excised from the credits; no writer's name at all appeared on the screen. Then, when the film won the Writers Guild Award and it looked as though *The Friendly Persuasion* was a shoo-in for an Academy Award for Best Screenplay, credited or uncredited, the Motion Picture Academy ruled that under no circumstances could a blacklisted writer be awarded an Oscar. The Academy had, however, overlooked the possibility of a writer winning under a pseudonym. . . .

By 1956 many of the self-exiled writers, directors, technicians, and actors were trickling back to Hollywood. Mexico was too far away for the exiles to keep tabs on the pulse of their industry. Besides, as Albert Maltz said: "To an artist his home country's audience is the most important."

When Robert Rich did not appear at the awards ceremony that night in 1956, and when the most vigorous efforts of the press to seek him out failed, the general assumption was that one of the blacklisted screenwriters had won the award. By remaining anonymous, the writer was taking a kind of bitter poke at the House Committee, the Producers Association, and the academy itself. But which screenwriter? Trumbo was contacted by the press and admitted to having penned several screenplays that had been nominated in recent years; but he wouldn't confirm or deny that Robert Rich was one of his nom de plumes. Instead, he waved them off to other members of the Hollywood Ten. Trumbo remained at the top of the list of possible writers not only because he was so prolific but because his works received so many awards. Both prior to and after the blacklist he received awards for *Kitty Foyle,* which was nominated for Best Screenplay; *A Guy Named Joe,* which received the Box Office Magazine Award; and *Thirty Seconds Over Tokyo,* which received not only the Box Office but the Parents Magazine Award and was one of the Ten Best in a Gallup Poll.

On Friday, January 16, 1959, CBS's Bill Stout of station KNXT in Los Angeles settled down for another routine interview in the station's Hollywood studio. His guest: Dalton Trumbo. While Stout's questions typically darted out like a snake's tongue at prey, Trumbo calmly explained his clandestine activities for the past several years, including the admission that he was Robert Rich. However, Trumbo did not make his claim until after the Academy of Motion Picture Arts and Sciences lifted their ban on giving recognition to persons accused or suspected of subversive activities by reason of invoking the Fifth or First amendments.

Dalton Trumbo's announcement marked the beginning of the end of the blacklist era. In 1970, Otto Preminger openly hired him to write the screenplay of *Exodus* and Dalton Trumbo saw his real name on the big screen again.

The blacklist had, however, inflicted wounds that sometimes never healed. Some members of the Hollywood Ten and other blacklisted artists never made it back. Albert Maltz didn't have a book published in the

United States for sixteen years. He is now back to writing, and lecturing. Ring Lardner, Jr., triumphed in his screenplay of *M*A*S*H*, as did Adrian Scott in *Midnight Cowboy*. Dalton Trumbo, of course, came back to receive the Writers' Guild's Laurel Award in 1970. By that time he was rejecting offers of less than $250,000 per screenplay.

Why did the blacklist have to happen at all? Why is there a need for a chapter titled "In Search of Robert Rich"? Many point to the meekness of the press. If they had questioned the likes of Thomas and McCarthy from the beginning, just as they questioned those involved in Watergate, the country would not have been so blighted. Perhaps Trumbo said it best, however, upon his acceptance of the Laurel Award: "There had been no villains or heroes or saints or devils in the blacklist days, only victims."

12

The Great Gods

The history of Spanish conquests in South and Central America incorporates fascinating records of the amazement with which Western Europeans viewed the cultures of those foreign nations. The accomplishments of the Incas overwhelmed the scribes of Pizarro's small army. They reported the incredible engineering feats of a people who had no written language and whose numerical system did not include the zero. There were other wonders to behold, many of which were puzzling to the traditional Western concepts of the invaders. For example, a system of paved roads linked the citadels of the Incan empire, yet no trace of a wheeled vehicle was discovered. Why, then, were paved roads constructed? Complex neurosurgery was performed that was advanced beyond any medical practice known in fifteenth-century Europe.

However admiring of the Incas' accomplishments, the Spanish adventurers in the New World chose to dismiss local culture as primitive and even worse, pagan. The twin goals of the occupying armies thus became the conversion of the population from heathen beliefs to Christianity and the plundering of all the gold in the kingdom.

A strange, and to me unexplainable, quirk of history facilitated the quest of the conquerors. Somewhere in the annals of Incan history there arose the legend of Viracocha. Viracocha was thought to be the first great teacher, a man-god descended from the heavens and carrying with him wondrous gifts of knowledge. He was compassionate and was skilled in farming and in medicine. We know few details of Viracocha, since the friars of Pizarro's forces were intent on wiping out all beliefs not rooted in Western Christianity. So Viracocha's origin is lost. I do not know where the belief began in a fair-skinned, red-bearded god who brought with him the seeds of all progress. Perhaps Viracocha was the embodiment of a wandering Phoenician trader. I have even, in moments of great fancy, pursued the notion that he might have been a lost spaceman who found respite from planetary wandering in the highlands of the Andes. Whatever his origin, I am struck by his similarity to other figures in the great lost civilizations of the Western Hemisphere.

The great man-god, bringer of civilization, exists for the Aztecs in the person of Quetzalcoatl and to the Mayas as Kukulcán. Each of these legends—Aztec, Mayan, and Incan—speaks of a certain white, bearded man who appeared as a stranger from afar and who lingered among the people, imparting the blessings and knowledge of civilization for which each was revered as the "traditional master-builder of civilization." They share, as well, a common fate: without warning, Quetzalcoatl, Kukulcán, and Viracocha disappeared, promising to return at another time.

Perhaps it was merely a coincidence that three separate, distinct civilizations had virtually identical culture heroes. But I found myself more than just a little intrigued.

The man-gods had disappeared as mysteriously as they had come. Anthropologists and archaeologists are unable to say with certainty who these mysterious men were, where they came from, or where they went when they left. Yet, Incan, Aztec, and Mayan legends all contain mention of the fair-skinned, bearded men. The analogy is considered truly remarkable in light of the fact that there are no traces of direct communication among any of these civilizations. Moreover, on that continent, where beards and fair skin were unknown, could any natives have invented the legends?

It was a marvelous story, most certainly a myth, or so I thought, at least prior to my trip to a few of the Central American archives. I felt there was more to the myth than just the primal meanderings of story-tellers. It was the classic, archetypal, missing-person story—the strange disappearances of unidentified heroes who were venerated as gods in three separate, distinct cultures.

During one of the *In Search of. . .* expeditions to Central and South America I met and spoke with a host of anthropologists and archaeologists about the three legends I had found in the course of my research. Some archaeologists flatly declared that these three culture gods had never existed except in the minds of the myriad Indians who had worshipped them; others believed that there could have been several genuine heroic men who were given these names at different points in the Indians' history and that in time all of their deeds came to be attributed to a single figure. But I was not satisfied with such pat answers.

I may well be a romantic and a dreamer, but I know that legends have more than once been proved to have their basis in facts. Therefore, I find it hard to believe that in a region where fair skin and beards were totally alien, Indians would have or could have dreamed up such heroes. It seems to me more likely that the tendency would be to invent a hero in one's own image, one's own likeness. Yet, not one but three distinct cultures speak of a fair-skinned, dark-bearded man-god, dressed in flowing robes, who came from afar and bestowed a wealth of information from which each civilization flourished to great heights of culture, art, agriculture, and architecture. The teachings of these man-gods enabled primitive Indians in grimly inhospitable regions to shape magnificent civilizations of soaring pyramids and splendid palaces. Who were these strange, wondrous men?

One of the first pre-Hispanic Middle American races was the Mayas. Lurking in the vast, mysterious, hot forests of the old Mayan empire, I found the tradition of Kukulcán, the gentle king-god. Mayan legend tells of the hero Kukulcán, who had come to Chichén Itzá about 1100 A.D., an exile from the city of Tula in the north. The Mayas threw him in the sacred well as a sacrifice, but when he did not drown, the Mayas fished him out and gave him the rank of a god. He ruled over them, becoming the most powerful leader in Yucatán. His name meant "feathered serpent," and everywhere in Mayan territory statues of feathered serpents abound. Suddenly, at the height of his power, he disappeared mysteriously, with the promise to return.

Carved images of Kukulcán show him resembling a white man and portraits have him wearing a beard, while the Mayas themselves were olive-skinned and beardless.

Chichén Itzá, in northern Yucatán, was the center of the later Mayan culture. Jutting from corners and enscrolled on columns are carvings of feathered serpents. I was immediately struck by the lifelike quality and the sheer number of the representations. Kukulcán, whoever he was, was a very real and important presence in Mayan life.

The Mayas themselves left a record shrouded in mystery. They flourished for at least fifteen centuries, and between 250 and 900 A.D. they carved a gloriously advanced civilization. Then suddenly, inexplicably, it was over. Cities were abandoned, populations declined, and the jungle reclaimed its reign over the land. No one knows why the Mayan empire vanished. Many reasons have been gingerly proposed (cataclysmic forces of nature, epidemics, etc.), but none has been able to answer the riddle of what destroyed the Mayas.

I thought that the answer to Kukulcán/Quetzalcoatl/Viracocha's identity could become clearer if I made a brief survey of the people over whom they had ruled. Oddly enough, it seemed that both the accomplishments and the fates of each of these vanished civilizations were inextricably linked to the sudden appearance and disappearance of their respective "master-builders of civilization." Each civilization attributed its achievements and level of advancement to the teachings of its strange, fair-skinned god. When the invading bearded Spanish platoons arrived in the sixteenth century, many of the Indians in Yucatán as well as in Mexico and in Peru mistook them for the returning gods. The beliefs were so strong that the Indians made the Spanish conquest extraordinarily easy.

Why else would a people who had reached the pinnacle of cultural achievement have laid their lives so trustingly in the hands of unknown newcomers? And why shouldn't the Indians have believed and trusted the bearded Spaniards? Hadn't the Indians benefited from the complex culture that their fair-skinned, bearded gods had left behind? The Mayas' accomplishments are today likened in extent and wonder to those of the early civilizations of Asia and the Mediterranean.

A thousand years before Columbus, the Mayas reigned in columned palaces. They were practicing an astronomy so precise that their ancient calendar was as accurate as the one we use today. They plotted the courses of celestial bodies and their priests predicted both solar and lunar eclipses. They calculated the path of Venus—an elusive planet—with an error of only fourteen seconds per year. They originated a complex writing system and pioneered the mathematical concept of zero.

The Mayas claimed that they learned these things from Kukulcán. Their highly advanced nation was a product of his teachings. They in fact were his descendamts.

The sixteenth-century chronicler Torquemada wrote: "The people of Yucatán reverenced this Quetzalcoatl, calling him Kukulán and saying that he came to them from the west, that is from New Spain [Mexico], for Yucatán is eastward therefrom. From him it is said that the kings of Yucatán are descended who call themselves Cocomes, that is to say 'judges or hearers.'"

A judge or hearer was set apart from the rest of the race. He would have come from a region unknown. Some historians believe he could have been a traveling colonist from the great Scandinavian expeditions. Were Quetzalcoatl, Kukulcán, and later Viracocha one and the same man? Or were they three different men?

Even though Yucatán is far removed from the Mexican plateau, recent excavations at Tula (a few miles north of Mexico City) have clearly established a connection. In fact, Chichén Itzá had been called a grandiose duplicate of Tula. It is now an accepted fact that Toltec Tulans conquered Mayan Chichén Itzá in the tenth century and brought along the belief in Quetzalcoatl and/or Kukulcán. Thus, the three mysterious strangers might have come from a single source.

Of course, there are other valid possibilities. In 1885 Edward Herbert Thompson, the "Schliemann of Yucatán," set out to locate the then only fabled city of Chichén Itzá. He succeeded not only in locating the city but in converting myth into fact when he excavated the Sacred Well of Death and managed to dredge up the bones of young girls. Ancient Mayan legend had told of virgins who had been thrown into the well as human sacrifice to appease the gods. This story, like many others, had been relegated to the realm of fable and fancy. But Thompson proved that some of the myths were facts.

Thompson found an elaborate tomb at Chichén Itzá that he believed to be the tomb of the great priest Kukulcán. The find also supplied Thompson with what he considered proof for his original theory—that the Mayas were survivors of lost Atlantis. Perhaps Kukulcán and his followers were Atlanteans?

I have a theory of my own. Couldn't three different

bearded, fair-skinned colonists from the same advanced civilization appear at three different times in
the desert of Mexico, the jungle of Yucatán, and the
mountain-rimmed Altiplano of Peru? Couldn't they
each have brought the people food, energy, security,
and surplus manpower on a scale previously un-
dreamed of, and couldn't they have taught them the
same arts and technologies, which would later diverge
somewhat in the hands of the three different em-
pires? And then perhaps certain unknown, external
considerations (maybe a master plan) eventually made
all three leave by their own volition with a promise to
return, which apparently has never yet been kept.

While various speculations were being advanced in
the nineteenth century concerning the origins of the
Mayas, another Central American race was being re-
discovered—the Aztecs of Mexico. William H. Prescott in 1843 published his book *The Conquest of
Mexico,* which made use of forgotten documents left
by the Spanish conquistadores.

It seemed that the Aztecs, like the Mayas, had built
temples, palaces, and great cities. Their language was
nothing like that of the Mayas, but clearly they had
one similar belief, for the Aztec chief Montezuma's
final surrender to Cortes was due to his relentless
conviction that the fair-skinned, bearded, Quetzalcoatl
had returned in the person and form of the Spanish
invader. Thus, the end of the Aztec empire was a
tragic and bizarre case of mistaken identity.

When the ill-starred Montezuma sat facing Cortes
in a splendid palace and spoke of a "certain lord" who
had led his people from foreign parts to the land of
Mexico and then returned to his native land "where
the sun rises" (could this have been a reference to another planet?), we can be sure Montezuma was referring to Quetzalcoatl.

One of the first Spanish historians was Father Ber-
nardino de Sahagún, a Franciscan missionary. Sahagún sought out the learned men of the village and

asked each to paint in Aztec picture-writing as much as he could remember of Aztec history. Sahagún recorded the following story of Montezuma's first encounter with Cortes:

"Montezuma straightened himself to his full height and standing close before Cortez, addressed him thus: 'O Lord, our Lord, with what trouble, what fatigue have you journeyed to reach us, have arrived in this land, your land, your own city of Mexico, so sit on your mat, your stool, which I have been guarding for you this while. Your vassals, the old kings, my ancestors are gone after they too had kept ready your mat. Would that one of them could rise from the dead and astonished, see what my eyes truly see, for in no dream do they see your face. . . . For the kings, my ancestors told that you would appear, that you would return to sit on your mat, your stool. Now it has come true; you have returned. . . . Welcome to this land. Rest now. You are tired. . . . Rest in your palace.' "

And so Cortes and his band of conquistadores did just that. The Aztec empire vanished and with it their fables and beliefs. Thanks to a few missionaries like Sahagún, some minute fragments of Aztec history still remain.

Those historical fragments tell us that there was indeed a Quetzalcoatl who was king of the Toltecs, of whom the Aztecs are direct descendants. Quetzalcoatl was the prophet. A treasured Aztec legend claimed, "In all crafts and artifices/ Skilled were they as wondrous workmen./ And in Quetzalcoatl all these had their beginnings;/ In him all were manifested./ He was the master workman who taught them/ All their trades and artifices. . . ."

Quetzalcoatl soon departed but promised to return in One Reed year. One Reed year occurred at irregular intervals. Two One-Reed years had passed and Quetzalcoatl had not returned. The next One Reed year was 1519. It was a strange coincidence that Cortes managed to land on the very day of that year when he was expected. His appearance matched the Aztecs' expectations—fair-skinned and bearded: Cortes could be no one but Quetzalcoatl.

It is clear that Quetzalcoatl/Kukulcán figured indelibly on the memories of the Aztecs, Toltecs, and Mayas. Perhaps the gods never existed at all. Perhaps imaginative storytellers made them up by sheer coincidence. But sheer coincidence is not easy to back up. The likelihood that these three men had the same origin is more plausible, but this view still refutes the possibility that three separate men could have arrived in reality rather than merely in symbol. It cannot be denied that three different bearded white missionaries from an advanced civilization *could* have been sent at three different times. Consider the Incan story of Viracocha.

Today, in the mountain-studded Altiplano of Peru, the story of Viracocha is but a mere echo of a name long forgotten. But back in the days of pre-conquest America, when Pizarro and his men came ashore near Tumbes, the northernmost coastal city of the Incas' realm, they were greeted by this name. "Viracocha" has arrived. The message filtered back through the jungle. Viracocha, the gentle bringer of civilization, had returned as he had promised.

Pizarro and his bold companions found themselves in a flourishing empire of absolute and despotic power. The Incan kingdom was a militaristic welfare state that controlled the destiny of every citizen—quite unlike the loosely knit Aztec confederation that Cortes had smashed eleven years before. As Pizarro and his army marched along to conquest, they noted the well-engineered roads, vast irrigation projects, temple-pyramids, and swarming cities.

Yet it was only six months after Pizarro's troops had landed that they were able to capture the last Incan lord, Atahualpa, whom they held for a fabulous golden ransom. Promising the Incan ruler his freedom upon delivery of an enormous fortune, Atahualpa ordered the large treasure room filled with gold. The

Spaniards had no intention of freeing the Incan ruler quite so easily. Having received their millions in ransom, the Spaniards in brutal treachery tried Atahualpa on false charges and then granted him his choice of the manner of death. The Incan empire fell to the Spaniards. Another glorious civilization vanished. And, strangely enough, the name "Viracocha" could be heard echoing in the distance. Was there a link between the Viracocha cult and the sudden collapse of the Incas?

Atahualpa was a forceful young warrior. He ruled an empire that stretched twenty-five hundred miles along the Pacific, including what are now Ecuador, Peru, and Bolivia, as well as part of Chile. The population that he controlled numbered three and a half million. Why did Atahualpa succumb so easily? Did he, like Montezuma, fall victim to a case of mistaken identity?

Within hours after the Spaniards had disembarked, the native couriers were hiking up the Andes with full reports for the Incan lord. Bearded white men had arrived from over the sea. Viracocha had returned.

The god of civilization, Viarcocha, the legends said, was a holy man from the sea. They said that Viracocha had passed out of sight over the same sea when his work of creation was completed. In another version, the holy man preached a farewell sermon, promising that someday he and his helpers would revisit his people. Finally he spread his cloak on the sea, stood upon it with his followers, and departed over the water.

Pizarro and his men took advantage of the Incas' belief in Viracocha. Having heard the same tale of an ancient man-god in Mexico, they knew that they were in luck—for the Spaniards had also heard that in the vast regions of Yucatán, Mayan legend spoke of a bearded white man-god who promised to return. In Mexico, Central America, and now again in Peru, the conquistadores had come upon people of more advanced cultures, and in each case pre-Hispanic native legends attributed this higher civilization to bearded white gods. The story was not unique. It very well could have been true.

Even though there is still no universally accepted theory regarding the identity and the eventual disappearance of Kukulcán/Quetzalcoatl/Viracocha, one cannot deny their overriding presence and predominance in three separate cultural legends. Moreover, I cannot help but recognize the analogous way in which each of the man-gods was linked to the sudden appearance and eventual disappearance of these ancient, lost civilizations. No one can explain the sudden collapse of the mighty Aztecs or the fierce militaristic Incas and finally the mysterious retreat of the glorious Mayas. Their kingdoms flourished while Europe was in the Dark Ages. And then suddenly they vanished. The stories of their gods all but disappeared with them.

All we do know is that these three gods were believed to have brought civilization to these early Americans. They came with a mission and then disappeared as mysteriously as they had come, promising to return at some future date. So loved and revered were these man-gods that the people eagerly awaited their arrival. So real were these man-gods that the natives kept their memories alive throughout the centuries. And so when the Spanish invaders arrived, the Indians greeted them with trust. They could be none other than Viracocha and his followers returned. But the bloody, black truth has long since been recorded. The gods had not returned. I wonder now if the Mayan legend of apocalypse and redemption will hold true—if in the year 2011 A.D., on Christmas Eve, the old cycle will end and Kukulkán will again appear.

Bibliography

Chapter 1   Richard Halliburton

Clapp, Jane, *Vanishing Point*. New York: Scarecrow Press, 1961.

Halliburton, Richard, *The Royal Adventures of Richard Halliburton*. Indianapolis: Bobbs-Merrill, 1947.

——. *His Story of His Life's Adventures as Told in Letters to His Mother and Father*. Indianapolis: Bobbs-Merrill, 1940.

——. "A Half a Mile of History," *Reader's Digest*, October 1937.

——. "The Tokyo of 15 Years Ago." *China Weekly Review*, April 15, 1939.

——. "I Swam the Hellespont," *Asia*, May 1927.

Halliburton Papers, Princeton University Library.

Hanemann, H.W., "Richard Halliburton Plays Polo," *The Bookman*, March 1930.

Harrington, Mildred, "Dick Halliburton Followed the Royal Road of Romance," *American Magazine*, October 1926.

Root, Jonathan, *Halliburton—The Magnificent Myth*. New York: Coward, McCann & Geoghegan, 1965.

Time, "Innocent Abroad," July 8, 1940.

Chapter 2   Percy Fawcett

Churchward, Robert, *Wilderness of Fools*. London: G. Routledge and Sons Ltd., 1936.

Dyott, George, *Manhunting in the Jungle*. Indianapolis: Bobbs-Merrill, 1930.

Fawcett, Brian, *Ruins in the Sky*. London: Hutchinson, 1958.

Fawcett, P.H. Col., *Lost Trails, Lost Cities*. New York: Funk and Wagnalls, 1953.

——. "The Calahuaya's Curse," *English Review*, November 1933.

Fleming, Peter, *Brazilian Adventure*. The Press of the Readers Club, New York, 1942.

——. "Fawcett and Co.," *The Spectator*, April 10, 1953.

Life, "The Strange Case of Col. Fawcett," April 30, 1951.

Literary Digest, "To Rescue a Diety of Brazilian Indians," May 1928.

Saturday Review, "Fastness of the Equator," January 30, 1932.

Time, "Fawcett of the Mato Grosso," May 25, 1953.

Chapter 3   Amelia Earhart

Burke, John, *Winged Legend.* New York: G.P. Putman's Sons, 1970.

Drake, Francis and Katherine, "First Lady of the Air," *Reader's Digest,* May 1951.

Dreher, Carl, "The Lady Vanished," *The Nation,* March 20, 1967.

Elliott, Lawrence, "The Mystery of Amelia Earhart's Last Flight," *Reader's Digest,* July 1957.

Ferris, Helen, *Five Girls Who Dared.* New York: Macmillan, Inc., 1931.

Flying, "Amelia Earhart Lives," March 1971.

Georner, Fred, *The Search for Amelia Earhart.* Garden City, New York: Doubleday & Co., 1966.

———. "I'll Find Amelia Earhart," *Argosy,* February, 1967.

Grinker, Roy, *Men Under Stress.* Blakiston, Pa., 1945.

Hamill, Pete, *"The Cult of Amelia Earhart." Ms,* September 1976.

Klaas, Joe and Joseph Gervais, *Amelia Earhart Lives.* New York: McGraw-Hill, 1970.

Montague, Richard, *Ocean Poles and Airmen.* New York: Random House, 1970.

Putman, George, *Soaring Wings.* New York: Harcourt Brace Jovanovich, 1939.

Time, "Sinister Conspiracy," September 16, 1966.

U.S. Navy, "The Flight of Amelia Earhart."

U.S. News and World Report, "New Disclosures in Amelia Earhart Mystery," July 24, 1967.

Chapter 4   Michael Rockefeller

The Art of the Asmat New Guinea, New York: The Museum of Primitive Art, 1962.

Desmond, James, *Nelson Rockefeller, A Political Biography.* New York: Macmillan, Inc., 1964.

Gardner, Robert and Karl Heider, *Gardens of War.* New York: Random House, 1968.

Gerbrands, A.A., *Wow-Ipits.* The Hague: Mouton and Co., 1967.

Goodwin, John, "Where Is Michael Rockefeller," *Argosy,* October 1968.

Hastings, Peter, "Among the Asmatters," *New Guinea and Australia the Pacific and South-East Asia,* June/July 1968.

Kutz, Myer, *Rockefeller Power.* New York: Simon and Schuster, 1974.

Look, "Michael Rockefeller's Own Story," January 29, 1963.

Machlin, Milt, *The Search for Michael Rockefeller*. New York: G.P. Putnam's Sons, 1972.

Mann, Milton and Joan, *New Guinea*. Tokyo: Kodansha Intl. Ltd., 1972.

Matthiessen, Peter, *Under the Mountain Wall*, New York: The Viking Press, 1962.

Morris, Alex Joe, *Nelson Rockefeller*. New York: Harper and Row, 1960.

The New York Times, 1960: July 7; 1961, April 5, October 25, November 20–28, November 30, December 2, December 3, December 6, December 13, December 21, December 22, December 23; 1962: January 31, June 13, September 9, September 11, September 16.

Newsweek, "Father and Son," December 4, 1961.

Oui, "Is This the Man Who Ate Michael Rockefeller?" April 1977.

Rockefeller, Michael, *The Asmat of New Guinea*. New York: The Museum of Primitive Art, 1967.

Stolley, Richard, "So Bad Even the Bloody Trees Can't Stand Up," *Life*, December 1, 1960.

Time, "Search for Michael," December 1, 1961.

Chapter 5 The Romanovs

Alexandrov, Victor, *The End of the Romanovs*. London: Hutchinson, 1966.

Anastasia, *I Am Anastasia*. New York: Harcourt Brace Jovanovich, 1958.

Grey, Ian, *The Romanovs*, Garden City, New York: Doubleday and Co., 1970.

Literary Digest, "The Arrest and Exile of the Romanovs," March 9, 1918.

Newsweek, November 1, 1976.

O'Connor, John, *The Sokolov Investigation*. New York: Robert Speller and Sons, 1971.

Sublette, Bill, "Anastasia Calls Book a Mess . . . ," *The Daily Progress*, October 28, 1976.

Summers, Anthony and Tom Mangold, *The File on the Tsar*. New York: Harper & Row, 1976.

Telberg, G.C., "Last Days and Death of the Russian Emperor and His Family," *Saturday Evening Post*, August 7, 1920.

Chapter 6 Martin Borman

Eliott, John Brenday, *Hitler and Germany*. New York: McGraw-Hill, 1968.

Farago, Ladislas, *Aftermath, Martin Bormann and the Fourth Reich*. New York: Simon and Schuster, 1974.

McGovern, James, *Martin Bormann and the Fourth Reich*. New York: William Morrow, 1968.

Newsweek, "Mixed Motives," September 13, 1971.

Newsweek, "Swastikas West," November 4, 1974.

Samuels, Gertrude, "Wanted: 1000 Nazis Still at Large," *The New York Times,* 1965.

Sognnaes, Reider, "Post-Mortem Identification of Martin Bormann," *The Criminologist.* London: 1975.

——. "Dental Proof of Martin Bormann's Death," *Scanodont.* Stockholm, 1975.

Stevenson, William, *The Bormann Brotherhood.* New York: Harcourt Brace Jovanovich, 1968.

Trevor-Roper, H.R., *The Bormann Letters,* London: Widenfeld and Nicolson, 1954.

——. "The Last Word on Adolph Hitler," *Colliers,* January 6, 1956.

Wiesenthal, Simon, *The Muderers Among Us.* New York: Bantam Books, 1967.

Chapter 7   James Hoffa

Esquire, March 1975.

Dobbs, Farrell, *Teamster Power.* New York: Monad Press, 1973.

Farley, Oscar, *Hoffa, The Real Story.* Briarcliff Manor, New York: Stein & Day, 1975.

James, Ralph and Estelle, *Hoffa and the Teamsters.* New York: Van Nostrand Reinhold Co., 1965.

Mollenhoff, Clarke and Zigg, "Jimmy Hoffa the Man Who Outsmarted Himself," *Look,* May 13, 1958.

Newsweek, March 23, 1964.

Raskin, A.H., "Why They Cheer for Hoffa," *The New York Times Magazine,* November 9, 1958.

Stanecki, Jerry, "It Gets Dark Every Night," *Playboy,* December, 1975.

Velie, Lester, "Why James Hoffa Had to Die," *Reader's Digest,* December 1976.

——. "The Riddle in the Middle of America's Most Powerful Union," *Reader's Digest,* December 1955.

Chapter 8   D. B. Cooper

Aviation Week and Space Technology, December 6, 1971.

Hubbard, David. *The Skyjacker.* New York: Macmillan, Inc., 1971.

Newsweek, "Quantum Leap," December 6, 1971.

Newsweek, "An Instant Legend," January 31, 1972.

Richards, Leverett, "Alive or Dead Skyjacker Pioneer Came Out Loser," *The Sunday Oregonian,* November 14, 1976.

Science Digest, "What Makes a Skyjacker," January 1972.

Science News, "Psyching the Skyjacker," February 12, 1972.

Seattle Times Magazine, "D.B. Cooper, Is He at the Bottom of Lake Merwin or Walking the Streets," October 3, 1976.

Time, "The Sick Skyjacker," November 13, 1972.

———. "The Bandit Who Went Out into the Cold," December 4, 1971.

Chapter 9   Jesus Christ

Anderson, Hugh, *Jesus.* Englewood Cliffs, New Jersey: Prentice-Hall, Inc., 1967.

Aron, Robert, *Jesus of Nazareth.* New York: William Morrow and Co., 1962.

Black, Matthew, *The Scrolls and Christianity.* New York: Allenson, 1969.

Campbell, Joseph, *The Hero with a Thousand Faces.* Princeton, New Jersey: Bollingen Series XVII, 1949.

Conzelmann, Hans, *Jesus.* Philadelphia: Fortress Press, 1973.

Coughlan, Robert, "Who Was the Man Jesus?," *Life,* December 25, 1964.

Cross, Colin, *Who Was Jesus?,* New York: Atheneum, 1970.

Kazantzakis, Nikos, *The Last Temptation of Christ.* New York: Simon and Schuster, 1960.

Lawrence, David H., *The Man Who Died.* New York: Random House, 1959.

Merrill, Selah, D.D., *Galilea in the Time of Christ.* Piccadilly, London: The Religious Tract Society, 1891.

Paton, Lewis, *Jerusalem in the Bible Times.* London: University of Chicago Press, 1908.

Phipps, William, *Was Jesus Married?* New York: William Morrow and Co., 1962.

———. *The Sexuality of Jesus.* New York: Harper & Row, 1973.

Schweitzer, Albert, *The Quest for the Historical Jesus.* New York: Macmillan and Co., 1968.

Schneemelcher, Wilhelm and Edgar Hennecke, editors, *New Testament Apocrypha.* English translation by R. McL. Wilson. Philadelphia: The Westminster Press, 1963.

Smith, Huston, *The Religions of Man.* New York: Harper & Row, 1958.

Suetonius, *Lives of the Caesars.* Cambridge: Harvard University Press.

Tacitus, *Annals.* London: Oxford University Press, 1960.

Chapter 10   Aimee Semple Macpherson

Bahr, Robert, "The Disappearance of Aimee," *TV Guide,* November 6–12, 1976.

Bissel, Shelton, "Vaudeville at Angelus Temple," *Outlook,* May 23, 1928.

Comstock, Sarah, "Aimee Semple Macpherson," *Harper's Magazine,* May 23, 1928.

Darst, Sephen, "The Theology of Joy," *Nation,* November 1, 1971.

Keatley, Vivien, "Siren of the Sawdust Trail," *Coronet,* August 1957.

Macpherson, Aimee Semple," Four-Square," *Sunset,* February 1927.

Ross, Ishbel, *Charmers and Cranks.* New York: Harper & Row, 1965.

Ryder, Warren David, "Aimee Semple Macpherson," *The Nation,* July 28, 1926.

Thomas, Lately (pseudonym for Robert Steele), *The Vanishing Evangelist.* New York: The Viking Press, 1959.

Chapter 11   Dalton Trumbo

Belfrage, Cedric, *The American Inquistion 1945–1960.* Indianapolis: Bobbs-Merrill Co., 1973.

Cook, Bruce, *Dalton Trumbo.* New York: Scribner's, 1977.

Lasky, Jesse, Jr., *Whatever Happened to Hollywood.* New York: Funk & Wagnalls, 1973.

Trumbo, Dalton, *Time of the Toad.* Harper & Row, New York, 1972.

Chapter 12   The Great Gods

Landsburg, Alan, *In Search of Ancient Mysteries.* New York: Bantam Books, 1974.

Prescott, William, *The Conquest of Mexico.* New York: The Modern Library, 1931.

Thompson, Edward, *People of the Serpent.* New York: Houghton Mifflin Co., 1932.

ABOUT THE AUTHOR

ALAN LANDSBURG is a successful film and television producer, heading up his own production company in Los Angeles, California. He was instrumental in bringing the von Däniken phenomenon to the attention of the American public through TV by producing "In Search of Ancient Astronauts." Alan Landsburg is also the author of *In Search of Ancient Mysteries* and *The Outer Space Connection.* He is currently working on a weekly television series, "In Search of . . . ," which has been on the air since September 1976. *In Search of Missing Persons* and five other books on extraterrestrials, magic and witchcraft, myths and monsters, lost civilizations, and strange phenomena, are based on this series.

OTHER WORLDS
OTHER REALITIES

In fact and fiction, these extraordinary books bring the fascinating world of the supernatural down to earth from ancient astronauts and black magic to witchcraft, voodoo and mysticism—these books look at other worlds and examine other realities.